Drawn by J Duncan

Engraved by P Christie

CITY OF MONTREAL FROM THE CANAL.

HOCHELAGA DEPICTA;

OR THE

HISTORY AND PRESENT STATE OF THE ISLAND AND

CITY OF

MONTREAL.

Mc Tavish's Monument

MONTREAL

WILLIAM GREIG

1839.

HOCHELAGA DEPICTA

THE

EARLY HISTORY

AND

PRESENT STATE

OF THE

CITY AND ISLAND OF MONTREAL.

WITH NUMEROUS
ILLUSTRATIVE ENGRAVINGS.

EDITED BY
NEWTON BOSWORTH, F. R. A. S.

MONTREAL:
WILLIAM GREIG, ST. PAUL STREET.

MDCCCXXXIX.

COLES CANADIANA COLLECTION

Originally published in 1839
by William Grieg,
Montreal.

Facsimile edition published
by COLES PUBLISHING COMPANY, Toronto
© Copyright 1974.

TO

HIS EXCELLENCY

SIR JOHN COLBORNE, K.G.C. &c. &c.

GOVERNOR-GENERAL

OF

BRITISH NORTH AMERICA,

TO WHOSE

WISE, EQUITABLE, AND PROMPT ADMINISTRATION,

IN A SEASON OF PECULIAR DANGER,

THE PROVINCE OF LOWER CANADA

IS UNDER

GREAT AND LASTING OBLIGATIONS,

This Volume

IS, WITH PERMISSION, MOST RESPECTFULLY DEDICATED,

BY HIS OBLIGED AND OBEDIENT SERVANT,

W. GREIG.

MONTREAL,
1st June, 1839.

ABOUT THE AUTHOR

Newton Bosworth (? - 1848) was the second pastor of the first Baptist church in Montreal, located on St. Helen Street. His church was important then as the centre from which the Baptists first sought to establish their church in Canada. Bosworth was deeply involved in evangelizing work, which was soon abandoned in Quebec under pressure from French Catholics. After that, he was re-assigned to a church in Paris, Upper Canada, where he served for the rest of his life. He was a frequent contributor to the Canada Baptist Magazine and Missionary Register, perhaps the best newspaper in Canada at the time. Bosworth died in Paris in 1848, nine years after publication of this book.

Toronto, 1974

PREFACE.

In a conversation with my friend, the Publisher, on the former and present state of Canada, he suggested the idea of the following work, and requested me to undertake it. I did not then see the possibility of doing so ; but afterwards a temporary cessation of part of my ministerial duties, afforded me an increase of leisure, and enabled me to comply with his wish. Desirous of looking more particularly into the history of my adopted country, the researches I had occasion to make for this purpose were attended with much interest and gratification to me. I marked, as was natural, with more attention than when, at a distance from the spot, I read the accounts as matters of general information, the events and circumstances connected with the discovery, acquisition, and advancement of this important part of the British dominions. But in committing the result to writing, even on the limited scale which the plan of this work allows—rather, perhaps, the more so on account of that limitation,—I found more difficulty than I at first expected. The minor points of the history were in different accounts so discordant, that with my natural aversion to uncertainty, and perhaps a too fastidious desire to reconcile what will not admit of agreement, I was often longer, and more perplexed, in adjusting these points than those who have not employed themselves in similar pursuits would readily imagine. The main facts, however, are sufficiently well attested; and of these I have endeavoured to embody as many as my range would allow in the slight sketch I have given of the introductory history.

In obtaining the Topographical information, many hours were sometimes spent in seeking for that which a few minutes would suffice to put into writing; not from any unwillingness on the part of those who had information to give, but from the very nature of the case. The gentlemen to whom enquiries were directed, are entitled to my own thanks, and those of the Publisher, for the courtesy and readiness with which those enquiries were answered. At first, it was intended to present to each a distinct acknowledgment; but the number has so increased, that it is hoped they will accept this general expression of obligation.

It is natural for every man of ordinary curiosity and discernment, when he comes into a new country, and especially if he mean to reside in it, to desire to know something of its past and present state; and a portion of his time may be lawfully employed in gratifying this desire. The knowledge thus obtained, is capable of being applied to various useful purposes; and more so by the Christian than by any other person. He may often see the finger of God in controlling events, where others discern nothing but the operations of natural causes, or the developements of human agency and design.

N. B.

Montreal, June 1, 1839.

PREFACE.

The appearance of the work has been delayed beyond the time mentioned in the original prospectus, by causes over which the Publisher had no control ; but the delay has been rather serviceable than otherwise, by increasing the accuracy of the descriptions, and affording an opportunity of sketching the history of the two Rebellions.

In every first attempt of this kind, it is almost inevitable that defects and inaccuracies should occur. Both the Editor and the Publisher will, therefore, be obliged by such hints as shall contribute to the improvement of the work in a new edition.

CONTENTS.

CONTENTS.

CONTENTS.

LIST OF PLATES.

HOCHELAGA DEPICTA.

CHAPTER I.

DISCOVERIES OF COLUMBUS, AND OTHER NAVIGATORS.
ARRIVAL OF JACQUES CARTIER AT HOCHELAGA.

THERE is in man a natural propensity to enquire into
the origin of every thing with which he has any connection,—to trace the rise and progress of each discovery,
art, and invention, by which the circle of knowledge is
extended, or the happiness of nations and individuals
increased. In accordance with this almost universal
sentiment, the first of any series of events is usually an
object of peculiar interest, and their gradual evolution,
up to a certain point, scarcely less so. Thus, standing
where we may, watching the tide of human affairs,
while the onward prospect encourages hope and animates
exertion, the retrospective view yields another kind of
pleasure nearly as intense, and perhaps equally beneficial
and satisfactory.

Nor is this insatiable curiosity, on other grounds, a
vain or useless feeling. The history of the past is often
useful to illustrate the present, and regulate plans for
the future. Even the failures which have attended the

investigations and projects of men are so many beacons to warn us against danger and error, and guide with more safety our movements and enquiries. Whatever idea is formed of history, whether, with the late Mr. Fox, we consider it as simply " telling the tale of other times," or, in conformity with the more magnificent designation of earlier writers, view it as " philosophy teaching by example," the study of it is not less rational than entertaining, nor less instructive than delightful.

That the discovery of the New World should have created an unusual sensation in the Old, is amongst the most natural of all consequences. Yet, after the first surprise and curiosity had subsided, and the extravagant expectations that prevailed had been disappointed, the interest of these distant regions was for a time so diminished in Europe as to occasion surprise to us, who know to what a degree of importance the Western World has arisen, and can observe the bearing of its interests upon the destinies of the other quarters of the globe. But little more than three centuries have elapsed since the spot on which we are now writing, and the City whose history we are about to describe, was totally unknown to the rest of the world. It was just in the situation, with respect to the Eastern hemisphere, which Virgil assigns to the now famed inhabitants of our " father land," in local reference to the shores of Italy :

ET PENITUS TOTO DIVISOS ORBE BRITTANNOS.*

As both the Parent State and the rising Colony have been in circumstances of equal obscurity in past, though

---

* It is not improbable, as some critics have suggested, that the poet had in his eye the notion that Britain was once united to the Continent, and had been separated from it by some convulsion of nature ; but the fact of its comparative obscurity in ancient times is sufficiently prominent to justify the allusion in that sense of the expression.

different ages, it may not be presumptuous, and it is certainly not unpatriotic, to indulge the hope that the latter may emulate the former in deeds of excellence and glory, and both long unite their energies for the benefit of the world.

It has been affirmed that he who discovered America was not in quest of new lands, but only purposed to explore a new way to lands already known. To what extent both these ideas were entertained distinctly in the mind of Columbus, it is not easy now to determine with precision ; but that it was one main object of his pursuit to discover, by sailing westward, a shorter, or at least an easier and more uninterrupted, passage to the rich countries known by the name of the East Indies,. will not admit of a doubt. The long and tedious journeys over land to the tropical regions rendered it very desirable, if it could be realized, to obtain a readier access to the trade which, even at that time, had enriched several of the commercial nations of Europe.

Columbus was born about the middle of the fifteenth century, and entered early, as a navigator, into the service of the Portuguese, who were most actively engaged in mercantile and commercial pursuits. The spirit of discovery which had been some time in operation, led Columbus, during his frequent voyages, to reflect upon the possibility of reaching the Eastern World by a different route from any that had been taken, and, after many enquiries and much study, even to suppose that by sailing westerly he should more readily approach the farther boundary of the country which he sought, than by any other course. Filled with this idea, and desirous also of distinguishing himself by the discovery of other lands which his meditation and researches led him to expect in his passage, he applied for aid, in the first place, to the Senate of his own country, Genoa; but without success.   His next application was to the court of Portugal, with no better result.   On the part of the King it was followed by a breach of good faith; for while he rejected the proposal of Columbus, he meanly endeavoured to supplant him in the object of it by sending out an expedition of his own, which, however, returned without making any discovery.   His final resort was to Spain, then under the separate Government of Ferdinand of Arragon, and Isabella of Castile.   The King refused to countenance the design, but Her Majesty, more wise and liberal, after several years delay, consented to patronize it, furnishing the means for accomplishing the voyage from her own treasury, and actually selling her jewels to supply the deficiency of the national resources; thus associating her own name with that of Columbus in the imperishable glory of this memorable expedition.   Our own country, however, has some claim to a share of this honour; for Columbus having sent his brother Bartholomew to England, to interest the King, Henry VII., in favour of his plan, that sagacious monarch, having examined his proposal and approved it, entered into an agreement with Bartholomew, in 1488, to carry it into execution; but Columbus himself was then in treaty with Isabella, and four years afterwards, when he was just upon the point of relinquishing all hopes from that quarter, and renewing his application to England, Isabella decided in his favour.

On Friday, the 3d of August, 1492, Columbus sailed from Palos, a port of Andalusia in Spain; and on the 12th of October, to his unspeakable gratification, he made his first discovery in the New World.   This was one of the Bahama Islands, called by the natives Guanahaui, named by Columbus St. Salvador, and afterwards Cat Island by the English.   He landed the same day, took possession of the island in the name of the Spanish Sovereigns, and assumed the titles of Admiral and Viceroy, which had been assigned to him before he sailed from Europe. Leaving the island after a few days examination, he passed on to another a few leagues distant, where he landed on the 16th, and named it Conception. On the 17th he reached another, which he called Ferdinanda: in modern maps it is named Exuma. Pursuing his voyage, he discovered the island called by the natives Samoet, by Columbus Isabella, and by more recent navigators Long Island. After cruising some time among the Bahamas, he discovered on the 24th of November the important island of Cuba, and, on the 5th of December, Hispaniola or St. Domingo, now called Hayti. Here he built a fortress, and leaving thirty-nine men in possession of it, he sailed for Spain on the 4th of January, 1493 ; arrived, after a stormy and dangerous voyage, at the mouth of the Tagus on the 14th of March, and at mid-day on the 15th, entered the harbour of Palos, whence he had sailed the preceding year ; " having taken not quite seven months and a half to accomplish this most momentous of all maritime enterprizes." He was received at Court, whither he was accompanied by six of the native Indians he had brought with him, with all the honour and admiration which such splendid discoveries naturally called forth ; and, what was still more gratifying to him, an order was immediately given for a second expedition on a larger scale than the former. On the 25th of September, 1493, he sailed from the bay of Cadiz, and steering further south than in the former voyage, he fell in with what are now called the Caribbee or Leeward Islands. After visiting several of these, he spent some time in regulating affairs at the places he formerly discovered, and returned to Spain in 1496. A third and a fourth voyage were afterwards undertaken, in which **Columbus** made various other discoveries ; in the former the island of Trinidad, and the adjacent coast of South America, which he saw for the first time in 1498; and in the latter, which commenced in 1502, a considerable part of the northern coast of the same continent.

It is remarkable that, from the commencement to the end of his illustrious career, Columbus tenaciously adhered to the opinion that the lands he had discovered were either parts of the Eastern World he was in pursuit of, or were in some way connected with it ; or that, by sailing among them and branching off as appearances might suggest, he should ultimately discover a passage to the object of a desire so long and so fondly cherished. So completely had this idea taken posses- sion of his mind, that no labours or disappointments were sufficient to dislodge it. Had it not been for this mistake, it is reasonable to believe he would have been even more successful than he was, and have left less for other navigators to accomplish. In consequence of this notion, the countries which he had found were called *The Indies* by Ferdinand and Isabella in their ratifica- tion of the powers granted to Columbus ; and though the error has been detected the name has been retained, and the appellation of *West Indies* continues to be given to the country, and that of *Indians* to its aboriginal inhabitants. The true passage to the East Indies by the Cape of Good Hope was ascertained, in 1498, by Vasco de Gama, in the service of the Portuguese.

But although Columbus found not all he sought, the grandeur of his conceptions, and the skill and persever- ance he displayed in the execution of them, have placed him upon the highest pinnacle of nautical fame; and though, intent upon nobler objects, he gave not his own name to the world he revealed to others, the gratitude and admiration of mankind will not suffer his true honour to be lost, but whenever they think upon America, will call to mind the name of its discoverer with feelings of reverence and affection.

While the Spaniards were thus actively engaged in the research after new countries, the English were not inattentive to the progress of maritime discovery. Henry the Seventh, who, it has been stated, gave the first encouragement to the plans of Columbus, issued a commission to John Cabot and his son Sebastian, natives of Italy, to engage in the then favourite pursuit of a North-west passage to the East. The continent of *North* America was one of the fruits of this expedition. The adventurers discovered Newfoundland early in June, 1497, and, after exploring a part of the Gulf of St. Lawrence, they took a westerly course, and then proceeded to coast the main land as far as latitude 67° 50′ north. The following year they returned to England. The date usually assigned for the discovery of Canada is April 5, 1499. In 1502 Hugh Elliott and Thomas Ashurst, merchants of Bristol, obtained a patent from Henry to establish Colonies in the countries recently discovered by Cabot. In the following reign, Henry VIII. fitted out another expedition, which sailed in 1527, but was not attended with any important discoveries.

About this period some individuals in France turned their attention to these new countries, and we have accounts of their fishing for Cod on the Banks of Newfoundland, and along the sea-coast of Canada, in the beginning of the century. About the year 1506, a Frenchman, named Jean Denys, drew a map of the Gulf of St. Lawrence; and two years after, Thomas Aubert, a ship-master of Dieppe, carried over to France some of the natives of Canada. But it was not until

1523, in the reign of Francis I., that any thing on an extensive scale was undertaken by this nation, or patronized by its Government.   In that year the enterprising monarch just named sent four ships under the command of Verazzano, a Florentine, to prosecute discoveries in this country. Of his first voyage no particulars are known. He undertook a second in the following year, with one ship only, in which he is said to have explored a great part of the coast of the present United States, and of British North America. A third expedition is spoken of by some historians, in which Verazzano is stated to have been massacred with all his crew by the natives ; but the greater probability is, that he left the service of the King of France when that monarch was a prisoner in the hands of his great rival Charles V., of Spain, and that he spent his latter years in his native land.*

The success of the French having excited the jealousy of the Kings of Spain and Portugal, to whom the Pope, in acccordance with the ecclesiastical maxims of those days, had confirmed the possession of America, Francis, not acknowledging this right to exclude him from a share, and facetiously remarking that he " would fain see the article in father Adam's will, which bequeathes that vast inheritance to them," resolved not to be deterred from prosecuting his discoveries. Verazzano had given to the countries he had visited the name of New France, *La Nouvelle France*, an

* See the evidence on this point in Hawkins's *Picture of Quebec.* We take the opportunity of referring with pleasure to this well-written and meritorious work. The writer has taken great and laudable pains to investigate and compare authorities, and has often succeeded in his attempts to reconcile or correct the contradictory accounts that have descended to us of early voyages to theWestern World. If we might suggest what appears to us would be an improvement in this interesting volume, we would recommend a different arrangement, in some places, of excellent materials most skilfully and judiciously prepared. So much talent is but rarely shewn in works of this nature.

appellation which afterwards comprehended the Canadas. Philippe Chabot, Admiral of France, represented to the King the advantage of establishing a Colony in his new dominions, and introduced to him Jacques Quartier or Cartier, a native of St. Malo, who had been engaged in the cod fishery, as a person eminently qualified for this service. He sailed on the 20th of April, 1534, " with two ships of three score tons a-piece burthen, and sixty-one well-appointed men in each." He reached Newfoundland in twenty days, passed through the straits of Belleisle, traversed the Gulf of St. Lawrence, approached the continent at the *Baye des Chaleurs*, which he so called on account of the great heat of the summer, proceeded to Gaspé or Gachepé Bay, where he erected a cross with the Fleurs-de-Lys of France, to secure possession in the name of its King, and persuaded two of the natives to accompany him to France, where he arrived in September the same year.

This celebrated navigator calls for more especial notice at our hands, inasmuch as he was the first who explored the shores of Canada to any considerable extent, and was the very first European who became acquainted with the existence of Hochelaga, and pushed his way through all obstacles till he discovered and entered the village which occupied the very spot where now stands the city we are about to describe.

Through the influence of the Vice-Admiral of France Cartier obtained a new commission more extensive than the former, and sailed with three vessels, the *Great Hermina*, the *Little Hermina*, and the *Hermerillon*, on the 19th of May, 1535. The vessels having been separated by tempestuous weather, re-united on the 26th of July on the coast of Newfoundland. Proceeding to the Gulf and coasting along the north shore, they came, on the 10th of August, to " a goodly great

Gulf, full of islands, passages, and entrances towards what wind soever you please to bend." This day will ever be memorable* in the history of Canada; for it being the festival of St. LAWRENCE in the Romish Church, Cartier gave that name to the bay in which he was sailing, and it was afterwards extended to the whole of the Gulf and the noble stream which flows into it. On the 15th he discovered an island to the south, which he named Assumption, in honour of the day: it is now known as Anticosti, agreeing somewhat in sound with its Indian name Natiscotec. Continuing his course, he examined the shores on both sides the river, and held communication with the inhabitants, in which he was assisted by the two natives whom he had taken to France on his previous voyage. He soon entered the river Saguenay, and a few days after made the *Isle aux Coudres*, so called from the excellent filberts which he found there. Feeling an increasing interest in his progress, he pursued it with unabated ardour, and soon reached an island, which, from its beauty and fertility, especially from the number of wild vines growing there, he named the Isle of Bacchus, now the Island of Orleans. Here he was visited by "the Lord of Canada," whose name was Donnacona; and having afterwards found a safe harbour for his vessels, he moored them in the Port de St. Croix, in the river St. Charles, and was here again visited by Donnacona, who came with five hundred of his attendants to welcome his arrival into the country. The residence of this chief was at Stadacona, which occupied a portion of the space on which Quebec now stands.

* As it will be also, for a very different reason, in the history of the country of which Cartier was a native. On the 10th of August, 1792, the Parisian mob broke into the Palace, menaced the lives of the Royal Family, and murdered several of the Swiss guards; the prelude to innumerable cruelties and much bloodshed.

The discoveries hitherto made by Cartier, numerous and surprising as they were, so far from satisfying his ambition, served only to excite his desire for still greater achievements. Stadacona, as it did not bound his curiosity, so neither did it limit his progress. Having learned, while here, that there existed a place of much greater importance, at a considerable distance up the Great River of Canada, he determined to advance in pursuit of it. Neither the lateness of the season, nor the representations of those about him, could divert him from his object, and he commenced his voyage in the *Hermerillon,* with two long boats, provisions, and ammunition. The scenery on both sides of the river delighted him with its beauty, and the natives cheerfully supplied him with what they could procure to supply his necessities. The chief of the district at Hochelai, now the Richlieu, paid him a visit, and presented to him a child of his own, about seven years of age. At Lake St. Peter, the party were obliged, by the shallowness of the water, and their ignorance of the deeper channel, to leave the pinnace, and betake themselves to their boats. On the second of October, 1535, they effected a landing about six miles from the town, below the current of St. Mary. Here they were met by more than a thousand of the natives, who received them with every demonstration of joy and hospitality. Cartier returned these civilities by distributing among the people such small presents as the taste or the fancy of these simple children of nature taught them to value. The next day, having obtained the services of three natives as his guides, Cartier, with a number of his own men, entered for the first time the Indian village of Hochelaga,* the germ or nucleus of the present city of

---

* Part of the *river* was also distinguished by this name,—sometimes, and perhaps originally, spelled and pronounced HOSHELAGA.

Montreal.   After a short stay among these hospitable
strangers, he returned to his boats, and proceeded on
his passage back to winter at St. Croix.

CHAPTER II.

PRIMITIVE CONDITION OF HOCHELAGA—NAME CHANG-
ED TO "MOUNT ROYAL"—COMPANY OF ONE HUN-
DRED PARTNERS—CANADA TAKEN BY THE ENGLISH,
1629—RESTORED, 1632.

THE present inhabitants of this city would find it as difficult to recognise its "local habitation" as its "name" from the following description of its ancient state. The way to the village was through large fields of Indian corn. Its outline was circular; and it was encompassed by three separate rows of palisades, or rather picket fences, one within the other, well secured and put together. A single entrance was left in this rude fortification, but was guarded with pikes and stakes, and every precaution taken against siege or attack. The cabins or lodges of the inhabitants, about fifty in number, were constructed in the form of a tunnel, each fifty feet in length by fifteen in breadth. They were formed of wood covered with bark. Above the doors of these houses, as well as along the outer rows of palisades, ran a gallery, ascended by ladders, where stones and other missiles were ranged in order for the defence of the place. Each house contained several chambers, and the whole were so arranged as to enclose an open court yard, where the fire was made. The inhabitants belonged to the Huron tribe, and appear to have been more civilised than their neighbours. Being devoted to husbandry and fishing, they seldom wandered from their station. They received the Frenchmen with courtesy, feasted them after the manner of their tribe, and presents were reciprocally exchanged. The sight of the Europeans struck them with astonishment: their fire-arms, their trumpets, their dress, their long beards (fashionable in that age), were all sources of wonder and conjecture to the natives. They constantly interrogated their guests, who on their part were also desirous of learning all they could; but as neither party could understand the language of the other, and as they could only converse through the medium of signs, very little information was received or imparted.

Cartier appears to have been regarded by these simple people as a being of superior order, capable, at least, of curing diseases at his pleasure; for, during his stay, he was surprised to see the chief of the village brought towards him, and who, pointing to his limbs, testified by signs that he suffered pain of some kind, and wished to be healed. The gesticulations of the chief were imitated by his attendants, and presently afterward a number of other persons were brought in, who were either ill, or decrepid from old age. Touched by this display of confiding simplicity, Cartier did what he could to soothe their minds, and, as the Catholic historians relate, filled with holy fervour, recited as devoutly as possible the opening passage of the Gospel according to St. John. He then made the sign of the cross upon the sick, distributed chaplets and images of the *Agnus Dei* amongst them, impressing them with the belief that these things had much healing virtue. By the same authority we are informed that, though he disclaimed the power they ascribed to him, he recited to them with a loud voice the sufferings of the Saviour, though to what purpose we do not perceive, if they understood not his language. At all events, he prayed fervently with them, and for them, that the Almighty would not suffer these poor idolaters to remain under the power of error, and in the darkness of infidelity. We are told that the whole was listened to with respectful attention and great interest; and we can easily believe that a flourish of trumpets at the termination of the ceremony " delighted the savages beyond measure."

Having seen all that he deemed worthy of notice in the city, Cartier proceeded to examine the mountain in its vicinity. It was even then, according to his account, tilled all around, and remarkable for its fertility. He was particularly enchanted with the magnificent and beautiful view presented to him from the summit of its eastern promontory; and so splendid a panorama of " thirty leagues" radius must have given him a lofty and gratifying idea of the country he had been exploring. In honour of the King, his master, he gave to the elevation the name of MOUNT ROYAL, which, with a singular change in its terminational adjective, has been since extended to the city itself, and to the whole of the Island and District in which it is situated. When the change took place does not appear. It retained the original name at least till 1690, as it is termed Mount Royal by Major Walley in his official journal for that year.* By the view which he had from the mountain he was induced to consider the village below him as a favourable site for a French settlement; but he lived not to see his idea realized, nor was it acted upon till about a century after he had formed it.

A great multitude of the inhabitants accompanied him

---

* See the Journal in Smith's History of Canada, vol. 1, pa. 96.

to his boats, and even assisted such of his men as they perceived to be fatigued with their march, by carrying them upon their shoulders ; appearing to be grieved with the shortness of their stay, and following their course along the banks of the river. On the 11th of October they rejoined their companions at St. Croix, were again visited by Donnacona, and returned the visit at Stadacona, about three miles distant from their port. The inhabitants appeared docile and tractable, and their houses well stored with every thing necessary for the approaching season. Cartier and his companions, however, suffered much in their retreat, for, being unaccustomed to the rigours of a Canadian winter, and but scantily supplied with proper food and clothing, they were nearly all attacked by the scurvy, and twenty-five of their number died. Being advised to use a decoction of the spruce fir *(Pinus Canadensis)*, since well-known as a powerful anti-scorbutic, they complied with the advice, and soon recovered their health. Cartier, beginning to entertain some suspicion of the Indians, by the arrival of some young hunters of the tribe, " lusty and strong men" whom he had not seen before, seized Donnacona, the interpreters, and two of the chief inhabitants, whom, with a few other natives, he carried with him on his return to France the ensuing spring.

Though the common people of France were but little elated with the result of this expedition, attaching but a slight value to a country which yielded no abundance of gold and silver, the representations of Cartier, supported and confirmed by the testimony of Donnacona, who had frequent interviews with the King, and aided by the good sense of several persons about the Court, had such an effect, that he determined upon sending him out on a third voyage. François de la

Roque, Lord of Roberval, a gentleman of Picardy, intent upon gain and discovery, was appointed to the command of the expedition, under the titles of Viceroy and Lieutenant of Canada, &c.; and Cartier, as pilot, was placed second in command, with the title of Captain General. Roberval, who undertook to equip two additional ships at his own expense, not being ready at the time appointed, Cartier sailed without him on the 23d of May, 1541, with five vessels, and full powers to make discoveries and settlements in Canada. Roberval did not follow him till the next year, 1542, when he sailed from Rochelle on 16th of April, with three large vessels, having on board two hundred persons, as settlers, both men and women, among whom were several gentlemen of quality. This combined expedition did not yield much either of knowledge or of success to the French in Canada. The accounts indeed of these voyages are inconsistent and unsatisfactory. It seems, however, pretty certain, that, though Cartier, on his return to St. Croix, was kindly received and apparently welcomed by the natives, he soon found reason to suspect that they were averse to any further intercourse with the French, and to their settlement in the country. This might arise, as it probably did, from their learning on enquiry that Donnacona was dead, and that the other natives would not return, and from their fear, not an unreasonable one, that others would in like manner be torn by force from their native soil. Feeling uncomfortable in his position, he removed a few leagues farther up the river St. Lawrence, where he laid up three of his ships, and sent the other two back to France, with letters to the King. He ordered two forts to be built, one at the bottom of the cliff, and the other on the point above: the latter he named Charlesbourg Royal. Leaving the Viscount de Beaupré in command, he proceeded to visit the Saults or Rapids above Hochelaga. On his way he left two boys with his friend the chief of Hochelai, for the purpose of learning the language. The Saults, which are now called the Sault St. Louis, he was unable to pass in his boats. He found the inhabitants friendly, received from them provisions, and exchanged presents with them; but could not divest himself of the fears and suspicions which had arisen in his mind, and for which he found afterwards additional reasons. He passed the winter at Cap Rouge, where he had erected the fort above named. As he had received no tidings of Roberval, he resolved to return to France; and on his passage, putting into St. John's, Newfoundland, he met the Viceroy with provisions and new settlers. He endeavoured in vain to persuade Cartier to remain in Canada. To avoid an open quarrel, the latter weighed anchor in the night and proceeded on his homeward voyage. This is to be regretted, as, with the assistance of Roberval, he might have strengthened his position in the country, and probably effected a permanent settlement. Cartier made no subsequent voyage to Canada; but died soon after his return to France, having sacrificed his fortune in the cause of discovery. Roberval, notwithstanding his discouragements, proceeded to the station which Cartier had left, where he endeavoured to secure himself and his new settlers by enlarging the fortifications. Having passed the winter here, he left thirty men in the fort, and proceeded to explore the province of Saguenay; but the particulars of the expedition are not known. He returned to France in 1543, and for six years took no further interest in Canada, being engaged in the service of his patron Francis I., in his war with the Emperor Charles V. On the death of the French King, he resumed his former career, and associating with himself his brother Achille, a brave warrior, named by Francis *Le Gendarme d'Annibal,* he embarked again for Canada in 1549, with a numerous train of enterprising young men. They were never heard of afterwards, the whole being supposed to have perished at sea. By this misfortune all hopes of supporting an establishment in Canada were for a time destroyed ; and during fifty years no measures were taken for succouring the descendants of the few French settlers who had remained in the country.

Toward the end of that period, in 1598, the Marquis de la Roche, a native of Brittany, was appointed by Henry IV., of France, his Lieutenant General in Canada. His commission is the first that makes provision for partitioning the discovered lands into Seigniories and Fiefs, to be held under the feudal tenure, and as a compensation, when required, for military service in the field. Having resolved to examine the country, before carrying out many settlers, he only brought with him about sixty persons, some of them of ruined fortunes, and others convicts taken from the prisons. He landed forty on Sable Island, a place then totally unfit for colonization. He next reconnoitered the neighbouring coast of Acadia, now called Nova Scotia, and having collected all the information he deemed necessary, he returned to France, being prevented by tempestuous weather from taking back the persons he left on Sable Island. Seven years of continued suffering had reduced the number of these poor creatures to twelve, when a vessel sent to their relief took them back to France just as they were resigning themselves to despair. The King had the curiosity to see them in their wild dress of skins as they landed, and presented each of them with fifty crowns and full pardon. The captain had robbed them of several valuable skins, which they recovered, by law, with damages. La Roche was not destined to repeat his voyage, for his private misfortunes detained him in France, where he fell a victim to disappointment and chagrin, soon after his return.

In the year 1600 Henry granted to M. Chauvin, a naval officer, a commission for an exclusive trade with Canada, and other powers similar to those of La Roche. He was joined by Pontgravé, a skilful navigator and merchant of St. Malo. They made two profitable voyages to Tadoussac, near the mouth of the river Saguenay, where they carried on an extensive trade of furs with the Indians, who gladly bartered their most valuable skins for mere trifles. Chauvin died in 1603, and was succeeded by De Chatte or Chaste, Governor of Dieppe, who founded a company of merchants at Rouen, in order to establish the trade on a liberal and efficient scale. Dying soon afterwards, without having himself visited Canada, Pierre du Guast, Sieur Demonts, an officer in the court of France, was appointed to succeed him, with a commission of greater extent than had before been granted, entitling him to authority from Virginia to the Esquimaux River, or from latitude 40° to 54°, and empowering him to grant lands between latitude 40° and 46°. He was of the reformed religion, and was allowed the free exercise of it for himself and his friends, but prohibited from establishing any other than the Catholic worship among the native inhabitants. This gentleman and his predecessor De Chatte, though they had not opportunities of doing much for Canada, by their personal services, contributed very effectually to its future prosperity, by their successive appointment of the celebrated Samuel Champlain to a share in the enterprize. He was a native of Saintonge, and acquired, by three years service in the West Indies, as a Captain in the Navy, a reputation for bravery and skill. His personal qualities, his fine talents, his comprehensive views, animated by energy and patriotism, peculiarly fitted him for the office to which he was appointed; and enabled him, after many years of ineffectual effort on the part of those who went before him, to place the affairs of the colony in a more prosperous condition than had been previously known. He first sailed with Pontgravé in 1603, and, leaving their vessels at Tadoussac, they ascended in a lighter boat as far as Sault St. Louis. The situation of Quebec even then appeared to him a most eligible site for a future colony; but he did not visit the Indian settlement of Hochelaga, which appears to have dwindled from the comparative importance it possessed when visited by Cartier in 1535, to a place of no moment; indeed, according to another account, " the village of Hochelaga was now no more."*

Demonts returned to France in 1605; but was, in consequence of complaints and representations from persons concerned in the Fisheries, who stated that he interfered with their occupation, deprived of the commission which had been granted him for ten years. In 1607 it was renewed to him for one year, during which Pontgravé was despatched to Tadoussac, and Champlain, with a commission of Lieutenant under Demonts, sailed for the express purpose of establishing a settlement on the St. Lawrence, above Tadoussac. As he ascended the river, he carefully examined the shores, and at length fixed upon a spot near the Indian village, Stadacona, where, on the third day of July, 1608, he laid the foundation of the present city of QUEBEC, one year after the settlement of Jamestown in Virginia was

---

* Jeffery's History of French Dominions in America. Fol. 1760,

founded by Captain Newport, and one hundred and sixteen years from the discovery of America by Columbus. Huts were soon erected, a store house built, lands cleared and sown with wheat and rye, and a few gardens made, to ascertain the quality of the soil, which proved to be excellent. In these wise and prudent measures Champlain had in view not merely the interests of a petty trade, but also the establishment of a prosperous colony and extensive empire in the Western World. In a subsequent measure, however, he acted not with his usual sagacity, and brought upon the country a large train of disastrous consequences. The infant establishment soon attracted the curiosity of various tribes of Indians. The Mountaineers, who inhabited the lower part of the St. Lawrence,—the Algonquins, who occupied its shores from Quebec to Montreal,—the Hurons, whose principal residence was on Lake Huron,—and other less considerable tribes,— who were all engaged in war with the Iroquois, solicited and obtained the assistance of the French. Champlain, without reflecting upon the mischief he was introducing, not only supplied them with fire-arms, and instructed them in their use, but even joined them in their wars against the powerful Iroquois or Five Nations. In this thoughtless manner began the ruinous contests between the French settlers and the Iroquois, who soon obtained the support of the English and Dutch colonists ; and continued their predatory and cruel warfare with little intermission, notwithstanding the conciliatory efforts of the Jesuits, for nearly a century, until the final subjugation of Canada by Great Britain, in the year 1760.

Having passed the winter in his new settlement, Champlain ascended the river as early in the spring of 1609 as the weather would permit, for the purpose of exploring the interior of the country of which he had taken possession. He was both delighted and astonished with what he saw, as he advanced, of the beauty and fertility of the regions he visited: he discovered the beautiful Lake which has ever since borne his name; he returned to Quebec in the autumn; and, leaving the settlement under the command of Pierre Chauvin, he sailed for France, where he was well received by the king, who was pleased with the prospect of advantages to be expected from the new establishment. Canada was henceforth included in the general appellation of New France, which had already been given to the other French possessions in North America.

The following year, 1610, he returned to Canada, accompanied by Portgravé, who was charged with the improvement of the Fur trade, while Champlain was to attend to the general affairs of the colony. As an example of very quick sailing, in the then imperfect state of navigation, it is recorded that he performed the voyage from Harfleur in France to Tadoussac, in the singularly short space of eighteen days. In 1612 Letters of Incorporation were obtained for certain merchants of St. Malo, Rouen, and Rochelle, who had formed themselves into a company for trading to Canada. The ever vigilant Champlain not only pressed upon this Society the necessity of sending out more settlers, but stated also, in strong terms, the want of spiritual agency to instruct them in the principles of religion. By his representations four Recollets were prevailed upon to leave France for this country, and they were the first priests who settled here. He repeated his voyages to France to promote the interests of the rising colony, and in one of them brought out his family to reside with him. The Company was by no means active or efficient in seconding his efforts, either

by protecting the settlement from the attacks of the
Indians, or supplying the wants of the settlers; and
was, on account of its negligence in these essential
points, deprived of its charter, which was transferred to
two brothers of the name of De Caen.   Champlain
having erected a temporary fort on the site of the
Castle of St. Lewis, in 1621, rebuilt it of stone and
fortified it in 1624; and, as soon as it was finished,
again visited France to obtain succours.   The Duke
de Ventadour, Henry de Levi, having purchased the
Viceroyalty from his uncle the Duke de Montmorenci,
and being very desirous of converting the Indians to
the Catholic faith, sent over with Champlain three
Jesuits and two lay brothers, men of exemplary character, to accomplish this great object.   They joined
the Recollets, already at Quebec.   The Caens directed
their chief attention to the Fur trade, but being Hugue-
nots, and therefore of a different religion from the Duke,
and not likely to favour his measures, the Cardinal
Richelieu, Prime Minister of Louis XIII., revoked the
privileges that had been granted to them, and encouraged the formation of a company to be composed of a
great number of men of property and credit.   A
charter was granted to them in 1627, under the title of
" The Company of One Hundred Partners" or Associates.   The Company engaged, first, to transport
emigrants, artificers, and farmers to Canada, to the
number of sixteen thousand,—to lodge and feed them
during three years, and ultimately to locate them on
farms cleared to a certain extent, and to furnish them
with wheat for sowing; secondly, that the emigrants
should be native Frenchmen and Catholics, and that no
stranger or heretic should be introduced into the
country ; thirdly, to support three priests in each
settlement during the first fifteen years of its existence.

In return for these services the king made over to the Company the whole of New France and Florida, with power to appoint judges, build fortresses, cast cannon, confer titles, and take what steps they might think proper for the protection of the colony, and the fostering of commerce; giving them at the same time the complete monopoly of the fur trade. The Company were allowed to import and export all kinds of merchandise and other commodities, free of duty; and gentlemen, both clergy and laity, were invited to a share in the concern, which they readily accepted, till the number of partners was completed. This was a favourite scheme of Richelieu's; and Charlevoix, who describes it at length, speaks of it in terms of great applause, as calculated, had it been strictly adhered to and wisely executed, to render New France the most powerful colony of America. The combination of clergy in this new association gave it decidedly a religious character; and on this account it has been stated that the primary object of the Company was the conversion of the Indians to the Catholic faith, and the secondary an extension of the fur trade and of commerce generally, and the discovery of a passage to China.

The plan of improvement, thus determined upon, met with a temporary interruption, and was threatened with utter destruction, by the breaking out of a war between France and England in 1628, which in the following year transferred the possession of Canada from the former to the latter power. Charles I. gave to David Kertk, a French refugee, a commission authorizing and commanding him to conquer Canada, in consequence of which, after some offensive operations at Tadoussac, he appeared with his squadron before Quebec, and summoned it to surrender; but he was answered in so spirited a manner, that he judged it prudent to retire. The following year, 1629, his two brothers, Louis and Thomas, with a superior armament, were more successful, and the capital of New France, with all its dependencies, fell into the hands of the English ; but so little value did they set upon their new acquisitions that they readily restored them to France at the peace of St. Germain en Laye on the 29th of March, 1632. Champlain had been taken prisoner and conveyed to France, but he returned to Canada, and resumed his government of it, in 1633. He continued to administer the affairs of the colony with singular prudence, resolution, and courage, until 1635, when he died, after a residence of nearly thirty years, in Quebec, leaving behind him a name highly honoured and respected by all parties. The French historians represent him as a man of superior talents, and of upright intentions ; active, enterprising, and vigilant ; and cherishing so warm a zeal for the propagation of religion, that it was a common saying with him,—" that the salvation of one soul was of more value than the conquest of an empire."

With all the advantages, however, which France enjoyed for colonization, under the direction of so wise a man, so tardy was the progress of her affairs in this quarter of the world, that at the period of which we are writing, the whole of her available possessions in Canada consisted of the fort of Quebec, surrounded by some inconsiderable houses, and barracks for the soldiers, a few huts on the Island of Montreal, as many at Tadoussac, and at other places on the St. Lawrence used as trading and fishing posts, and a settlement, just commenced, at Three Rivers.

CHAPTER III.

SETTLEMENT OF THE ISLAND OF MONTREAL—MAI-
SONNEUVE, GOVERNOR—CANADA BECOMES A ROYAL
GOVERNMENT—REMARKABLE EARTHQUAKE—WEST
INDIA COMPANY.

IT has been stated, in the preceding Chapter, that
several Priests from France had arrived, and were
settled at Quebec, for the purpose of propagating the
Roman Catholic religion among the Indians in the
colony; and though several of them returned to their
native land on the cession of the country to the English,
they came back to Canada when the French had
regained possession of it, for the purpose of resuming
their labours. By these first missionaries it was soon
perceived that the occupation and defence of the Island
of Montreal, was an object of the greatest importance,
rendered indeed imperative, if they wished to retain
their authority in the Island, by the wars of the
Iroquois; but the Company were unwilling to second
their views in this respect. It fell, therefore, to the lot
of private individuals to accomplish this design. Several
persons in France, powerful from their connections and
full of religious zeal, formed themselves into a Society
consisting of thirty-five members, for the purpose of
colonizing the Island. It was proposed that a French

village should be established, and be well fortified to resist a sudden irruption of the natives ; that the poorer class of emigrants should there find an asylum and employment, and the rest of the Island be occupied by such friendly tribes of Indians as had embraced Christianity, or wished to receive religious instruction ; and it was hoped that in time the sons of the forest might become accustomed to civilized life, and subsist by cultivating the earth. The greater part of the Island had been granted to Messrs. Charrier and Le Royer ; but whether disposed of by them, or forfeited, to the Crown does not appear from any official record that has been preserved.* The king, however, ceded the whole of it, in 1640, to the association, who took formal possession of it at the conclusion of a grand mass which was celebrated on the occasion in a tent. The following year M. de Maisonneuve, one of the associates, brought out several families from France, and was appointed Governor of the Island. On the 17th of May, 1642, the spot destined for the city was consecrated by the Superior of the Jesuits, who also dedicated a small chapel, hastily constructed, in which he deposited the host. This ceremony had been preceded, three months before, by a similar one in Paris, where all the associates went together to the church of Notre Dame ; those of them who were priests officiated, and all of them supplicated the " Queen of Angels" to take the Island under her protection. The ceremony, at Montreal, was celebrated on the 15th of August, the day observed by the Romish Church in honour of the Assumption of the Virgin Mary ; a great number both of French and Indians were present, and nothing was omitted which it was supposed would give to the natives a lofty idea of the Christian religion. Thus, "a few houses," as Bouchette observes, "built close together in the year 1640, on the site of the Indian village of Hochelaga, was the commencement of the city of Montreal, or, as it was first named, Ville Marie."

On the evening of this memorable day, Maisonneuve visited the Mountain. Two old Indians who accompanied him, having conducted him to the summit, told him that they belonged to the nation which had formerly occupied the country he beheld. "We were," said they, "a numerous people, and all the hills which you see to the East and to the South were peopled by us. The Hurons drove from thence our ancestors, some of whom took refuge with the Abenaquis, some with the Iroquois, and some remained with their conquerors." The Governor urged the old men to invite their brethren to return to their hunting grounds, assuring them that they should want for nothing, and that he would protect them from every attack of their enemies. They promised to do so; but it does not appear that they were successful. This incident, in conjunction with the prospect before and around him, might well awaken feelings of no ordinary interest in the bosom of the Governor. The unbounded tract that opened itself to his view, discovered to him dark, thick, and deep forests, whose height alone was a proof of their antiquity. Numberless large rivers came down from a considerable distance to water these immense regions. Every thing in this rude part of the New World appeared grand and sublime. Nature here displayed such luxuriancy and majesty as commanded veneration; and a thousand wild graces far more striking than the artificial beauties of European climates.

In the year 1644, the whole of this beautiful domain became the property of the St. Sulpicians at Paris, and

c 3

was by them afterwards conveyed to the Seminary of
the same order at Montreal, in whose possession it still
remains.

The circumstances attending the foundation of the
new settlement were thus far encouraging ; and notwithstanding its exposure on all sides to the inroads of
the bold, crafty, and revengeful Iroquois, it daily
improved in commerce and magnitude ; and many years
elapsed before any serious thoughts were entertained of
fortifying it.   The European inhabitants were so
accustomed to place confidence in their own bravery
and military skill, that it was difficult for them to be
convinced of the necessity of enclosing the town with a
strong and durable defence ; and their comparative
poverty rendered them less able to erect a fortification
than to display their courage in the field.   The Iroquois,
perceiving the defenceless state of the place, and, above
all, envious of its growing importance, renewed their
attacks with increasing vigour and frequency ; so that
the new inhabitants of Montreal were at last persuaded
of the necessity of guarding themselves against the
often meditated surprises of their enemies.   An order
to enclose the town was therefore given by the Chevalier de Calliers, brother to the celebrated statesman of
Ryswick.   At first, and for nearly forty years
afterwards, this barrier consisted of only slight palisades
surmounted by a bastion, and a defective redoubt built
on a little hill in the centre of the town, which served
as a bulwark, and which was terminated by a small
square.   But so simple a defence, not promising to the
town and its inhabitants that security which was so
essential to their prosperity and happiness, it was
afterwards encompassed with the more powerful safeguard of a wall of masonry, not very substantial,
however, but only sufficient to overawe the numerous

tribes of Indians whose jealous attention had been drawn towards the place, or to guard against any sudden attack which they might be disposed to make upon it. This wall was fifteen feet high, with battlements; having six or seven gates, large and small. Being thus enclosed and defended, the inhabitants soon began to pursue their different avocations with a spirit, a confidence, and an alacrity which excited sanguine expectations of the future prosperity of the settlement. Nor were these expectations disappointed. The fur trade was the first which the Europeans carried on in Canada. It was begun and regularly established at the French colony at Tadoussac, a port situated thirty leagues below Quebec. The town of Three Rivers became a second mart for this traffic; but in process of time the fur trade centered almost entirely in Montreal, to which place almost all the inhabitants carried their furs, and exchanged them for European merchandise. The skins were brought in canoes, which began their movements in June each year. The number of Indians who resorted to the city increased, as the reports of those who visited it extended the knowledge of what was doing there. The account of the reception they had met with, the sight of the things they had received in exchange for their goods, all contributed to increase this traffic; so that whenever they returned with a fresh supply of furs, a new nation or tribe generally came with them. Thus, by degrees, a kind of fair was opened, to which the several tribes of the continent resorted. The fair was held annually from the beginning of June till the latter end of August. Many solemnities were observed, at which the Governor assisted, and guards were placed to preserve good order among such a concourse of different savage nations, all of whom were extremely fond of spirituous liquors, and

when intoxicated committed great excesses. Whatever
benefits, in the way of trade, these natives of the woods
derived from their connection with Montreal, the
introduction of the use of ardent spirits among them is
an evil which they have had abundant reason to deplore.

In a journal kept by the Jesuits, of the affairs of the
colony, there is an account of the price of commodities,
which affords some points of comparison that may be
interesting to the reader. It is stated that wood for
fuel was this year, 1647, publicly sold: the price was
one shilling and three pence, Halifax currency, per cord.
The price of bread was fixed at seven pence halfpenny
for a loaf of six pounds weight. The price of labour
was one shilling and three pence per day, exclusive of
board and lodging. A servant's wages were, by the
year, four pounds three shillings and four pence, and a
pair of shoes. Eels were sold in the market for one
farthing per hundred: 40,000 had been taken that year
from August to November.

While the French settlements were improving in
Canada, those of England on the eastern shores of
America were also making progress; and a union
seemed desirable to prevent that rivalry, or moderate
the effects of it, which is almost sure to take place
between nations so contiguously situated and engaged in
a similar pursuit. The French Governor, M. de
D'Aillebout, in 1648, proposed to the New England
colonies an alliance between them and the French, one
object of which was an engagement to assist each other,
when necessary, in making war against the Five
Nations. However desirable the English colonies might
have been, on other accounts, to form such an alliance,
the condition respecting the Indians was not acceptable
to them, and the negotiation was broken off. Of what
effects this union, had it taken place, would have been

productive, it is impossible to conjecture ; but it is evident that the failure of the proposition must have had an important bearing upon the events which followed, first in the continued rivalry of the two nations, then in the frequent wars between them, and lastly in the subjugation of the whole country to the power of Britain.

The prosperity of the City and Island of Montreal continued to increase. As early as the year 1657, a large part of this property, even at that period valuable, was cleared and settled, under the direction of the Abbe Quetus, who had arrived from France, with authority from the Seminary in Paris for that and other purposes essentially connected with the welfare of the Province. Among other important services, he founded the Seminary of St. Sulpice at Montreal for the conversion of the Indians, and for promoting the settlement of the whole domain. As soon as the members of the order residing here had taken possession of their property, they forwarded the design of establishing a hospital for the sick, in which they were assisted by munificent donations from several persons in France. In 1662, the Seminary was enlarged by further endowments, for the purpose of providing a sufficient number of young men for the priesthood, and of supplying the new parishes with cures.

The Company of One Hundred Partners, though attentive to their own interests in rigidly guarding their monopoly and all its exclusive privileges, had been all along regardless of the general welfare of the colony. Applications to them in favour of public improvements were, for the most part, treated with neglect. At length, in 1663, the proceedings of the Company had become so obnoxious, that the king of France, Louis XIV., under the direction of the great Colbert, then his

Prime Minister, decided upon the immediate resumption of his rights, and erected Canada into a Royal government, with civil authority and jurisdiction, according to the laws and usages of the Mother Country. This change from an ecclesiastical mission to a temporal government was followed by the happiest effects in the civil regulation and military protection of the colony, and in the rapid extension of agriculture and commerce.

This was an eventful year to Canada. In the early part of it an earthquake, attended with some extraordinary circumstances, is recorded to have happened here. Some of the accounts, indeed, are presented in a manner so exaggerated, as to give it the appearance of a supernatural phenomenon, and have naturally induced some persons to doubt the truth of the narration. The following description, though sufficiently singular and striking, is far less extravagant than some others yet extant. It is taken from a manuscript in the Jesuits' College at Quebec.

" On the fifth of February, 1663, about half past five o'clock in the evening, a great rushing noise was heard throughout the whole extent of Canada. This noise caused the people to run out of their houses into the streets, as if their habitations had been on fire; but instead of flames or smoke, they were surprised to see the walls reeling backwards and forwards, and the stones moving, as if they were detached from each other. The bells sounded by the repeated shocks. The roofs of the buildings bent down, first on one side and then on the other. The timbers, rafters, and planks, cracked. The earth trembled violently, and caused the stakes of the palisades and palings to dance, in a manner that would have been incredible had we not actually seen it in many places. It was at this moment every one ran out of doors. Then were to be seen animals flying in every direction, children crying and screaming in the streets; men and women, seized with affright, stood horror-struck with the dreadful scene before them, unable to move, and ignorant where to fly for refuge from the tottering walls and trembling earth, which threatened every instant to crush them to death, or sink them into a profound and unmeasurable abyss. Some threw themselves on their knees in the snow, crossing their breasts and calling on their saints to relieve them from the dangers with which they were surrounded. Others passed the rest of this dreadful night in prayer; for the earthquake ceased not, but continued at short intervals, with a certain undulating impulse, resembling the waves of the ocean; and the same qualmish sensations, or sickness at the stomach, was felt during the shocks, as is experienced in a vessel at sea.

" The violence of the earthquake was greatest in the forests, where it appeared as if there was a battle raging between the trees; for not only their branches were destroyed, but even their trunks are said to have been detached from their places, and dashed against each other with inconceivable violence and confusion—so much so, that the Indians, in their figurative manner of speaking, declared that all the forests were drunk. The war also seemed to be carried on between the mountains, some of which were torn from their beds and thrown upon others, leaving immense chasms in the places from whence they had issued, and the very trees with which they were covered sunk down, leaving only their tops above the surface of the earth; others were completely overturned, their branches buried in the earth, and the roots only remained above ground. During this general wreck of nature, the ice, upwards of six feet thick, was rent and thrown up in large pieces, and from the openings, in many parts, there issued thick clouds of smoke, or fountains of dirt and sand, which spouted up to a very considerable height. The springs were either choked up, or impregnated with sulphur—many rivers were totally lost; others were diverted from their course, and their waters entirely corrupted. Some of them became yellow, others red, and the great river of St. Lawrence appeared entirely white, as far down as Tadoussac. This extraordinary phenomenon must astonish those who know the size of the river, and the immense body of water in various parts, which must have required such an abundance of matter to whiten it. They write from Montreal, that, during the earthquake, they plainly saw the stakes of the picketing or palisades jump up as if they had been dancing; and that of two doors in the same room, one opened and the other shut of their own accord; that the chimneys and tops of the houses bent like branches of trees agitated with the wind; that when they went to walk, they felt the earth following them, and rising at every step they took, sometimes sticking against the soles of their feet and other things in a very forcible and surprising manner.

" From Three Rivers they write, that the first shock was the most violent, and commenced with a noise resembling thunder. The houses were agitated in the same manner as the tops of trees during a tempest, with a noise as if fire was crackling in the garrets. The shock lasted half an hour, or rather better, though its greatest force was properly not more than a quarter of an hour; and we believe there was not a single shock which did not cause the earth to open either more or less.

" As for the rest, we have remarked that, though this earthquake continued almost without intermission, yet it was not always of an equal violence. Sometimes it was like the pitching of a large vessel which dragged heavily at her anchors; and it was this motion which occasioned many to have a giddiness in their heads, and qualmishness at their stomachs. At other times the motion was hurried and irregular, creating sudden jerks, some of which were extremely violent; but the most common was a slight tremulous motion, which occurred frequently with little noise. Many of the French inhabitants and Indians, who were eye-witnesses to the scene, state that a great way up the river of Trois Rivieres, about eighteen miles below Quebec, the hills which bordered the river on either side, and which were of a prodigious height, were torn from their foundations, and plunged into the river, causing it to change its course, and spread itself over a large tract of land recently cleared; the broken earth mixed with the waters, and for several months changed the colour of the great river St. Lawrence, into which that of Trois Rivieres disembogues itself. In the course of this violent convulsion of nature, lakes appeared where none ever existed before: mountains were overthrown, swallowed up by the gaping, or precipitated into adjacent rivers, leaving in their places frightful chasms or level plains; falls and rapids were changed into gentle streams, and gentle streams into falls and rapids. Rivers in many parts of the country sought other beds, or totally disappeared. The earth and the mountains were entirely split and rent in innumerable places, creating chasms and precipices whose depths have never yet been ascertained. Such devastation was also occasioned in the woods, that more than a thousand acres in our neighbourhood were completely overturned; and where but a short time before nothing met the eye but one immense forest of trees, now were to be seen extensive cleared lands, apparently cut up by the plough.

" At Tadoussac (about 150 miles below Quebec on the north side) the effect of the earthquake was not less violent than in other places ; and such a heavy shower of volcanic ashes fell in that neighbourhood, particularly in the river St. Lawrence, that the waters were as violently agitated as during a tempest.   Near St. Paül's bay (about 50 miles below Quebec on the north side), a mountain about a quarter of a league in circumference, situated on the shore of the St. Lawrence, was precipitated into the river, but, as if it had only made a plunge, it rose from the bottom and became a small island, forming with the shore a convenient harbour, well sheltered from all winds.   Lower down the river, towards Point Alouettes, an entire forest of considerable extent was loosened from the main bank, and slid into the river St. Lawrence, where the trees took fresh root.

" There are three circumstances, however, which have rendered this extraordinary earthquake particularly remarkable : the first is its duration, it having continued from February to August, that is to say, more than six months almost without intermission !   It is true, the shocks were not always equally violent.   In several places, as towards the mountains behind Quebec, the thundering noise and trembling motion continued successively for a considerable time.   In others, as towards Tadoussac, the shock continued generally for two or three days at a time with much violence.

" The second circumstance relates to the extent of this earthquake, which we believe was universal throughout the whole of New France, for we learn that it was felt from L'Isle Persée and Gaspé, which are situated at the mouth of the St. Lawrence, to beyond Montreal, as also in New England, Acadia, and other places more remote. As far as it has come to our knowledge, this earthquake extended more than 600 miles in length, and about 300 in breadth. Hence 180,000 square miles of land were convulsed in the same day, and at the same moment.

" The third circumstance, which appears the most remarkable of all, regards the extraordinary protection of Divine Providence which has been extended to us and our habitations; for we have seen near us the large openings and chasms which the earthquake occasioned, and the prodigious extent of country which has either been totally lost or hideously convulsed, without our losing either man, woman, or child, or even having a hair of their heads touched."*

Perhaps to the majority of readers the most singular part of this account may appear to be the unusual length of time during which the earthquake, with occasional interruptions, continued. Upon the whole, however, as here stated, it is not more incredible than many facts upon record in the history of the world, which, resting upon testimony not more complete, have been admitted without hesitation. Besides, there are geological phenomena, and appearances in the physical aspect of the country, which render it probable that such events have actually occurred.

The affairs of the colony were, for a time, embar-rassed, and its prosperity checked, by its union, in 1664, to the other territories of the French West India Company, which thus became possessed of Canada, Acadia, and Newfoundland, conceded to them *en Seigneurie*, to be governed by the laws and ordinances

---

* See Montgomery Martin's *History of the British Colonies*, Vol. III. pa. 9: a very valuable and instructive work, recently published in five large volumes, 8vo., full of interesting details respecting the British Colonial possessions in every part of the world.

of the empire. The Company held this territory for
ten years, when, finding themselves unable to manage
the complicated objects of their charter, they resigned it
to the Crown. In the interim, however, some improvements were effected; for the Indians having made
peace with the French in 1668, the inhabitants began
to extend their settlements and cultivate their new,
lands. The officers and soldiers employed in the
preceding wars had grants of land made to them : to
the former were given Seigniories, according to their
rank; and this will account for the French names
which they bear to this day. A free trade had also
been granted; and from all these favourable circumstances arose a great increase to the prosperity of the
colony. The number of men, however, greatly exceeded that of the women; and the government took
a method to supply the deficiency, at which some of
our readers will smile. Several hundred females were
sent from France to Canada; and on their arrival, an
advertisement was published to let the people of the
country know that a supply had been sent over, and
that " such as had the means of supporting a wife
should have their choice. The collection consisted of
tall, short, fair, brown, fat, and lean. The notification
had been made but a few days, when so great was the
demand, that in less than fifteen days the whole of the
females were disposed of. As soon as the marriage
ceremony had taken place, the Governor General
distributed oxen, cows, hogs, fowls, salted beef, and
some money, to the married people."* In order still
further to encourage the settlement of the colony, and
to promote marriage among the people, the king of
France proposed certain bounties to be paid. On the

* Smith's History of Canada, vol, I. page 55.

marriage of males of the age of twenty and under, and females of the age of sixteen and under, the king ordered a present of twenty-five livres in each case ; and a pension of three hundred livres to be annually paid to parents having ten children born in wedlock, and four hundred livres to such as had twelve. To the same end, His Majesty directed that a pecuniary fine should be imposed upon such parents as did not marry their children before the ages above mentioned.*

* Ib. vol. I. page 59.

CHAPTER IV.

GOVERNMENT SETTLED—CONTESTS BETWEEN THE
FRENCH AND ENGLISH—PERFIDY OF LE RAT.

As on the final resumption of the government of
Canada, by the Crown of France, a Governor, Council,
and Judges were established on a more permanent and
effectual plan than heretofore, by the appointment and
authority of the king himself, the affairs of the colony
thence assumed a national character, and must be
treated more in connection with political parties and
events. The progress of colonization on the eastern
shores of the continent, especially in New England and
New York, naturally produced a collision in matters of
trade, and not seldom occasioned political jealousy
between the two powers most intimately concerned in
them. The province of New York originally belonged
to the Dutch, from whom it had received the names of
New Holland and New Belgia. The English having
acquired possession of it in 1664, were desirous of
turning their acquisition to the best account, and with
this view they sought and obtained by degrees a large
portion of the fur trade. Many of the Indians brought
their skins to New York, where they sold at a higher
price than in the French colony; and the English,

either afraid of the encroachments of the French, or desirous of extending their own territories, or more probably influenced by both these considerations, sought every opportunity of gaining the alliance of the Indians. After many attempts, and frequent disappointments and changes, they at length succeeded in gaining the Iroquois or Five Nations to their interest. These restless and turbulent tribes were often made serviceable to the interests of the English, whom they assisted in repressing the incursions of the French, who had often shown a desire to weaken or expel them as rivals, and in extending their commerce. Between the English and the French colonies, contiguously situated as they were upon the same continent, and whose parent-states were often at war, it was inevitable that occasions of discord should arise, and that more active hostilities should often take place. During these contentions, prolonged through the greater part of a century, many deeds of valour were performed, many sufferings were endured, many cruelties were committed, and many incidents occurred, which, in an extended history of Canada, would require to be narrated at length, but which, in a topographical work like that now before the reader, can only be occasionally alluded to or described, as they bear upon the subject immediately in view. As the French settlement increased in extent and rose in power, it assumed offensive operations on the New England frontier. The jealousy of the British colonists was roused, and both parties, aided alternately or partially by the Indians, carried on a destructive and harassing border warfare. In 1674 the whole French population, including converted Indians, did not exceed eight thousand; but, by the aid of their native allies, whom they were more expert in conciliating, they for many years maintained their position, and even gained

upon their less skilful but persevering neighbours.
The Hurons and other powerful tribes on this side the
St. Lawrence were generally in alliance with the
Canadians, as the French settlers now began to be
called, and were often persuaded to take a part in their
martial operations, whether offensive or defensive ; but
sometimes they suffered from the jealousy or the
treachery of these untamed and irregular allies, of
which the- following is an instance. The French had
often made attacks upon the Iroquois, as allies of the
English, and were in their turn often annoyed by them.
At length, both parties desired peace, and a treaty was
set on foot for this purpose, when an extraordinary
character appeared among the Indians of the Huron
tribe, possessing talents of no common order, and
equally distinguished for cunning and perfidy. His
name was Kondearouk, but was more familiarly known
in the history of those times by the title of Le Rat.
As chief of the Michillimakinac Hurons, he was dis-
pleased that the French Governor-General, Denonville,
should attempt to make peace with the Iroquois without
consulting the Hurons his allies, and therefore determined to put an end to the negotiation. With this view
he marched with a chosen band towards Cataracuoy,
now Kingston, where he learned that the Governor-
General was waiting at Montreal for the ambassadors
and hostages to conclude the treaty, and was told that
it was the desire of the French that they might pass
unmolested. Disregarding this wish, he lay in ambush
for them, killed some of them, and made others prisoners.
When charged with having violated good faith, by
taking captive an ambassador, he affected surprise, and
pretended that the French had authorized him to do so.
Then releasing all his prisoners, except one whom he
kept, as he feigned, in lieu of one of his men who had

been killed, he proceeded with his prisoner to Michilli-makinac, where he so represented matters as to induce the French commandant to put the unhappy man to death. His next step was to set at liberty an old Iroquois, who had been some time a prisoner at that place, enjoining him to return to his own countrymen, and acquaint them that while the French were amusing the natives with sham negotiations, they were daily putting them to death. This master-piece of dissimu-lation had the desired effect, by furnishing the Iroquois with a plausible pretext for breaking off the treaty. Not satisfied with this result of his treachery, Le Rat urged his countrymen, and even stimulated the Iroquois to aid him in an attack upon Montreal: the colonists were taken by surprise, a thousand of them slain, and the houses, crops, and cattle on the Island destroyed.

Such exercises of severity were not, however, in those turbulent times, confined to the people *called* " savages," but were occasionally resorted to even by the more civilized inhabitants of Canada. The French, having received reinforcements from Europe, sent a strong force in February, 1690, to Schenectaday, who massacred the greater part of the Indians residing there; and are said to have perpetuated such cruelties upon those whom they took prisoners, as one is very unwilling to believe.* This massacre had the effect of inducing the Iroquois and other nations to become more closely attached to the English; and the French were compelled to act on the defensive, and keep within their own territory. They had, however, erected several forts on the St. Lawrence, and in other parts; and given various indications of a hostile design; and the English at Albany were at first so much alarmed, that

* Colden, page 78, quoted in Martin, III. 18.

they prepared to abandon the country. At this crisis the New England colonies came to a mutual understanding, and formed a coalition for their self defence. Commissioners were sent to New York, and a mission to London, explaining their views, and soliciting aid. An expedition against Canada was accordingly undertaken in 1690, under Sir W. Phipps; and Quebec was attacked both by land and sea, but not at the same time. The attempt was unsuccessful, the assailants being defeated by the Sieur de Frontenac, and compelled to retreat to Boston. Encouraged by this success Frontenac adopted the aggressive policy, and endeavoured, by means of the fur-traders and his own forces, to extend the dominion of France. He even meditated the conquest of New York; but the peace of Ryswick, in 1697, put a stop, for a short period, to the ravages of war.

The parent states having recommenced hostilities in 1702, America became again the scene of contest. Frontenac died in 1689, and was succeeded by the Marquis de Vaudreuil, who, in 1708, carried his operations into the British frontier settlements, having persuaded the Iroquois to neutrality. The New Englanders prepared to attack Montreal, but the withdrawment of some troops into Europe induced them to desist from their purpose. The English, in 1709, reduced Acadia, now Nova Scotia. The peace of Utrecht took place in 1703, and Vandreuil availed himself of it to strengthen the fortifications of Quebec and Montreal. The population of the former city, in 1720, was 7,000, and that of Montreal 3,000. Ten years of peace very much improved the trade and resources of Canada: nineteen vessels cleared from Quebec in 1723, and six merchant ships and two men of war were built in the colony during this period.

Vaudreuil died in October, 1725, and was succeeded the following year by the Marquis de Beauharnois, a natural son of Louis XIV. He was able and ambitious; and increased the jealousy of the English colonists against France. The war in 1745 led to the reduction of Cape Breton. At the treaty of Aix la Chapelle in 1748, commissioners were appointed to settle a boundary line between the British and French territories in North America; but the Canadian government acted so arrogantly in this business, that the Indians, being also alarmed, united more vigorously with the English for the utter expulsion of French authority from this Continent.

In 1752 the Marquis du Quesne de Menneville arrived as Governor of Canada. To restrain the British he built a fort on the Ohio, called after his own name; and in the vicinity of it the British erected another which they called Necessity, and placed under the command of the afterwards celebrated Washington. Meantime hostilities commenced between the two powers, in Europe; and troops were sent from France to reinforce Quebec. Du Quesne resigned his government in 1755, and was succeeded by the Marquis de Vaudreuil de Cavagnal, the last French Governor in Canada. He defeated General Braddock in one of the defiles of the Alleghany Mountains. Washington, on whom the command devolved on the death of the General, succeeded in rescuing the remainder of the British army, who were afterwards joined by 6,000 provincials under Johnson and Shirley. This and the two following years the French arms continued to be successful. Fort St. George yielded to their attack, and the English prisoners, amounting to nearly 2,000, were brutally massacred on their march to Fort Edward, by the Indian allies of the French. This monstrous

deed excited the strongest feeling both in England, and
through British America, and contributed to hasten the
downfal of the French dominion in Canada.

CHAPTER V.

THE year 1759 is, and ever will be, memorable in the annals of this Colony. The French, perceiving that the English were in earnest in their designs upon Canada, sent strong reinforcements to their garrisons. The campaign opened with great vigour. Canada was to be invaded at three different points under Generals of high talent. The forces intended to act against Quebec were under the command of the heroic General Wolfe, who had taken Fort Louisburg and subdued the Island of Cape Breton the preceding year. Wolfe's army, amounting to about 8000 men, was conveyed to the vicinity of Quebec by a fleet of vessels of war and transports commanded by Admiral Saunders, and landed in two divisions on the Isle of Orleans the 27th of June. The French commander, Montcalm, made vigorous preparations for defence. He arranged his army of about 12,000 men, between the river of St. Charles and the Falls of Montmorenci, to oppose the landing of the British forces, which, in their attack upon his entrenchments, were repulsed. Wolfe at first doubted from this failure whether any thing could be

E 1

effected in the present season ; but afterwards, rousing
his brave and ardent spirit, and calling a council of war,
he resolved upon the bold and hazardous enterprise of
ascending the heights of Abraham, and attacking the
city in that direction.   The plan was executed with
admirable skill and determination.   The result is well
known : the chiefs on both sides fell, and left behind
them honourable names.   Wolfe died on the field of
battle, in the arms of victory; and Montcalm in the
city, to which he had been carried, thankful that he
should not live to see the surrender of the place.   The
battle on the Plains of Abraham was fought on the
13th of September, 1759; and five days afterwards, on
the 18th, Quebec surrendered to the British arms.
The details of this memorable exploit belong to the
history of that city,* but the glory of it will remain to
distant ages, and every Briton especially, on looking
back to the Ministry which projected and the General
who achieved it, will reflect with delight

> " That CHATHAM'S language was his mother tongue,
> And WOLFE'S great name compatriot with his own."

   In the following spring the French army which had
been collected in the neighbourhood of Montreal, under
the command of the Chevalier de Levi, marched to
Quebec for the purpose of attacking and regaining it ;
but without success.   A reinforcement from England
arrived just in time to save the city ; and de Levi broke
up his camp, and retired with precipitation towards
Montreal.   Vaudreuil, the Governor, finding the whole
of the Canadas in danger, determined to take his last
stand on behalf of French dominion, in this city ; and

---

* The principal of these events are given with lively interest and effect, by
the competent pen of Dr. Fisher, in Hawkins' *Picture of Quebec.*

hither he called in all his detachments, and concentrated his remaining strength. He enlarged the fortifications for the defence of the town, and converted sloops into armed vessels. Meantime General Murray, with as many troops as could be spared from Quebec, advanced towards the point of attack, notwithstanding the obstructions which the enemy threw in the way of his progress up the river; and General Amherst with the army from Oswego, approached in an opposite direction: both armies took post near the city on the same day, September 6, 1760. Colonel Haviland, with a strong detachment, lay on the south shore of the St. Lawrence, opposite to Montreal. ' Vaudreuil, perceiving that defence was hopeless, on the morning of the 7th proposed terms of capitulation; and on the 8th, the city surrendered, and was taken possession of by the British troops in the name of his Britannic Majesty. A few days afterwards, the French troops were sent down to Quebec, and thence to France, not to serve again during the war. Thus was the last, decisive act in the conquest of Canada performed without firing a gun, or shedding blood.

The terms on which the city was surrendered to the British were expressed in fifty-five articles, of which the most important were the following: That immediately after signing the capitulation, the English troops should take possession of the gates of Montreal; that the French should lay down their arms, and not serve during the war, but should go out by the gate of Quebec with all the honours of war; that the militia should return to their homes without being molested; that the Marquis Vaudreuil should not be obliged to leave the city before a certain day, and no person to lodge in his house till he left it; that the most convenient vessel that could be found should be appointed to carry the

Marquis to France; that two ships should carry the
Chevalier de Levi, the principal officers, &c., provided
the officers should faithfully deliver up all the charts
and plans of the country ; that the free exercise of the
Catholic and Roman Religion shall remain entire ; that
the Chapter, Priests, Curates, and Missionaries should
retain a perfect liberty to exercise the functions of their
curés, in the parishes of the towns and countries ; that
the communities of Nuns should be preserved in their
constitution and privileges, should continue to observe
their rules, be exempted from lodging any military, and
not be interrupted in their religious exercises, for which
purpose safeguards should be given them, if desired ; that
all the communities and all the priests should preserve
their moveables, the property and revenues of the seigniories, and all other estates which they possessed in the
Colony, of what nature soever they might be, and the
same estates should be preserved in their privileges,
rights, honours and exemptions ; that all classes should
preserve the entire peaceable property and possession of
their goods, moveable and immoveable, merchandizes,
furs, and other effects ; that the archives of the Supreme
Council of Quebec, and of the whole royal jurisdiction
of the country, should remain in the Colony ; and that
care should be taken that none of the Indians should
insult any of the subjects of the French King.

The form of taking possession was as follows. The
capitulation having been signed at break of day, the
troops marched into the town in the following order—
1st. A twelve pounder, with a flag, and a detachment
of the Royal Artillery, commanded by Colonel Haldi-
man ; 2. Grenadiers of the line, by Colonel Massey ;
3. Light Infantry, by Colonel Amherst ; each party
preceded by a band of music. The eldest Ensign in
General Amherst's army attended to receive the colours

of the French regiments. Having thus obtained peaceable possession of this important city, and brought the war in Canada to a happy termination, the General on the next day, the 9th of September, issued the following General Orders, which, as they formed the first public document promulgated in the name of Great Britain over her newly acquired territories, cannot fail to be perused with interest, and are worthy of being preserved in a sketch of Canadian history :—

" Camp before MONTREAL, September 9, 1760.
Parole,—King GEORGE,—and CANADA.
The General sees, with infinite pleasure, the success that has crowned the indefatigable efforts of His Majesty's troops and faithful subjects in America. The Marquis de Vaudreuil has capitulated ; the troops of France in Canada have laid down their arms, and are not to serve during the war ; the whole country submits to the dominion of Great Britain. The three armies are entitled to the General's thanks on this occasion ; and he assures them that he will take the opportunity of acquainting His Majesty with the zeal and bravery which has always been exerted by the officers and soldiers of the regulars and provincial troops, and also by his faithful Indian allies. The General is confident, that when the troops are informed that the country is the King's, they will not disgrace themselves by the least appearance of inhumanity, or by unsoldier-like behaviour, in taking any plunder, more especially as the Canadians become now good subjects, and will feel the good effect of His Majesty's protection."

On a review of this expedition, which brought such an immense accession of territory and of power to

Britain, it is singularly delightful to reflect upon the
comparatively slight effusion of blood and destruction of
life which attended its progress. Montreal, the last
important post, we have seen surrendered without a
blow. The humanity with which General Amherst
treated the conquered, both French and Indians, added
a high lustre to his conquest; and Sir William Johnson
deserves to be spoken of in terms of equal commendation,
with reference to the scenes in which he was engaged.

At the time of its surrender, Montreal was well
peopled : it was of an oblong form, surrounded by a wall,
flanked with eleven redoubts which served instead of
bastions. The ditch was about eight feet deep, and of a
proportionable breadth, but dry; it had also a fort or
citadel, the batteries of which commanded the streets
of the town from one end to the other. The plan of
the city, as it existed in 1758, while in possession of the
French, and which we have copied and reduced from one
published at the time, will shew these particulars very
distinctly. It should be recollected, however, that
Vaudreuil made some additions to the fortification in
the prospect of an attack by the British forces. The
town itself was divided into two parts, the upper and
the lower. In the lower, the merchants and men of
business generally resided; and here also were the place
of arms, the royal magazines, and the Nunnery
Hospital. The principal buildings, however, were in
the Upper Town, such as the palace of the Governor,
the houses of the chief officers, the Convent of the
Recollets, the Jesuits' Church and Seminary, the Free
School, and the Parish Church. The Recollets were
numerous, and their buildings spacious. The house of
the Jesuits was magnificent, and their church well-built,
though their seminary was but small. Several private
houses in Montreal, even at this time, made a noble

appearance, and the Governor's palace was a large fine building. The neighbourhood of the city contained many elegant villas ; and all the known vegetables of Europe were cultivated in the gardens attached to them.

By the terms of capitulation, which, under all the circumstances, were favourable to the conquered, not only the city and Island of Montreal, but the whole of the French possessions on the North American continent were surrendered to the British crown. The war between the two nations continued till the year 1763, when, by the treaty of peace concluded at Paris on the 10th of February, all these territories were formally ceded to Great Britain, much to the immediate benefit of the French inhabitants, and the improvement of the Colony at large.

While the negotiations, which issued in this treaty, were pending, an instance of malignant sagacity, which deserves to be recorded here, was displayed by the French minister, the Duké de Choiseul. The idea of relinquishing Canada was by no means palatable to the body of the people. The discontent at length rose to such a height that it reached the throne ; and the political opponents of the Duke in the cabinet did not fail to press it upon the Royal attention. The King sent for his Minister to remonstrate with him on the subject. The wily statesman, who looked far below the surface, and well understood the principles of human action, addressed his Majesty to the following effect :—

" We have now, Sire, but the one province of Canada* on the whole continent of America ; and the charge of maintaining it against such powerful neighbours as the English will not only exceed its value to us, but will

* The term was then used in a more extended sense than it is now.

open a door of perpetual hostility with England; whereas, ceding it at once to his Britannic Majesty will prevent these inconveniences, and find constant employment for the British nation. For, give me leave to tell you, Sire, that if the English ministry had as much wisdom as they ought to have, they would almost pay your Majesty a subsidy to retain it. Their colonies are now all flourishing, and will speedily be all insolent. They want the protection of the Mother Country no longer than while Canada is ours. They have for several years manifested a strong inclination for independence, and will assert that independence the moment a foreign enemy is removed from their back. The provinces, particularly of New England, cherish a deep abhorrence to Monarchial government. My advice, therefore, Sire, most humbly is, that the English mastiffs may have full liberty to worry one another. So long as Canada belongs to your Majesty, so long the British colonies will be dutiful to their Sovereign, because they will stand in need of his protection. But remove the want of that protection, and you remove their obedience instantly; from powerful friends, you turn them into most formidable enemies, of England, and rescue all Europe from the dictation of that power." The counsel was taken; and how far the main part of the prediction has been verified, need not here be told.

The interval between the capture ot Montreal, and the formal surrender of all the French possessions in America to the British crown, was employed by General Amherst in securing his conquests, and improving the condition of the inhabitants. He established a military government for the preservation of tranquillity, and divided the country into three districts,—Quebec, Three Rivers, and Montreal, placing General Gage at the head of the last. Within these districts he established several courts of justice, which were approved by the King, and remained in force till peace was restored and civil government established. If ever there was a people that had reason to rejoice in a change of masters, the French Canadians were that people. The conquest was a blessing to them. Under their former rulers— or rather owners, for they were despotically governed— they suffered much and enjoyed little. Peculation and fraud in the revenue enriched the few at the expense of the many. The feudal law was oppressive and degrading ; the criminal code was vague in its provisions, and capricious in its administration. Under the English Government some of these evils were at once removed or mitigated ; and the people in general were gratified with the change. To shew their sense of the benefits resulting from it, even at an early period, it may be sufficient to quote the address which was presented to the Governor on the death of George the Second, towards the close of the year 1760. All the French in Canada, of any distinction, went into mourning on the occasion.

" THE ADDRESS OF THE OFFICERS OF THE MILITIA, AND THE MERCHANTS OF MONTREAL, TO GENERAL GAGE, GOVERNOR OF THAT PLACE.

" Cruel destiny then has cut short the glorious days of so great and magnanimous a Monarch. We are come to pour out our grief into the paternal bosom of your Excellency ; the sole tribute of gratitude of a people who will never cease to exult in the mildness and moderation of their new masters. The General who conquered us has treated us more like victors than vanquished ; and has left us a precious PLEDGE [the meaning of Gage, in French] by name and deed of his goodness to us. What acknowledgments are we not bound to make for so many favours! They shall be for ever engraved on our hearts in indelible characters. We entreat your Excellency to continue to us the honour of your protection. We will endeavour to deserve it by our zeal, and the earnest prayers we shall offer up to the Almighty Being for your health and preservation."

The cession of Canada by the treaty of Paris early in 1763, and the announcement of peace in the colonies in the spring of that year, were followed by a proclamation issued in October from His Britannic Majesty, erecting four new civil governments in the newly-acquired territories, viz., those of Quebec, East Florida, West Florida, and Granada; and in November General Murray was appointed Captain General and Governor in Chief of the Province of Quebec, though the commission was not received and published in the Colony till the month of August the following year. By these means His Majesty declared his intention to assimilate the laws and government of the whole Province to those of the other American colonies and provinces already under His Majesty's Government, as far as could be done consistently with the conveyance and preservation of property. The liberties of the new subjects were thus far secured by the adoption, as far as practicable, of English laws, both civil and criminal :—and things remained in this state until the passing of the Quebec Act in 1774, when some changes took place in the former branch, or civil department of the laws, relative to the tenure and conveyance of property, in compliance with the wishes of the French inhabitants. Indeed, the anxiety of the British Government to promote the advantages of its new subjects, was so marked, that it is scarcely an exaggeration to affirm, as an able writer has done, that " previous history affords no example of such forbearance and generosity on the part of the conquerors towards the conquered—forming such a new era in civilized warfare that an admiring world admitted the claim of Great Britain to the glory of conquering a people less from views of ambition, and the security of her other colonies, than from the hope of improving their situation, and endowing them with the privileges of free men."*

Both the city and the island of Montreal partook of the benefits to which a return of peace, and improved institutions, were directly favourable ; yet not without some checks and interruptions, On Saturday the 18th of May, 1765, a fire broke out in the city, which in a few hours destroyed 108 houses and reduced 215 families to the greatest distress. A very interesting pamphlet, drawn up by a benevolent individual, was printed in London on this occasion, and circulated freely in behalf of the sufferers. A considerable sum was raised in England, and forwarded towards their relief. The first title of the pamphlet is *The Case of the Canadians at Montreal distressed by Fire ;* and underneath it, in a Vignette, a neat portrait of His Majesty George III., who contributed £500. The second title is MOTIVES *for a* SUBSCRIPTION *towards the relief of the sufferers at* MONTREAL *in* CANADA *by a dreadful fire,* &c. &c. These motives are presented in a great variety of forms, and urged with much benevolent importunity. It appears from an account attested by His Excellency the Hon. James Murray, Governor of the Province, that the loss amounted to more than one hundred and sixteen thousand pounds currency, equal to £87,580 sterling, and comprehended the following particulars :

* Political Annals of Canada : quoted in MARTIN.

Value in buildings, from a survey made on oath by Masons and
    Carpenters £31980 0 0
In Merchandise.. 54718 5 9
In Furniture and Apparel............................ 25261 12 6
In Cash, Plate, and Bills............................... 4814 0 3

        Currency....................... £116773 18 6

        Sterling....................... £87580 8 10

The pamphlet states, as " worthy of very honorable
notice, that these people were so tender of what they
evidenced on oath, that great numbers declared, some
time after, that they found their loss to be considerably
greater than the account they had sworn to."

The parts ravaged by the fire, and the extent of
distress it occasioned, may be seen from the following
statement :—

In St. François Street were burnt out ... ... 54 families.
    St. Paul Street, separating the Upper Town from
        the Lower... 87
In the Market Place.. 26
    Hospital Street. 1
    St. Louis Street... 15
    St. Eloix Street... 6
    St. Sacrament Street. 6
    St. Nicholas Street 1
    St. Ann Street. 1
    St. Ann Suburbs.. 10
    Grey Sisters' Hospital, Suburbs and houses nearest. 8

        In all... ... ... 215 families.

It was computed that, by this destructive fire, one
fourth part of the city was consumed, and about one
third part in value. The population of Montreal at this
period was about seven thousand. The fire broke out
in the house of one of the British inhabitants, named

Levingston, and was occasioned by hot ashes carried into the garret to make soap. The want of engines and the prevalence of a very high wind were favourable to the spreading of the conflagration, which was only stopped at last by pulling down a part of the Hospital Les Sœurs in Notre Dame Street, and some houses near it. By inspecting the plan of the city as it stood before the conquest, it will be perceived that the *Hospital General* of the *Grey Nuns* was without the wall, and separated from it by a rivulet (now covered); yet the wind was so strong and the flames so fierce, that several houses near it were destroyed. " Scarce was the sword well sheathed," it is affectingly remarked, " and the widow's tears dried up, when this conflagration happened. Under their former Governors...these people had experienced numerous calamities... They dreaded the same hard fate from us, but they were agreeably surprised by a different rule of conduct."*

Thankful for the relief afforded to them in this season of distress, the inhabitants cheerfully exerted themselves to rebuild their houses and retrieve their fortunes ; but they had scarcely recovered from their difficulties when they were again assailed by the same terrible visitant. On the 11th of April, 1768, a fire broke out in the stable of one of the sufferers in the late conflagration, in the upper town ; it soon reached the adjoining houses, and raged with incredible fury over that part of the town till five o'clock the next morning, when it partially subsided, but not until it had consumed ninety houses, two churches, and a large charity school. The sufferers lost nearly the whole of their effects, either by the fire or by theft. The number thus

* *Case of the Canadians*, pa. 34. A copy of the third edition of this work is in the Library of the *Natural History Society* of Montreal ; and the compiler of this volume is indebted to the Society for the loan of it.

reduced to poverty was very great, many of them having been burnt out at the last fire.

Another circumstance which, for a time, had an unfavourable effect in checking the prosperity of Canada, was the conduct of Bigot, the Intendant or financier of the King of France : the consequences resulting from it were for some years severely felt. Having the entire management of the finances of the Colony, he and his dependants had the opportunity, which they eagerly embraced, of plundering the colonists in every direction. The expenses of the civil and military establishments were supported by a paper currency termed Card money. This was so faithfully redeemed during thirty years, that it enjoyed unlimited credit; and not only enabled Bigot to carry on his system of extortion and peculation, but for a long time to conceal them from the Court. The French Monarch, by at length dishonouring the bills of exchange drawn by the Intendant to whom he had granted unlimited power, involved in ruin not only those who held this particular species of property, but also those who possessed any other paper currency, amounting, it is said, at the conquest, to four millions sterling. For this the unfortunate holders received only four per cent. of the original value. But better days were in reserve for Canada.

CHAPTER VI.

IMPROVEMENTS—ATTACK ON MR. WALKER—QUEBEC
ACT—AMERICAN WAR—MONTREAL TAKEN—EX-
TRAORDINARY PHENOMENON—CHOLERA.

THE confirmation of Great Britain in the possession of
Canada by the peace of 1763, gave an impulse to commercial enterprise ; and by the influx of British settlers
and British capital, the Colony received an accession of
wealth and energy, small indeed, at first, but which,
gradually increasing, gave in time a new character to the
population.   Trade was encouraged, both domestic and
with the Mother Country ; new lands were cleared, the
capabilities of the country more extensively explored,
and advances made in the improvement of political institutions, particularly in the administration of justice in
criminal cases.   The Canadian inhabitants began to enjoy a liberty they had never tasted before ; and the
British were careful to preserve here the liberty they
had enjoyed at home.   Montreal had its share in the
general and increasing prosperity.

On the 6th of December, 1764, an occurrence took
place which not only created a great sensation here, but
engaged the attention of the Government in Britain.
Mr. Thomas Walker, a Justice of the Peace in this city,

having, in the discharge of his official duty, exposed himself to the displeasure of an officer in the army who had been engaged in a dispute about lodgings, was violently attacked in his own house on the evening of that day. A party of persons in disguise entered the house ; and Mr. Walker, on rising from his chair, received a wound in his forehead from a broad-sword. Attempting to reach his bed-chamber, where his arms were deposited, he was attacked by five or six of the ruffians, and was so severely wounded and bruised that he sank down into a chair. On recovering himself a little, he struck at two of the party, but was soon overpowered by the rest, who not only attempted to throw him upon the fire, but wounded him severely on the head, which felled him to the ground ; and while he was in that situation one of the ruffians, kneeling down, cut off a part of his right ear, and endeavoured to cut his throat, which Mr. Walker prevented by his struggles. In consequence of this outrage the whole Province was thrown into the greatest possible alarm. The inhabitants of Montreal went armed in the streets, and " never went to dinner or to their homes without pistols before them." So lively was the apprehension of danger from the military, that whenever a soldier entered a shop to purchase an article, a pistol lying ready on the counter was presented at him, to prevent his committing outrage. As soon as this horrid assault was known in England, the King issued a proclamation, dated 29th March, 1765, offering a reward of one hundred guineas for the apprehension and conviction of any person concerned in the offence. The Governor of the Province, also, offered a reward of two hundred guineas, and Mr. Walker himself an additional one of one hundred guineas. Several persons were apprehended on suspicion of being concerned in this assault, truly called in the letter from the Secre-

tary of State to the Governor of the Province, " such
treatment as is a disgrace to all government;" some
were tried and acquitted ; but none who were actually
engaged in the transaction were apprehended, or, at
least, convicted of the crime. At length, however,
public confidence was restored, the pursuits of commerce and industry were extended, and the general
state of society improved.

By a proclamation issued on the 7th of October, 1763,
the King of England had declared that " all the inhabitants of the Province, and all others resorting to it,
might confide in his Royal protection for enjoying the
benefit of the laws of England." These were in general operation for some years, from that time ; but it
was not till the year 1774, that the first Act of Parliament was passed in relation to Canada. By this Act,
among other matters, a provision was made for the
better government of this part of the British dominions,
and vesting the authority in a Governor, aided by a
Council of not less than seventeen persons, and not
exceeding twenty-three, who had power to frame ordinances, but not to levy taxes except for making public
roads, and erecting a few local structures. By this
Act the English criminal law was preserved, but it was
ordained that in " all matters of controversy relative to
property and civil rights, resort should be had to the
rule and decision of the laws of Canada," except with
regard to " lands which had been or should be granted
in free and common soccage." The power of the
Roman Catholic clergy to enforce the payment of tithes
from the members of that church, was restored by this
Act : from the time of the conquest it had been left
optional.

Nothing particularly affecting the city of Montreal
occurred for several years : its inhabitants continued

to increase and to prosper.   At length the American
revolutionary war broke out.   The first general Con-
gress of what are now the United States was held at
Philadelphia on Monday the 5th of September, 1774.
Having in vain endeavoured to prevail upon the Canadians to join them in their opposition to the British
Government, they determined to invade the country.
After obtaining possession of Ticonderoga, Crown
Point, and St. John's, the Provincial forces advanced
towards Montreal.   A somewhat ridiculous attempt
was made upon, or rather projected against, the city.
An adventurer named Ethan Allen, who, without any
Commission from Congress, had a principal share in
the capture of the forts, was afterwards, under the
assumed title of Colonel, desirous to signalize his prowess,
and raise himself into importance, by surprising Montreal.   He undertook this rash enterprise at the head
of a small party, without the knowledge of the Com-
mander-in-Chief, or the assistance which he might have
procured from others.   On the 25th of November,
1775, being met at some distance from the town by the
Militia under the command of English Officers, and
supported by the few regulars who were in the place,
he was, as he might have foreseen, defeated and taken
prisoner, with nearly forty of his party.   Allen and his
fellow-prisoners were sent to England, but were some
time afterwards remanded back to America.   Montgomery, however, the General appointed by the Congress, was more successful.   He had a considerable
force, while there were but few British troops in Canada, and the principal part of them had been engaged in
the defence of St. John's.   General Carleton, with the
force he was able to collect, had been repulsed at
Longueuil, so that when Montgomery advanced upon
Montreal, he had only to take possession of the city,

which he did on the 13th of November, the naval force in the river being surrendered into his hands, and General Prescott, with the volunteers and soldiers who had taken refuge on board, becoming prisoners of war. Montgomery having found plenty of woollen manufactures in Montreal, took the opportunity of new-clothing his troops, who had suffered excessively from the severity of the climate, the badness of the roads, and the want of suitable clothing. Montgomery was afterwards killed in an unsuccessful attack upon Quebec. In the month of May the following year, 1776, reinforcements having arrived from Britain, under General Burgoyne, the Provincial troops abandoned the city and island of Montreal, which remained without interruption during the remainder of the war.

The tranquil state of Montreal for some years previous to the peace with the United States in 1783, and the activity that prevailed afterwards, were favourable to the interest of the city, which from that period has been gradually increasing both in extent and importance. An interval of thirty-six years of security was well improved; agriculture was extended; trade, in all its departments, flourished with a rapidity before unexampled; the Fur trade, especially, which always found its safest and most valuable depôt in Montreal, was resumed with a spirit and enterprise of the most promising characters, and an influx of emigration to the city and the surrounding country, took place, which was truly astonishing. At the commencement of this period the whole population of Canada scarcely exceeded ninety thousand souls; but within five years afterwards, about 1780, the amount was nearly double; and the population of Montreal was augmented in at least an equal ratio.

The King's Proclamation after taking possession of Canada, and his Commission to the Governor, were for

several years the only guides for the political regulation of the Colony. The Quebec Act, as has been
observed, was passed in 1774 : its object was declared to
be " for making more effectual provision for the government of Quebec," then including the whole of Canada.
After several years trial, this Act was found to be, in
many respects, inapplicable to the present state of the
Province, and failed therefore to give satisfaction to the
inhabitants. A plan better suited to existing circumstances, and intended to be as nearly analogous to the
British Constitution as the case would admit, engaged
the attention of the Ministry at home, and issued in the
Act of 1791, which has continued in operation ever
since. By this Act the Colony was divided into the
two Provinces of Upper and Lower Canada, and a
Legislature established in each. In pursuance of the
provisions of this Act, the first Provincial Parliament
of Lower Canada met at Quebec on the 17th of December, 1792, and sat till the 9th of May following. The
House of Assembly then consisted of fifteen English
and thirty-five Canadian Members. The session was
distinguished by great decorum and moderation through
the whole of the proceedings. The debate on the
Quebec Bill in the English House of Commons was
remarkable, as being the occasion on which a friendship
of five and twenty years between Mr. Burke and Mr.
Fox, was broken up by a difference of political sentiment.

His late Majesty King William IV. visited Canada
in the year 1787. He was then in command of the
Pegasus, 28 guns, one of the squadron under the command of Commodore Sawyer. He landed at Quebec
on the 14th of August; and on the 8th of September
made his entrance into Montreal, where, as Prince
William Henry, he was received and entertained with

all the honours due to his illustrious rank. On his return, having landed and passed some time at Sorel, he sanctioned the alteration of the name of that village to his own, William Henry. On the 10th of October he sailed from Quebec in his own ship.

In the year 1812, war was declared by the United States against Great Britain, and Canada was threatened with invasion. Several of the inhabitants of Quebec and Montreal were disposed to flee; but being roused to action by the Governor, Sir George Prevost, and the people at large, a general stand was made in defence of the country. All classes acted nobly on the occasion. Montreal was twice in danger; once in November, 1812, when the American General Wilkinson had brought his troops as far down as Prescott, with scarcely any British force to oppose him; but having wasted some time in delay, the troops from above advanced upon him, and the militia from below were again enabled to assemble. In the following spring the same General, at the head of more than 3,000 men, entered Lower Canada, on the western shore of Lake Champlain; but being repulsed at La Colle Mill, by Major Handcock, with an inferior force, he retired to the United States, and closed his military career. Had the city been taken, in either of these attempts, the whole of Canada would have been in danger. Peace was concluded on the 24th of December, 1814, and proclaimed at Washington and Quebec in February and March of the following year. The inhabitants of Montreal once more laid aside their martial implements and habits for the more congenial pursuits of industry and commerce.

A remarkable natural phenomenon, attended with no small degree of terror to many, occurred at Montreal in the year 1819. The account of it attracted so much attention, even in Europe, as to be made the subject of

an elaborate Essay read before the *Plinian Society* of
Edinburgh. On Sunday the 8th of November, dense
black clouds were diffused over the atmosphere, and
there fell from them a heavy shower of rain, which, after
it had been allowed for some time to rest, was found
to have deposited a substance, which to the eye, the
taste, and the smell, presented the resemblance of common soot. The sky, during the morning, occasionally
displayed a slight greenish tint, and the sun, through
the haze which surrounded it, appeared of an unusually
bright pink colour. Before evening, the weather cleared
up, and the next day was frosty. On Tuesday the 9th
a weighty vapour descended from a thick stratum of
clouds that seemed progressively to deepen in colour
and density. This was an awful day : the superstitious
were alarmed, and even the thoughtless were struck
with a mixture of astonishment and terror, at an appearance for which no one could account. At sun-rise the
clouds varied in colour, sometimes assuming a greenish
hue ; at others, a dark and almost pitchy black. The
sun, at that time, appeared of a dingy orange colour,
which at moments varied to a blood red, and at others
to a dark brown with but a slight degree of luminosity
remaining. Towards noon the darkness was so great,
that it was found necessary to have candles burning in
the Court House, the Banks, and most of the public
offices in the city. The gloom alternately increased or
diminished, according to the ascendancy of the wind,
which, during the day, was very fitful and change-
able. The inhabitants began now to express their surprise, and indulge their speculations, as to the probable
cause of so unusual an appearance. To some it appeared likely that a volcano had burst forth in the interior
of the Province, and that its smoke, vapour, and ashes
were now over the city. Even the Mountain near it,

by some travellers stated to be the extinct crater of a volcano, was by many of the credulous supposed to have resumed its operations; and the city itself at its base appeared about to undergo the fate of Pompeii or Herculaneum. By some an Indian prophecy was quoted to the effect that the island of Montreal would, at some period, be destroyed by an earthquake, while the opposite shores and the surrounding country should remain unhurt. Others supposed that some immense woods and prairies had been set on fire, and that the ashes were borne on the same winds which fanned the devouring flames. The few animals that were to be seen, hurried with horrid cries to their respective places of shelter; all species of cattle uttered mournful sounds, dogs particularly appeared to be restless, and all the prognosties of a coming storm were distinctly perceptible. Towards three o'clock a formidable body of clouds from the North East hurried over the town, and brought the obscurity to its climax. This was a moment of general awe—the crisis appeared now to have arrived. The stoutest held their breath, and became, like others, timid and fearful. One of the most vivid flashes of lightning that the oldest residents had ever beheld, was succeeded by a clap of thunder that was echoed and reverberated for some minutes. This was followed by others equally loud, which to the affrighted citizens felt like an earthquake, as many persons fell, from the trembling of the floor under their feet. Rain again fell of the same dark, sooty appearance as on the preceding Sunday. A momentary brightness succeeded; but the clouds again collected, and at four o'clock it was nearly as dark as ever. A flash of lightning was seen to strike the summit of the steeple of the Roman Catholic Parish Church; it seemed to have touched the ball at the foot of the cross, and continued playing and whirling a short

time around it, when it descended to the earth by the
rod. Suddenly the Tocsin or fire-alarm was sounded
from every bell in the city, and the streets resounded
with the cry of Fire ! The sky was completely veiled
in gloom, the Place d'Armes was crowded and continually swelling by the floods of people who poured in
from all the adjacent streets ; while, towering over the
heads of the immense throng, was to be seen the steeple
of the church, with its ball blazing like a meteor, and
throwing out from the foot of the cross with which it
was surmounted, a radiation of sparks rendered lurid
by the incumbent and surrounding haze : in the evening
it appeared like a lighthouse seen out at sea. By great
exertions the fire was extinguished : about a quarter of
an hour previously, the iron cross fell on the pavement
in front of the church with a tremendous crash, and
there broke into many pieces. A small piece that had
fallen before, lighted on the roof of the corner house in
the square, partly penetrated the roof, and there remained. The rain which had fallen during the day had
deposited larger quantities of soot than on Sunday, and
as it flowed through the streets it carried on its surface
a dense foam resembling soap suds. The evening again
became darker ; and thus ended a day which may be
classed among the *dies atri* of Montreal. The range
of this phenomenon must have been very extensive, for
several of its appearances were noticed at Quebec below,
at Kingston above, and in many parts of the United
States. A similar darkness is said to have occurred in
Canada in the year 1781, and the time of it is still
known by the name of the *dark Sunday*. The cause
of it is still unexplained.

The great distance of Montreal from the sea renders
a visit of any marine animals, a matter of very rare occurrence. About the middle of September, 1823, a

large whale found its way up the river St. Lawrence, till nearly opposite the city, where it continued to play for several days, not being able, from the shallowness of the water, to navigate its way down the river. Having attracted the notice of the inhabitants, several enterprising individuals put off in boats with some whale-fishing materials, in pursuit of it. At last, after nearly a week's exertion, it was harpooned by Captain Brush of the Tow-Steam-Boat. It was immediately dragged on shore, and exhibited in a booth fitted up for the purpose, for the gratification of the inhabitants. It was found to measure 42 feet 8 inches in length, 6 feet across the back, and 7 feet deep.

A serious riot occurred on the 21st of May, 1832, in consequence of political excitement in connection with the choice of a representative in the Provincial Parliament, for the West Ward of this city. Indications of tumult and danger having shewn themselves, and the civil force being unable to restrain the mob from acts of violence, the military were called in. The Riot Act having been read in vain, and the populace having commenced an attack upon the military by stones and other missiles, the troops were ordered to advance; but this having no effect, and the violence increasing, they were ordered to fire, which they did with fatal effect, three persons being killed, and several wounded. Although this measure put a stop to the progress of tumultuary outrage, it by no means allayed the ferment of the public mind. The Coroner's inquest could not agree upon a verdict; but a prosecution was instituted in the Court of King's Bench against the Magistrates who called out the military, and the officers who commanded. The Grand Jury, after a charge from the Chief Justice, and a patient investigation of the evidence, very properly ignored the bills.

The sensation which this unhappy event produced
had by no means subsided, when it was followed by
another still more terrible and alarming. The Asiatic
Cholera, the most fearful form of pestilence in modern
times, after extending its ravages from India through
various parts of Europe, made its appearance in Canada
in the early part of June this year. It first visited
Quebec; and very shortly afterwards, Montreal, diffus-
ing consternation and dismay among all orders of the
inhabitants. Many of them fled from the city, strangers
were afraid to approach it, business was at a stand, and
every one was either expecting his own death, or fearing
to hear that his friends and relations had been seized by
the destroyer.

The following table of *Weekly Returns* of deaths by
cholera in Montreal, will show the malignant character
of the disease, as it prevailed here:

Week ending	Deaths.
June 16, 1832	261
— 23, —	632
— 30, —	166
July 7, —	94
— 14, —	61
— 21, —	70
— 28, —	131
Aug. 4, —	136
— 11, —	101
— 18, —	79
— 25, —	68
Sept. 1, —	54
— 8, —	32
— 15, —	13
— 21, —	6
Total	1904

The greatest mortality was observed to occur about

the middle of June; on the 19th the burials amounted to the extraordinary number of 149.

The whole number of cases to the last date in the table was 4420, so that considerably more than one-third of the seizures proved fatal: three out of seven will give nearly the ratio. After this period but few cases occurred, the pestilence gradually declined, and in the beginning of the following month totally disappeared.

From a calculation made at the time, it was affirmed that a greater number of persons had been carried off by the Cholera in Lower Canada with a population of half a million, in three months, than in Great Britain, with fifteen millions, in six months.

Two years afterwards, in 1834, the same dreadful malady again visited the place. It did not commence so early as on the former occasion, nor was it either so violent in its character, so extensive in its ravages, or so productive of terror among the inhabitants at large. Some hundreds, however, fell victims to its stroke, during the fifty days of its continuance.

When at length, by the merciful Providence of God, this awful and calamitous scourge was removed, the spirit of enterprise and improvement returned in all its previous vigour; and the citizens of Montreal were by no means backward in their efforts to increase the accommodations and beauty of the city and its suburbs. A better style of building prevailed. Instead of the slight frame houses, or more substantial ones of rough stone, which were formerly erected, nearly all the recent structures, whether for private residence or mercantile stores, are formed of hewn stones in front, and many of them display considerable taste. Several lines of such erections adorn various parts of the city. The harbour has been improved, the streets are kept in better order, and an attention to convenience and comfort has become far more general than at any former period.

But every thing human is liable to change. A malignant influence, more extensive in its range, and more permanent in its effects, than the visitations of pestilence, had been long at work in this Province,—menacing, in no dubious tone, the peace, prosperity, and institutions of the land, the confidence of social life, and the stability of British connection. Seditious meetings had been held during the summer of 1837, in various parts of the District of Montreal, and on the 6th of November, a trifling skirmish between two rival political parties in the Place d'Armes, led the way to insurrections, and tumults, and at length to open rebellion.

GOVERNORS AND ADMINISTRATORS OF THE GOVERNMENT OF CANADA,

SINCE THE ERECTION OF THE ROYAL GOVERNMENT IN 1663.

French.

Sieur de Mésy	May 1,	1663.
Sieur de Courcelles	March 23,	1665.
Sieur de Frontenac	April 7,	1672.
Sieur de Barre	May 1,	1682.
Sieur Marquis de Nonville	April 15,	1684.
Sieur de Frontenac	May 15,	1689.
Sieur Chevalier de Callières	April 20,	1699.
The Marquis de Vaudreuil	Aug. 1,	1703.
The Marquis de Beauharnois	Jan. 11,	1726.
Sieur de la Jonquière	March 15,	1746.
Sieur Compte de la Galissioniere	June 19,	1747.
The Marquis du Quesne de Menneville	March 1,	1752.
Sieur de Vaudreuil de Cavagnal	Jan. 1,	1755.

English.

James Murray...	Nov. 21,	1763.
Paulus Emilus Irving, *President*.....................	June 30,	1766.
Guy Carleton, *Lt. Gov. and Commander in Chief.*	Sept. 24,	1766.
Guy Carleton, *Gov. in Chief.*.........	April 12,	1768.
Hector T. Cramahé, *President*......................	Aug. 9,	1770.
Guy Carleton..	Oct. 11,	1774.
Henry Hamilton, *Lt. Gov. & Commander in Chief.*	————	1774.
Henry Hope, *Lt. Gov. & Commander in Chief...*	————	1775.
Lord Dorchester, *Governor General*	————	1776.
Frederick Haldimand..................................	————	1778.
Alured Clarke, *Lt. Gov. & Commander in Chief.*	————	1791.
Lord Dorchester...	Sept. 24,	1793.
Robert Prescott..	————	1796.
Sir Robert S. Milnes, Bart. *Lieut. Governor.....*	July 31,	1799.
Hon. Thomas Dunn, *President*......................	July 31,	1805.
Sir J. H. Craig, K. B. *Governor General*.........	Oct. 24,	1807.
Hon. Thomas Dunn, *President*......................	June 19,	1811.
Sir George Prevost, Bart. *Governor General.....*	Sept. 14,	1811.
Sir G. Drummond, G. C. B. *Admin. in Chief...*	April 4,	1815.
John Wilson, *Administrator*...........................	May 22,	1816.
Sir J. C. Sherbrooke, G. C. B. *Gov. General...*	July 12,	1816.
Duke of Richmond, K. C. B. *Gov. General......*	July 30,	1818.
Hon. James Monk, *President*........................	Sept. 20,	1819.
Sir Peregrine Maitland.................................	————	1820.
Earl of Dalhousie, G. C. B. *Governor General...*	June 18,	1820.
Sir Frs. Nath. Burton, *Lieut. Governor*...........	June 7,	1824.
Earl of Dalhousie, G. C. B. *Governor General...*	Sept. 23,	1825.
Sir James Kempt, G. C. B. *Administrator*.........	Sept. 8,	1828.
Lord Aylmer, G. C. B. *Governor General*........	July 19,	1830.
Lord Gosford...	Aug. 24,	1835.
Sir John Colborne......................................	Feb. 27,	1838.
Lord Durham..	May 29,	1838.
Sir John Colborne......................................	Nov. 1,	1838.

CHAPTER VII.

TOPOGRAPHICAL DESCRIPTION—DISTRICT—COUNTY—
AND CITY—ECCLESIASTICAL EDIFICES.

The City of Montreal is the Capital of a district of the same name. The whole Province of Lower Canada is divided into five districts: three superior, Quebec, Three Rivers, and Montreal; two inferior, St. Francis and Gaspé. These are the judicial divisions of the Province, having Courts of superior and inferior jurisdiction. In the superior districts the jurisdiction of the Court of King's Bench is unlimited; but in the inferior it is circumscribed by the power of appeal in certain cases,—and all prosecutions for capital crimes must be carried on in the Courts of the superior districts.

DISTRICT OF MONTREAL.

Its boundaries are as follow: East by the North East boundary of the fief Dusablé or Nouvelle York on the North side of the St. Lawrence,—West by the County of St. Maurice,—South by the Counties of Yamaska, Drummond, and Sherbrooke,—West and Southwest by the Province of Upper Canada, the river Ottawa, and the western limits of the Province,—South by the Province line, lat. 45° N. from St. Regis to the river Connecticut, and thence by that river to its source in the high lands, thence by the North boundaries of the States of New York and. Vermont. It is the richest and most populous district of the Province. The soil is in general excellent, in some parts well cultivated, and in others capable of great improvement. The settled parts are mostly low and level, but mountainous towards the south, and in the vicinity of Hemingford and Bolton. On the north of the Lake of Two Mountains, a range of high lands traverses the district, striking west to the Grand Calumet on the Ottawa, and traversing that river. North of this ridge the country is more or less uneven and mountainous, and meets the range of high lands that divides the waters running into Hudson's Bay from those that empty themselves into the St. Lawrence. This district contains the city and island of Montreal, the towns of William Henry (Sorel), Laprairie, and Dorchester, beside numerous flourishing villages. Bounded for more than three hundred miles by the Ottawa, it is well watered by that river, and by numerous other streams and lakes, of which the following are the principal:

RIVERS.

North of the St. Lawrence.	South of the St. Lawrence.
Gatineau,	Richelieu,
Lievres,	Sorel,
Petite Nation,	Yamaska and its numerous
Rivière Blanche,	branches,
Rivière du Nord,	Montreal, L.
Mascouche,	Chateauguay and its numerous
Achigan,	branches,
L'Assomption,	La Colle,
Lachenaye,.	Magog,
Berthier,	Coaticook,
Chaloupe,	Missiskoui, part of
Du Chêne.	

LAKES.

North.	South.
White Fish,	Memphramagog,
Sables,	Tomefobi,
Kilarney,	Missiskoui Bay,
Temiscaming,	Scaswavinepus, part of
Lievres,	Yamaska Bay,
La Roque,	St. Louis,
Rochblave,	Two Mountains,
Pothier,	St. Francis,
Nimicachinqué,	Chaudière,
Papineau,	Chats,
Maskinongé.	Allumets.

COUNTY AND ISLAND OF MONTREAL.

The County comprises the whole of the Island, together with all the nearest islands which, in whole or in part, lie in front of it. The Island is divided into ten parishes, and contains several Seigniories through them. It sends six members to the Provincial Parliament, two for the county and four for the city of Montreal.

The Island of Montreal is the most considerable in the Province, and its superior fertility has acquired for it the appellation of the Garden of Canada. The general surface of the Island is level, with the exception of the mountain near the city: it is diversified, however, by those gentle ridges called Côteaux, which occur in various parts. The mountain, which is a very conspicuous object, consists of two distinct hills, between which passes one of the leading avenues into the city. There are roads by which the circuit of either mountain may be easily made, and which, from the many charms of its scenery, is a very favourite drive. The slopes of the mountain are wooded nearly to the summit, but towards the base the forest-trees have been succeeded

by orchards that produce apples, pears, and plums of
the choicest flavour; and it is worthy of remark that,
although the fruit of the Island is universally excellent,
all other parts of it yield to the vicinity of the mountain
in the luxuriance of the orchards, and the deliciousness
of the fruits they produce.

PARISHES.—The *Parish* of the *Town of Montreal*
comprehends the Côtes de la Visitation, St. Joseph,
Notre Dame, des Neiges, and St. Pierre, together with
parts of St. Paul and Ste. Catharine, the Isle St. Paul
at the mouth of the river St. Pierre, and Isle au Heron
lying off Côte des Argoulets. The road through Côte
des Neiges is well settled, and many of the buildings
present the appearance of an American village. There
is a chapel on the north of the road.

The *Parish* of *St. Laurent* contains the Côtes St.
Michael and St. Laurent, with one half of two ranges
of Notre Dame des Vertus. At some distance from
Côte des Neiges is the pretty village of St. Laurent,
containing a large Parish Church for Roman Catholics.

The *Parish* of *St. Geneviève* is situated at the north-
west extremity of the island, opposite to Isle Bizard.

The *Parish* of *Sault au Recollet* is handsomely
situated on the borders of Rivière des Prairies : it contains a small village, a fine church and presbytery, and
valuable corn and saw-mills. In front of the village of
Sault au Recollet are several small islands, which add
to its picturesque beauty.

The *Parish* of *Pointe Claire* extends from Côte de
Ste. Anne to Côte St. Remi, and includes the lower
part of Isle Perrot.

The *Parish* of *La Chine* comprises $2\frac{3}{4}$ leagues along
the St. Lawrence from Côte des Argoulets to Point
Clare, part of Côte St. Paul, and half of two ranges in
Côte de Notre Dame des Vertus. The Lachine Canal

is of vast utility in connecting the navigation above Sault St. Louis with the port of Montreal.

The *Parish* of *Point aux Trembles* extends along the St. Lawrence from the upper end of Isle Therese to the boundary of the Parish of Longue Point, including the Côte de la Point aux Trembles and part of Côte de St. Leonard. Pointe aux Trembles is a small village, containing thirty or forty houses, on the main road to Quebec. It is much frequented as a place of recreation by the citizens of Montreal.

The *Parish* of *Longue Pointe* includes part of Côte St. Martin north east, and extends north to the King's high-way which runs through the centre of the island.

The *Parish* of *Rivière des Prairies* contains only the Côte de St. Joseph, and extends two leagues along the Rivière des Prairies from the lower part of the island.

The *Parish* of *Ste. Anne*, at the upper end of the island, contains the extent between the River de l'Orme North, and the Côte de Point Clare South, and also the upper part of Isle Perrot.

CITY OF MONTREAL.

MONTREAL, the second city in political dignity, but the first in magnitude and commercial importance, in British America, is situated in Latitude 45° 31′ North, and Longitude 73° 34′ West. Including the suburbs it covers about 1020 acres, although within the fortifications the area did not much exceed 100 acres. Its local advantages for the purposes of trade, give it a decided superiority over every other place in the Province, and its climate, though severe, is more genial than that of Quebec. On approaching it either on the river from below, or in descending from Laprairie, the tall and elegant steeple of the English Church, the massive

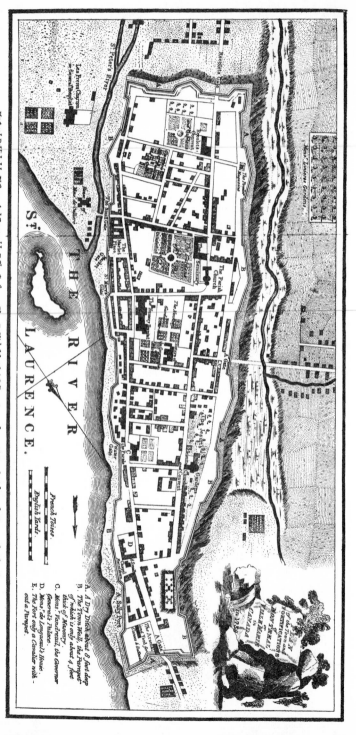

St. Peter's River

Les Peres Charcoins [illegible]

St. Laurens Gardens

THE RIVER ST. LAURENCE.

French Toises.

English Yards.

A. A Dry Ditch about 8 feet deep
B. The Town Wall, the Parapet of which is about 4 feet thick of Masonry
C. Mons. Vaudreuil, the Governor Generals Palace.
D. Mons. de Longueuil's House.
E. The Fort only a Cavalier without a Parapet.

Montreal Published by W. Gray, And Engraved by P. Stride from a Plan Published by Tho.s Jefferys Geographer to His Royal Highness the Prince of Wales. Jan. 1758 grandeur of the French Cathedral, the spires of other churches and chapels, the spreading mass of habitations in the suburbs, and the well-built and lofty stores in Commissioner Street, the stranger will be impressed with a very favourable idea of the city he is about to enter. If the entrance be by the Lachine road, a fine view of the city is presented just before descending the hill near the Tanneries, or the village of St. Henry; and another on coming along the road from Mile-end, north west of the city. In order to obtain an idea of the comparative magnitude of Montreal at the conquest and at the present time, the plan of the city as it then existed should be examined in connection with the modern map : the additional streets, stretching in every direction through the suburbs of St. Ann, St. Joseph, the Recollets, St. Antoine, St. Lawrence, and Quebec, will shew how the spirit of improvement has corresponded with the increasing prosperity of the city.

In the commencement of towns and villages, when no specific plan has been previously arranged, houses and other buildings will be erected where land can be obtained or convenience may dictate, without much regard to regularity or order ; and hence, in towns of any considerable standing, we generally find that the earliest streets are crooked and irregular. This may be seen in St. Paul Street in this city, which, by its contiguity to the river, presents great facilities for trade, and, with the space between it and the wharf, would be occupied in preference by men of business. It contains many excellent houses, which would be seen to more advantage, had the street been wider. It reminds one of some of the central streets in London, but without their fog and smoke. From St. Paul Street, downwards to the river, was formerly called the lower town, and the rest of the city the upper ; but though in some

of the cross streets there is an evident rising in the
ground, in others it is scarcely perceptible. The
principal streets are airy, and the new ones particularly
of a commodious width; some of them running the
whole length of the town, nearly parallel to the river,
are intersected by others generally at right angles. An
Englishman when he enters the city, and in his peram-
bulations through nearly the extent of it, is struck with
the French names by which nearly the whole formerly,
and the greater part now, of the streets are distinguished: the names of Catholic Saints, or eminent
Frenchmen, will meet his eye in abundance. The Rue
Notre Dame, extending from the Quebec to the
Recollet Suburbs, is 1344 yards in length, and 30 feet
broad. It is in general a handsome street, and contains
many of the public buildings. St. James Street, Craig
Street, and M'Gill Street, are of still greater width,
and when the yet empty spaces in each are filled up
with elegant houses, they will be ornaments to the town.
Should the first be extended in breadth in that part
called Little St. James Street, so as to form a line with
the other, it would be a noble street; but should Craig
Street be ever lined on both sides with houses like some
few that are in it, a still superior street might be formed,
in consequence of its more ample width.

The spirit of local improvement has long been in
active and efficient operation, and betrays no symptoms
of languor or decline. Those who knew the city seven
years ago, and have not seen it since, were they to visit
it now, would be surprised at the change, and be scarcely
able to recognise the places with which they were once
familiar. Beside a multitude of new and elegant houses,
in almost every part of the city and suburbs, large
spaces and several streets have been considerably
improved. The covering of the creek, or rather ditch,

CITY OF MONTREAL AS IT APPEARED IN 1803.

an offensive and dangerous nuisance, in Craig Street;
the levelling of M'Gill Street; the improvements in
Dalhousie Place, in the French Square, and Notre
Dame Street, and of thât part of St. Ann Suburbs
called Griffin Town, by which a large portion of
swampy land has been raised and made available for
building, may be adduced as specimens; but the particulars will be more fully noticed in their respective
places in the following descriptive account. The recent
houses are almost universally built of the greyish lime-
stone which the vicinity of the mountain affords in
abundance; the fronts of the same material, hewn and
squared; even the new stores and warehouses are
finished in the same manner, exhibiting an appearance
far more agreeable than those which were constructed
of the rough stones, made to fit as far as the mere
placing of them could do it, and their interstices filled
up with smaller stones and mortar. Many of the
houses are large, handsome, and in modern style, and
some of them display great taste in design. The
prevalent feature is a union of chasteness and elegance
in various proportions, with a commendable absence of
all meretricious style and ornament. The best houses,
and most of the churches, are covered with plates of tin,
a far better material for this purpose than the wooden
shingles which are frequently used, and though more
expensive in the first cost, are cheaper in the end, beside
the advantage of safety from fire when burning flakes
from neighbouring houses fall upon the roof.

In comparing the climate with that of Quebec, it may
be observed that in general the winter is shorter in
Montreal, and the cold not so intense. Fahrenheits'
thermometer in Quebec has sometimes descended to $31\frac{1}{2}$
degrees below zero, $= -28\frac{1}{4}$ Rèaumur, while in Montreal it seldom falls more than 22 degrees below

zero, = – 24 Rèaumur. In the latter city also the snow is seldom so deep, or remains so long, as in Quebec. As to the general state of the weather, it was observed, in the year 1831, that in Montreal there were 65 days of rain, 34 of snow, 168 of fine clear weather, and 98 of cloudy; and the same year at Quebec there were 160 days of rain, 56 of snow, 208 of dry weather, and 16 variable.

The favourable situation of Montreal enables her to command the trade of a considerable portion of the lower Province, and the greater part of the upper. With the United States also, and with Great Britain, an extensive commerce is maintained. Her position, indeed, is such as always to ensure a profitable connection with every part of the continent where business is to be done. By some persons it has been thought, however favourable the situation of Montreal is at present, it would have been better had the city been founded a little lower down the river, so that the difficulty of ascending the Current St. Mary might have been avoided. Should the original design of the Lachine Canal ever be carried into effect, some advantage might result from unloading vessels below the current. The aid of steam navigation, however, by which ships of all burdens may easily be towed up to the city, renders this a consideration of much less importance than it was formerly.

The civil government of Montreal is administered by Justices of the Peace, who are appointed by the Governor of the Province. They are at present forty-six in number, and have power to make certain assessments for defraying the necessary expenses of the city, and to enact and enforce such bye-laws for its regulation and advantage as are not inconsistent with the statutes of the realm. For a short period the municipal affairs of

Duncan Del.

Christie Sc.

FRENCH CATHEDRAL — PLACE D'ARMS.

the city were managed by a Mayor and Common Council. An Act passed the Provincial Legislature in 1832, forming Montreal into a Corporation, and transferring the authority from the Magistrates to the corporate body; but in 1836, the Act of Incorporation having expired, the Government again passed into the hands of the Justices of the Peace. The city is represented in the Provincial Parliament by four Members, the East and West Wards into which it is divided, returning two each. The period of service in the House of Assembly is four years. Under the Corporation the city and suburbs were distributed into eight wards, for the more convenient arrangement and dispatch of business. These are East and West Wards, the Wards of St. Ann, St. Joseph, St. Antoine, St. Lawrence, St. Lewis, and St. Mary. Another division of the city may be called the Military, according to which the battalions of militia, which are six in number, are collected from the portions of the city or suburbs in which they reside.

ECCLESIASTICAL EDIFICES.

PARISH CHURCH OF VILLE MARIE

OR, CATHEDRAL OF NOTRE DAME.

The first ecclesiastics who visited the Western world from Europe were two Jesuits, who were stationed as Missionaries at Port Royal in Acadia, now Nova Scotia, in 1611, under the direction of Père Coton, and through the encouragement of the Marchioness of Guercheville, a lady of the French Court, zealous to propagate the Catholic faith among the Indians of this continent. But the first who came to Canada were four Recollets, who were brought to Quebec by Champlain, in 1615, with the same design. They were, the Superior of the Mission, and the Fathers Joseph le Caron, Jean D'Olbeau, and Pacifique Duplessis. Three others, Jesuits, were sent out in 1625, by Henry de Levis, Duke of Ventadour, and three more were added in the following year. In 1636 there were fifteen Jesuit Missionaries in Canada. Those who settled in Quebec, assisted by the Queen of France, the Duchess of Aiguillon, and other benevolent individuals, formed several establishments in that city and the neighbouring country, for religious instruction, the relief of the miserable, especially the sick, and the tuition of the young.

Montreal, which was founded in the year 1642, as related in the third chapter, soon became the scene of similar operations. The chapel, which was a slight and hasty structure of wood, was by degrees improved and enlarged as the wants of the population required, and was at length succeeded by a more substantial erection of stone, in 1672. This stood in what is now called the French Square, or *Place d'Armes*, and occupied the middle of Notre Dame Street, standing quite across, so as to divide it into two nearly equal parts, and requiring travellers to pass half round the church to proceed from one part to the other. The belfry and steeple now standing in the square are the only remains of the former church. It was dedicated to the Virgin Mary, to whose protection, according to the usage of the Roman Catholic Church, the city was confided, and on this account received the appellation of Ville Marie. As the inhabitants increased in number, the church, even in its enlarged state, became too small, and the church of

Bonsecours was erected for their accommodation. The city continuing to prosper, especially after the Colony became British, further accommodation was needed ; and in the year 1824, the present magnificent Cathedral was commenced. On the third of September the corner-stone was laid; and it was so far completed as to admit of being opened for public worship on the fifteenth of July, 1829 ; when high mass was performed by the Bishop of Telmesse, and an oration delivered by the Rev. Mr. Quibler. The greater part of the Canadian Roman Catholic Clergy were present, and the solemnity was attended by Sir James Kempt, Administrator, the Staff, Corporations, and other public bodies, and upwards of eight thousand persons.

The edifice is a chaste specimen of the perpendicular style of Gothic architecture in the middle ages. Of this class of buildings, it has no superior on the continent of North America ; and when the plan is completed by the intended terrace along St Joseph Street, and the two lofty towers by which those in the front are to be surmounted, there will be nothing in this part of the world to be compared with it in plain and simple grandeur. Its only deficiency is an almost total destitution of ornament. The length of the church, from east to west, is 255 feet 6 inches, and its breadth from north to south, 134 feet 6 inches. The height of the flank is 61 feet from the flagging of the terrace to the eaves. There are six towers, so arranged that each flank presents three, and the east and west ends two each. Those on the principal or west front are to be 220 feet high. The space between the front towers is 73 feet, by 120 in height, crowned with an embattled parapet. The flanks and east towers are each 115 feet in height. There are five public and three private entrances to the first floor, and four to the galleries, so that an audience of ten thousand persons, the number for which it is seated, may assemble and disperse in a few minutes, without disagreeable pressure. The number of pews on the ground floor is 504, in the first gallery 373, and in the second 368; total number, 1244.

The eastern window at the high altar is 64 feet in height, and 32 in breadth. It is separated by shafts into five compartments, and sub-divided by mullions into 36 divisions. The windows in the flanks consist of one range, and those in the front are finished in the same style as the eastern window. The portal is formed by an arcade, consisting of three arches, each 19 feet by 49 in height. From this arcade are the entrances to the church; and over it is placed another of the same form in relievo, which connects the towers and piers. Between these are trefoil canopy-headed niches, intended for marble statues. It was a part of the original design to have a promenade between the towers 76 feet by 20, elevated 120 feet above the surface of the Place d'Armes, from which the spectator will have a delightful and extensive view of the River St. Lawrence and the surrounding country. The front towers are intended to contain clocks and bells, and to form observatories accessible by safe and easy flights of steps.

The floor, from the front entrance to the chancel, is a gently inclined plane of three feet in the whole length. There are seven spacious aisles in the same direction, and two crossing them at right angles, one of which leads to the flank doors. The pews are raised six inches above the aisles. There are seven chapels, so placed that all are seen from the front entrance. The high altar is nearly at the extremity of the nave: it is elevated in the chancel 2 feet 6 inches above the floor of the church, and is encompassed on three sides by semi-circular seats for the clergy, &c. The front of

the chancel is open, and is approached by an easy flight
of five steps, in the form of a double semi-reverse.   The
eastern window, high altar, and choir, will be seen from
the front door to great advantage, with a perspective
view of the side windows, altars, galleries, and the
groined ceiling, 80 feet in height.   The vaults of the
ceiling and galleries are supported in part by a double
range of grouped columns, 3 feet 4 inches in diameter:
from these spring the groins of the ceiling.   The pillars are of wood, and painted in imitation of clouded
Italian or American marble.   The hue accords with
the ceiling ; but the effect, though time may improve it,
is too glaring, and is evidently inferior to that which
stone pillars would have produced.   The facings of the
gallery trusses, and the greatest portion of the carpen-
ters' work, are painted in imitation of the oak finishings
in the Gothic Cathedrals of Europe.   The gallery
screens are in moveable pannels, and painted a crimson
colour : the railing, in front of them, imitates iron, and
produces an agreeable effect.

   There are recesses in the piers, between the windows
on the first floor, intended for family monuments, and in
the recesses of the windows are placed the confessional
screens. Suitable arrangements are made in the interior
for all the monuments and paintings that may be wanted ;
and at the sides of the high altar are places assigned for
twelve large historical paintings, which will occupy an
admirable light from their position.   The organ is placed
in the upper gallery over the front entrance ; the floor
in this part is elastic, and the organ projects six feet
beyond the line of galleries.   The choir screen is finished
in recessed seats for the clergy.   The pulpit and canopy
are attached to one of the pillars : the access to it is from
the first gallery.   It resembles in form that in the
Gothic Cathedral at Strasburg, in Germany.   The high

altar is a little in the florid style, and resembles in part that of St. Peter's at Rome. The Eastern window was intended to be filled with stained glass; but the funds were insufficient. The effect of the present substitute for it is too glaring, and will never be fully corrected until the original design is executed. It was intended to warm the church with heated air, from furnaces placed in apartments under the floor. At present it is heated by stoves.

The architect and superintendant was Mr. M'Donald; the master builders Messrs. Lamontagne and St. John, natives of Canada; Messrs. Redpath and Mackay, masons and stone-cutters, natives of Scotland; Messrs. Perry and Wetherilt, plasterers, natives of England; and Mr. Cox, carpenter, native of the State of New York.

A near view of this edifice from the Place d'Armes, of which it forms the Eastern boundary, and more distant views from different points of the ascent to the mountain in various directions, will convey to the observer a striking idea of its architectural character and imposing magnitude.

CHRIST CHURCH:

THE PROTESTANT EPISCOPAL CHURCH, IN NOTRE DAME STREET.

After the cession of the Canadas to Britain, many of the soldiers, when the troops were disbanded, preferred remaining here, and others attracted by the hope of commercial advantage, came over to this country, so that in a few years a considerable number of British were found among the settlers. Many of these were of the Episcopal persuasion, and naturally desired to

IEL S^T SCOTCH CHURCH

BONSECOURS CHURCH

CHRIST'S CHURCH (EPISCOPAL.)

procure clergymen from home to conduct public worship according to the practice of the Church of England in which they had been educated. The greater portion of these had settled in the towns ; and expressions of their desire having been forwarded to England, three clergymen were sent out together, and appointed to Quebec, Three Rivers, and Montreal. The Rev. Mr. Delisle, a native of Switzerland, was the first Protestant Episcopal Minister who settled in this city. When he arrived, there was no place of worship, and the people were not sufficiently numerous or affluent to build one : they readily obtained, however, the use of the Recollet Church at such hours as the society had not occasion to use it. There was then no Protestant Bishop at Quebec ; and in the year 1789, the Bishop of Nova Scotia came to Canada on a Diocesan visitation. The congregation, now much increased, applied to his Lordship for aid ; and soon afterwards obtained from Lord Dorchester, the Governor, the use of the church which formerly belonged to the Jesuits' College, and stood near the site of the gaol. Having fitted it up with pews, they attended divine worship in it for the first time, on Sunday the 20th of December, 1789.

The Provinces of Upper and Lower Canada were erected into an Episcopal See in the year 1793. Dr. Jacob Mountain was the first Bishop of Quebec, with power over the whole diocese. A fire broke out in an old building near the church, in the month of June, 1803, which so far injured the church itself as to render it useless for the purposes of worship. A meeting of the congregation was held within a few days, when measures were resorted to which issued in the erection of the present handsome structure ; in the mean time the congregation were accommodated with the use of the Presbyterian Church in St. Gabriel Street. The

Committee appointed were Dr. Mountain, the resident minister, son of the first Bishop of Quebec,—the Hon. James M'Gill, the Hon. Judge Ogden,—J. Frobisher, David Ross, Stephen Sewell, and J. A. Gray, Esqrs. A new church being resolved upon in preference to repairing the old, means were taken to raise a fund by the sale of pews and by application to His Majesty, the Archbishop of Canterbury, and the merchants in London who were interested in the trade of Canada. Two spots of ground were then at liberty ; one the vacant piece which adjoined the gaol, and was occupied as a garden for the Government house ; the other that lot in Notre Dame Street on which the old French prison stood formerly. The latter was preferred, being granted for the purpose by the then Lieutenant Governor, Sir Robert Shore Milnes. In addition to this lot the congregation purchased from Mr. Guy, for the sum of £500 currency, a strip of ground which ran along the rear of it, so as to admit of access to the church from Little St. James Street. A plan and specification by Mr. Berzey were selected, and a committee to direct the work immediately appointed. The contract was made in January 1805 with Messrs. Joseph Chevalier and Baptist Larochelle for the mason work, Messrs. Isaac Shey and D. Bent for the roof and covering, and Mr. Gilmore to superintend the building, and furnish the cut stone for it. The contractors began to prepare the materials, that the building might be commenced early in the spring. On the 21st day of June, the corner stone was laid with the usual formalities, by the Lord Bishop of Quebec, who came to Montreal for the purpose. Thus, after much effort, some disappointments, and many interruptions, an object of such interest to the Protestant Episcopalians of this place, was put into a train of accomplishment.

On a plate which is imbedded in the stone, there is the following inscription:

" Glory be to God."

" Of this sacred Edifice, raised upon Ground granted for that purpose by our most Gracious Sovereign George III. by the pious exertions of the Protestant inhabitants of this City, and dedicated to the service of Almighty God according to the establishment of the Church of England, this Corner Stone was laid by Jacob Lord Bishop of Quebec, on the 21st day of June, in the year of our Lord, 1805."

In a cavity formed in the stone to which the above Plate answers as a cover, there is a glass bottle hermetically sealed, and containing the following Coins and Medals, together with a roll of parchment, bearing an inscription, of which the undermentioned is a copy. In gold there is a Guinea of George III. bearing date 1792. A half Guinea, same reign, dated 1797. A third do. dated 1799. In silver there are a Shilling of George III. dated 1787. A Sixpence of the same reign, 1787. In copper there are One Penny George III. of 1797 ; a Halfpenny and a Farthing of the same King, dated 1799. Also a Halfpenny of George Prince of Wales, without date. Besides these there are two Medals, the one struck in commemoration of Lord Howe's victory of the 1st of June, 1794; and the other for Lord Nelson's defeat of the combined fleets of France and Spain, on the 5th of November, 1805. The inscription on the parchment roll, bears the names of the Building Committee, as follows :

" This Building was erected under the direction of the following Gentlemen, being a Committee chosen by the Congregation for that purpose. The Rev. Dr. Mountain, Edward William Gray, Joseph Frobisher, Robert Cruickshanks, John Platt, David Ross, Stephen Sewell, Esqrs, and Frederick William Ermatinger, Esq. Treasurer."

" Montreal, 25th June, 1805."

The funds hitherto obtained were insufficient to do more than finish the walls and the roof; and no further progress was made for some years. In 1808 the sum of £400 was received from merchants in England; and in 1810 the Imperial Parliament voted a grant of £4000 " towards finishing the Protestant Parish Church in Montreal"; but this was not received till 1812, and then with a diminution of nearly £800 currency, owing to a difference in the rate of exchange during the delay. In the spring of that year the carpenter's work of the inside and the plastering, were undertaken by contract, the former by Mr. John Try, and the latter by Mr. Thomas Phillips. On the 9th day of October, 1814, divine service was first performed in the new church. The organ was erected in 1816. It is a powerful and elegant instrument made by Mr. Thomas Elliot, of London. Its original cost was £1150 sterling, but with the expense of putting it up, and other charges, it cost nearly £1600 currency. The sum was raised by subscription. The following year Dr. Mountain died, and was succeeded by the Rev. John Leeds, who had previously acted as curate.

In the year 1817, application was made to the Legislature for an Act of Incorporation, but it was rejected. The Prince Regent was then applied to on the subject; and letters patent, bearing date the 12th of August, 1818, were issued, constituting this church a Parish Church and Rectory, and electing the Rector, Churchwardens, and other members for the time being, a body corporate for managing its temporal affairs.

The side galleries were erected the following year, being rendered necessary from the number of applicants for seats, owing to the great increase of the Protestant population of the city. Hitherto the church had neither a steeple nor a spire. Liberal offers for their erection were made, and both were added the same year, together with a clock, the donation of John Shuter, Esq. The stone work of the steeple was executed by Messrs. Surties and Muckle, and the wood work by Messrs. Clarke and Appleton.

The Church is 120 feet in length, by 80 in width, exclusive of the recess for the altar, which is 12 feet in depth by 40 in width. The windows are 14 feet in height, topped with a semi-circular arch with $3\frac{1}{2}$ feet nave—and 7 feet wide. The side walls are about 30 feet high. It is entered by three doors corresponding with the three passages which run along the body of the church from the entrance to the altar at the opposite end. The building recedes from the street, and is separated from it by a dwarf stone wall, surmounted by a handsome iron railing, with three neatly ornamented gates. The front is ornamented with pilasters support- ing a cornice and pediment of the Doric order of architecture. The tower is of stone, square and lofty, and from the top of it rises an octagonal prismatic spire of wood covered with tin. The height of the whole from the ground to the top is 204 feet. Surrounding the base of the spire on the top of the tower is a neat iron railing, which forms the front of a gallery or bal- cony, from whence there is an extensive view over the whole city and circumjacent country. On the top is a handsome vane, with an iron rod tastefully formed in open work, and cross pieces indicating the four cardinal points.

Of the interior, simplicity and neatness are the pre- vailing features, and where any ornament is introduced, it is in perfect unison with the style of architecture, and harmonizes with the rest. The pews are painted white, and capped with cherry wood—with the numbers neatly gilt on the doors. The side galleries are supported by the main columns, and the organ gallery at the end in which the choir sits, is supported by columns of the Corinthian order, very well executed. The pulpit is neat, and of a fanciful design, with a circular front : it is supported upon six columns of the Corinthian order, and ascended by two flights of circular stairs, meeting in a platform in the rear of it. The ceiling is divided into three compartments ; the centre one of which is a segment of a circle supported on three columns and two pilasters on each side, thirty-one feet in height. These are of the Corinthian order to correspond with the others, with their capitals and entablatures elegantly enriched—the capitals are cut in wood and the entablatures of stucco. In the circular ceiling are three handsome centre pieces of foliage work, 12 feet in diameter, each formed of stucco. The flat or level compartments of the ceilings on each side are supported by cross beams from column to column, and from these to the side walls this part is also relieved by pannels, and the soffits of these are supported on the side walls by rich freizes of elegant design and workmanship in stucco. The *tòut ensemble* is, upon the whole, well adjusted, with every attention to durability, correctness in design, and elegance of execution.

In the year 1818, the Rev. Mr. Leeds removed to Brockville, on exchanging with the Rev. John Bethune, D. D., who is the present Rector of Christ Church, having for his assistant the Rev. D. Robertson. The Rev. J. Ramsay is the minister of Hochelaga Chapel.

MONUMENTAL TABLETS in CHRIST CHURCH.

To the Hon, RICHARD CARTWRIGHT,
Member of the Legislative Council of Upper Canada.
Died 27th July, 1815, aged 57.

In Memory of the Hon. JOHN RICHARDSON, Merchant,
Member of the Executive and Legislative Councils of the Province;
a native of Portsoy, N. B., born 1775;
Died in this country on the 18th of May, 1831.
Erected by his Widow and Family.
A wing of the General Hospital, bearing his name, has been erected
to his memory,
By his fellow-citizens and friends, both in Canada and Great Britain.

———

To the Memory of the Rev. BROOK BRIDGES STEVENS,
Chaplain to the Forces, and Evening Lecturer in the Episcopal
Church.
By his exertions the Protestant Episcopal Church at Lachine
was erected.
His remains are deposited beneath the Altar there.
Died 13th May, 1834, aged 46.
Erected by the Congregation of the Church.

———

To MARY GRANT, wife of JOHN FORSYTH, Esq.
of Montreal, Merchant;
A native of Quebec. Died there 30th July, 1818, aged 41 years.
Erected by her Husband.

———

To Lieutenant-Colonel GORDON,
Commanding First Battalion of the First Royal Scots Regiment of
Foot.
Died 24th Sept. 1814, by a wound received from the Enemy at
Fort Erie, on 17th of the same month.
Erected by the Officers of the Battalion.

———

To MARGARET HATT, wife of JOHN JAMIESON, Esq.
Died at Savannah, in Georgia,
16th January, 1835, aged 24.

To ANNE GUY, wife of SAMUEL WENTWORTH MONK, Esq.
one of the Prothonotaries of the
Court of King's Bench, District of Montreal.
Died 13th August, 1834, aged 35.

THE CHURCH OF
NOTRE DAME DE BON-SECOURS,

IN ST. PAUL STREET.

The foundation of this Church was laid, in 1658, by the celebrated Sœur Marguerite Bourgeois, who intended to found here the Nunnery of the Congregation ; but, meeting with some obstacles, she visited France, whence she returned the following year with several young persons to educate, and proceeded to establish the Nunnery where it now stands, in Notre Dame Street. Some years afterwards, she was induced by the following circumstances to undertake the completion of the church. In her second visit to France in 1671, to obtain Letters patent for her institution, she was directed to the house of M. Pierre Chevrier, Baron de Fancamp, Priest, one of the first proprietors of the Island of Montreal, then resident in Paris. He had in his possession a small image of the Virgin, reputed to be endowed with miraculous virtue, brought by some other Priests, also associates of the company, from among the relics of their Chateau, where it had been preserved and honoured for at least a century. It was desired that this image should be removed to Montreal, and a chapel built for its reception. This, Sœur Bourgeois undertook to perform, and on her return, bringing with her the image, the inhabitants of Montreal with great zeal entered into her design. A solemn procession was made on the 29th of June, 1673, to lay the principal stones of the edifice, which was finished in 1675, and mass performed on the day of Assumption, August 15th. This was the first church built of stone in the Island of Montreal, the new Parish Church, then in progress, not being quite finished, when the Church of Bon-secours was opened. In 1754, it was consumed by fire, and not rebuilt till 1771, when its re-erection was resumed, and completed on the 30th of June, 1773.

It continued to belong to the Sisters of the Congregation, till it was disposed of, some years since, to the *Fabrique* of the parish ; and is now used in connection with the Roman Catholic establishment in this city.

THE SCOTCH CHURCH,

ST. GABRIEL STREET.

This Church and Congregation are connected with the Established Church of Scotland. When the Church was built, and for several years afterwards, it was the only one in this Province in connection with that Establishment, there being no building then erected in Quebec for the Members of that Church residing there. It was, in consequence, called the Scotch Church, the Protestant Presbyterian Church, or the Presbyterian Church of Montreal ; but for some time past, since two others have sprung up in this city, it is known by the name of the St. Gabriel Street Church.* Before it was built, the Congregation assembled in the Recollet Church.

The ground on which it stands, was purchased from the late Mr. Hypolite Hertel, with the exception of

* Extracted from the Church-book, by favour of the Committee.

twelve feet in breadth, which was granted by Government from the Champ de Mars, in 1792. The Church was built the same year, by Messrs. Telfer and M'Intosh, Masons. Its size is 60 feet by 48, and it will seat 750 persons. A part of it is assigned to the use of the troops, when any Scotch Regiments are quartered here. The bell in the steeple of this Church is said to be " the first Protestant bell sounded in Canada."

On opening the Church, in 1792, the pulpit was occupied by the Rev. John Young, from Schenectady, the first Minister, who remained with the Congregation till 1802, when he was succeeded by the Rev. J. Somerville, who held the office twenty years, resigning it in 1822, on an annual allowance from the Church and Congregation. The Rev. Henry Esson became his assistant in 1817, and his successor when he retired. The Rev. Edward Black was chosen assistant to Mr. Esson, and remained in that office eleven years, when he left St. Gabriel Street, in 1833, and afterwards occupied the Church built for him in St. Helen Street.

WESLYAN CHAPEL G? S? JAMES ST?

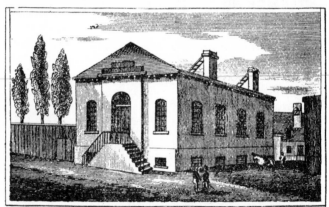

WESLYAN CHAPEL S? ANN'S SUBURB.

JEW'S SYNAGOGUE

CHAPTER VIII.

ECCLESIASTICAL EDIFICES, CONTINUED—METHODIST CHAPELS—JEWS' SYNAGOGUE—AMERICAN PRESBY-TERIAN CHURCH——CONGREGATIONAL CHURCH—SCOTCH SECESSION CHURCH—ST. ANDREW'S CHURCH—ST. PAUL'S CHURCH—BAPTIST CHAPEL.

BRITISH WESLEYAN METHODISTS.

The Wesleyan Methodists have three Chapels in Montreal. The first occupied by them was erected in 1809, and was situated in St. Joseph Street, with a house adjoining for the resident Minister. This building is at present occupied as an Exchange, and News Room.

The original Chapel being found too small, a lot of ground was purchased in St. James Street, on which the present elegant building was erected in 1821. It is of cut stone, and the architecture is of the Grecian Doric order, with a portico corresponding. It is galleried all round, and has a fine organ. The basement story is spacious, and is appropriated to the Sunday School. It is justly considered as one of the most beautiful edifices of the kind in the city, and has a convenient house adjoining, for the resident Minister, called the Mission House. The late Daniel Fisher, Esq. was a munificent contributor to the erection of the building, and the Trustees have placed a neat monument in the Chapel to his memory and "as a tribute of respect to departed worth." The Chapel will seat about 1000 persons, and the cost of the erection was £5,500.

Another Chapel, built and occupied by the Wesleyan denomination, is situated in the St. Ann Suburbs. It is a neat stone building, erected in 1833, with a basement story for a School. It will seat 450 persons.

The third Chapel occupied by the Wesleyans is situated in the Quebec Suburbs, and will seat about 300 persons.

Connected with these Chapels are six Schools, in which from 500 to 600 children receive weekly instruction.

The resident Ministers at this time are, the Rev. R. L. Lusher, and the Rev. J. P. Hetherington.

JEWS' SYNAGOGUE.

The Synagogue, situated at the upper end of Chenneville Street, St. Lawrence Suburbs, is a fine specimen of the Egyptian style of architecture. The front is of cut stone, and adorned with a handsome portico with two columns. The interior of the building is remarkably neat, fitted up with benches, which are occupied by the male part of the congregation. The gallery is supported by four handsome pillars, and is assigned to the female part of the congregation: the whole tastefully painted throughout. Opposite to this, also in the Egyptian style, is a very beautiful mahogany Ark, over which are placed the Ten Commandments, in Hebrew characters, cut in white marble.

The expense of the building was raised by private subscription, principally amongst persons professing Judaism in this city. The largest donation was given

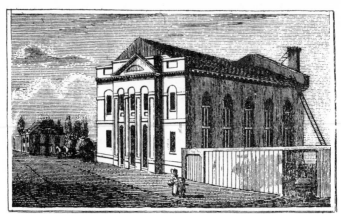

AMERICAN PRESBYTERIAN CHURCH.

CONGREGATIONAL CHAPEL

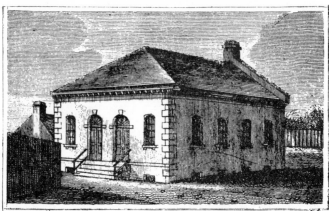

Duncan Delt.

SCOTCH SECESSION CHAPEL

Christie Sculpt.

by the late Mrs. Francis Michaels, of this city, amounting to £575 currency.

This Synagogue is the only one in British North America.

AMERICAN PRESBYTERIAN CHURCH,

ST. JAMES STREET.

The American Presbyterian Congregation was organised in December, 1822. The individuals who composed it were originally members of the St. Andrew's Congregation. Feeling themselves aggrieved by certain measures there pursued, they seceded, and formed themselves into a body, with a name significant of their national origin. For a considerable time, the Congregation thus formed was destitute of any house for public worship, and of course subject to great expense and inconvenience, in procuring temporary accommodations. After some delay, a piece of ground, advantageously situated, was procured, and the corner stone of the present edifice was laid in June, 1825. In the winter of 1826 the stated religious services of the Sabbath were commenced within the walls of the new building, although it was in a very unfinished state.

While struggling with the expense incident to the erection of so large an edifice, the Congregation had procured the services of a young clergyman of great piety and talent, the Rev. Joseph S. Christmas. He remained with them until June, 1828, having been then Pastor four years. He was then compelled, by the state of his health, to resign his pastoral charge.

After an interval of more than a year, the present Pastor, Rev. G. W. Perkins, commenced his services, and was regularly installed in the month of May, 1830.

The Congregation, originally small and often diminished by emigrations from the city, has yet greatly increased, and is now one of the largest Protestant Congregations in Montreal.

For some years past, the Sabbath Schools connected with this Congregation, and taught by its members, have contained nearly 500 pupils. At present there is a Free School connected with this Church, which gives gratuitous instruction to a large number of children. It was sustained for two years at an expense of One Thousand Dollars, by members of the Congregation; but now receives aid from Government.

CONGREGATIONAL, or INDEPENDENT CHURCH,

ST. MAURICE STREET.

The Congregational cause began in this city in the year 1831. The Rev. Richard Miles, recently in connection with the London Missionary Society, in South Africa, arrived in Montreal from England in September of that year. He found several members of this denomination without a Church or Minister of the order they preferred, and desirous of attempting the formation of a Church and Congregation in accordance with their principles. At their solicitation, he commenced his public ministry on the first Sabbath of October, in a School-room hired for the purpose. Soon thereafter, a larger and more commodious Room in the Mansion House, College Street, was obtained and fitted up to accommodate an increasing Congregation.

On the 6th July, 1832, fifteen individuals, including the Minister, the whole of whom had been members in good standing of Congregational Churches, formed themselves into a Church of Christ, after unanimously and solemnly adopting the following Declarations as the basis of their union and fellowship:

" 1. We, regarding each other as brethren and sisters in the Lord, do hereby form ourselves into a Christian Church of the Congregational or Pædobaptist order, professing the doctrines of faith in unison with those contained in the Assembly's Shorter Catechism, and usually denominated Calvinistic.

" 2. We do hereby resolve, in the strength of Divine grace, to walk with each other as a Christian Church in all the Commandments and Ordinances of the Lord."

The need of a more suitable and permanent edifice for public worship was early felt, and measures were adopted to supply it. After much effort and self-denial on the part of the infant cause, a suitable piece of ground was purchased in St. Maurice Street, at a heavy expense, and arrangements were made to proceed with the work. The foundation stone was laid in the month of July, 1834, and the building was finished and opened for public worship on the second Sabbath of February, 1835.

It is an exceedingly neat and well finished structure, having an elegant portico of the Doric order, and appropriate iron railing in front. The interior is at once comfortable and elegant, seating about 400, without galleries. There is a large School-room underneath, in which the usual Week Evening Services are held, and where a School of about 100 children assemble on the Lord's Day. The whole building, above and below, is lighted with gas. The cost was £1700.

In August, 1835, the Rev. R. Miles announced his intention to resign the pastoral charge of the Church and to proceed to a Missionary station in the country In October, the Rev. H. Wilkes, A. M., of Edinburgh, was invited to recross the Atlantic, and take the oversight of the Church.   Early in the year 1836, the Colonial Missionary Society, in connection with the Congregational Union of England and Wales, was formed ; and, being desirous of obtaining the services of a competent individual to act as their Corresponding Agent in the Canadas, Mr. Wilkes accepted this appointment, and also complied with the call of the Church.   He arrived with his family in August, 1836 ; and having spent some time in a journey through Upper Canada, on the business of the Colonial Mission, he commenced his stated labours in Montreal on the first Sabbath in October, 1836.   Mr. Wilkes is the present Clergyman.

The Church is connected with the Congregational Union for Lower Canada, which consists at present of thirteen Churches and Ministers.   The Congregational Union of Upper Canada consists of ten Churches and Ministers.   These bodies are in correspondence with the several Congregational Unions in Great Britain.

SCOTCH SECESSION CHURCH,

IN LAGAUCHETIERE STREET, ST. LAWRENCE SUBURBS.

Many of the Emigrants from Scotland, connected with the Secession Church in that country, when writing to their friends at home complained of the religious destitution in which they felt themselves here, and feeling still an attachment to the Church in which they had been educated, requested that some Ministers of that communion might be sent out.

At length the United Associate Synod undertook a mission to the Canadas, and in 1832 sent out several Missionaries.   All proceeded to Upper Canada, except the Rev. Mr. Robertson, who remained in Montreal, where he designed to form a church. His prospects of success were encouraging, but after a few months residence he was suddenly cut off by cholera, to the general regret of his friends.

In 1833, the Rev. Messrs. Murray and Taylor were sent out, and directed to form a church at Montreal, which they accomplished ; and soon afterwards the latter gentleman received an invitation to undertake the pastoral charge. At that time the Congregation met in Mr. Bruce's school room in M'Gill Street. This was soon found too small ; and the temporary use of the American Presbyterian Church was requested, and freely and gratuitously granted, at such hours as it was not needed by its own congregation.

In the following year the present building was commenced. Many difficulties were encountered by the Society in its feeble state ; but by the help of God they were all surmounted. In addition to what was raised in the city, contributions were received from the parent Church, and from Christians in the United States. The Church is a plain, but substantial building. It was intended to be two stories high, but the return of the cholera that year occasioned the work to be hastily finished. Its appearance suffers by the diminution of height, but it is a commodious place of worship, and will seat conveniently about 480 persons. The Church consists of 200 members, and the usual audience is about 400. There is a Sabbath School connected with the Church, in which from 80 to 90 children are instructed by 16 or 17 teachers. A Library is attached to the School, and another to the Church for the use of the Congregation, from which many advantages have already resulted.

The site may in one respect be deemed unfavourable, as being at too great a distance from the city ; but it

K 1

was originally chosen from a regard to the destitution of the neighbourhood, many of the inhabitants of which have reason to rejoice in the selection. The Rev. W. Taylor is pastor of the Church.

ST. ANDREW'S CHURCH,

IN ST. PETER STREET.

This Church, now in connection with the Established Church of Scotland, was commenced in the year 1805, and finished in April, 1807, at a cost of about £1500. It is a plain and substantial building of stone, 70 feet by 51 without, comfortably fitted up, and capable of containing with ease 760 persons. Galleries were erected in 1816, at an expense of £400. A Sabbath School is conducted in the Church, at which from 60 to 70 are generally in attendance; and a Theological Library is established for the use of the Congregation.

The Society was formed in the year 1804, and assembled for worship in a large private room, under the pastoral care of the Rev. Robert Easton, from Hawie, Roxburghshire, who continued in that office after the Church was built, until 1824, when he resigned his charge in consequence of the increasing infirmities of age and ill health: his declining days were made comfortable by a liberal allowance from the church. Both Mr. Easton and the original congregation belonged to the Burgher Secession in Scotland, and considered themselves to be in connection with the Associate Reformed Synod in that country; but this connection not being formally acknowledged by the Synod, on the proposed resignation of Mr. Easton, the congregation resolved to procure a Minister of the Church of Scotland, " and none else." The Rev. John Burns, A. M., succeeded

S^T PAUL'S SCOTCH CHURCH

S^T ANDREW'S SCOTCH CHURCH

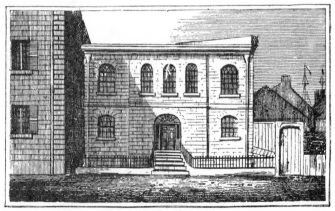

BAPTIST CHAPEL

Mr. Easton, and the congregation from that time became connected with the Established Church of Scotland. Some of the members, not being satisfied with this change, withdrew, and built a separate place of worship, known as the American Presbyterian Church. Mr. Burns continued Minister of St. Andrew's Church for nearly two years, when on succeeding to some landed property in Scotland, he returned to his native country. He was succeeded, in 1826, by the Rev. Dr. Mathieson, from Dumbarton, who is the present incumbent.

ST PAUL'S CHURCH,

IN ST. HELEN STREET.

This is also in connection with the Established Church of Scotland. The Congregation for whose use it was erected originally formed a part of that assembling in St. Gabriel Street. It is a chaste and elegant building of cut stone, and was erected by Mr. John Wells of this city, from a plan by Mr. Thompson, Architect, from London, who resided here some years. The Church is 71 feet in length by 53 in width. In the centre of the front, which is entirely Gothic, are two large octagonal buttresses, and small square ones at the ends. The buttresses terminate with pinnacles; the parapets* are embattled, and the whole is surmounted by open Gothic balustrades. The flanks are pierced by five large windows on each side, fifteen feet high, by five wide. The interior of the building is Grecian; and underneath is an extensive cellar, seven feet three inches high, with vaulted ceiling. The ground upon which it stands is a part of that which was formerly attached to the Jesuits' College.

* The lateral parapets are now removed,

K 2

The whole expense of erection, including the purchase of the ground, as appears from the Committee books, was.. £3569 8 8

That of the adjoining School House.... 436 15 2

The funds were partly raised by voluntary contributions, and partly borrowed. The trustees are, the Hon. P. M'Gill, and J. Redpath, and Joseph Ross, Esquires.

The Church was opened for Divine service on the 26th day of August, 1834, by the Rev. Dr. Black, the present incumbent. A meeting of the pew-holders was held in the Church on the 8th of April, 1835, when the first Temporal Committee was elected. Though not imposing by its magnitude, the Scotch Church in St. Helen Street is richly entitled to commendation as one of the most beautiful and ornamental edifices in the city.

BAPTIST CHAPEL,

ST. HELEN STREET.

The members of the Baptist denomination who successively took up their residence in this city, though differing from many other Christians only on the ordinance of Baptism, were naturally desirous of forming a religious Society, agreeably to their own views ; but no opportunity of doing this occurred till the year 1831. They had attended the ministry of Mr. Denham, for some months, in the years 1829 and 1830 ; and afterwards that of the Rev. John Gilmour, who, deeming it his duty to leave his charge in Aberdeen, Scotland, to preach the Gospel in Canada, arrived in Montreal, in the month of September. He succeeded Mr. Denham in the occupation of the school-room in which the congregation were in the habit of meeting.

The few members of the Baptist denomination then

in the place of course attended his ministry, and, aided by other Christian friends, resolved to build a chapel for the worship of God. In the spring of the following year, 1831, the building was begun; and finished and ready for public worship in September of the same year. It was immediately occupied by the Congregation to which Mr. Gilmour was preaching, and now belongs to the members in fellowship, represented by trustees, authorised by an act of the Provincial Legislature to hold property on their account.

The Chapel is built of cut stone; it is a neat and comfortable place of worship, capable of seating 400 hearers, with provision for the erection of galleries when required. The cost of its erection was £1200, including the lot of land on which it is built.

There is a Sunday School supported by the Church assembling here, held in the basement story of the building, which place is likewise used as a lecture room for the week-day services. The School averages in attendance of from 50 to 60 scholars.

The Church is in connection with the Ottawa Baptist Association, which at present includes nine Churches and eight Ministers.

K 3

CHAPTER IX.

ECCLESIASTICAL AND OTHER EDIFICES.——THE PRIESTS'
FARM——THE BISHOP'S CHURCH——RECOLLET CHURCH
——GENERAL HOSPITAL——ST. ANN'S MARKET——
NATIONAL SCHOOL.

THE PRIESTS' FARM

Is situated on the side of the Mountain, a little to the left of the road leading to Côte des Neiges and St. Laurent. It consists of extensive gardens and orchards, and several acres of land which are cultivated as a farm for the benefit of the Seminary, to which it belongs. The buildings are substantial and commodious, and occupy a position which commands a lovely view of the city, the River St. Lawrence, and the fine country in front. They are in summer the weekly resort of the professors and pupils of the Seminary and College; and nothing can be better adapted for exercise, and recreation from sedentary employment. They march to and from the place in regular order, and are generally accompanied by a band of music, formed from amateurs of their own body. The place was formerly known by the appellation of the *Château des Seigneurs de Montreal*, but now frequently called *La Maison des Prêtres*.

PRIEST'S FARM

BISHOP'S CHURCH & RESIDENCE

Duncan Del.

RECOLLECT CHURCH.

Christie Sculp.

ST. JAMES'S, or the BISHOP'S CHURCH,

IN ST. DENIS STREET.

When the Rev. Jean Jacques Lartigue was consecrated Suffragan of the Bishop of Quebec, under the
title of Bishop of Telmesse, some difficulties arose as to
the exercise of certain prerogatives.   These difficulties
induced the personal friends of M. Lartigue to unite
with him in erecting a church as the locality of his See.
The land for this purpose was granted by the Hon.
D. B. Viger, and the expense of building the church
and the adjoining residence and school-house, was obtained principally from the contributions of Roman
Catholic inhabitants of Montreal and its vicinity.   The
church was erected in 1824, and is capable of containing
3000 persons.

In 1836, Montreal was erected into a Bishopric.
Bishop Lartigue is now Titular Bishop of Montreal.
He took possession of his See on the 8th September,
1836, and St. James's Church became his Cathedral.

RECOLLET CHURCH,

IN NOTRE DAME STREET.

The property of the Recollets, on the extinction of
that order in Canada, having come into the possession
of the British Government, that part on which their
monastery stood, and the adjoining land in the city of
Montreal, was conveyed to the Hon. Mr. Grant, in
exchange for the Island of St. Helen, which previously
belonged to that gentleman.   The number of Irish
Catholics having much increased by emigration, and
there being no separate place of worship of sufficient
magnitude for their use, the Fabrique purchased of Mr.
Grant the church and some adjoining buildings.   The

present front of the church was built of materials from
the old Parish Church in the Place d'Armes, when it
was taken down in 1830.   In the Recollet Church the
Irish Catholics assemble on the days of service appointed
by authority, and form a numerous congregation.   Adjoining to the church on the north is an Orphan Asylum,
and at the east end a School for the children of Roman
Catholic parents.   The Rev. Mr. Phelan is the officiating
clergyman of this church.

GENERAL HOSPITAL,

IN DORCHESTER STREET.

The various charitable institutions connected with the
Roman Catholic establishments of this city, were several
years since found inadequate to the increasing wants of
the population, either from their own limits, the restric-
tion of admission to particular cases, or the reluctance
of the Protestant part of the inhabitants to enter them.
On all these accounts a new establishment, of a more
general and extensive character, became desirable.   The
increase of emigration, too, which, since the termination
of the war in 1815, brought to our shores vast numbers
of persons who were incapable of reaching their destination, being overtaken by sickness on their passage, or
detained by poverty on their arrival, and unable to procure either support or medical attendance from any
funds of their own, made an urgent appeal to the benevolent inhabitants of our cities, and prompted them to
devise means for the relief of these miserable exiles.
An association of females in Montreal, designated as the
Ladies' Benevolent Society, was formed expressly for
the relief of the indigent emigrants, who were sought
out and relieved with an assiduity which cannot be too

GENERAL HOSPITAL.

Sᵗ ANNS MARKET

NATIONAL SCHOOL

highly commended. The concern for these objects soon became so general among the inhabitants, that, in 1818, a fund of £1200 was raised to relieve the wants of these sufferers and the poor of the city ; and a soup kitchen was opened, where these philanthropic ladies personally superintended the distribution. But more than this was needed ; and the ladies pressed upon the attention of the Committee entrusted with the disbursement of the money collected, the cases of the sick, who needed, but were not able to procure, medical aid. Dr. Blackwood, a young gentleman who had retired from the army in which he had been a surgeon, and some other medical gentlemen of the city, agreed to give their professional assistance, provided a house could be obtained where the most necessitous cases of sick poor could be relieved. The late Isaac Winslow Clark, Esq., then Deputy Commissary General, and an active member of the Committee, obtained from the Governor, the Duke of Richmond, a quantity of condemned barrack bedding. A small building, of four apartments, in the St. Joseph Suburbs, was then hired, and called the *House of Recovery.* Small as it was, and inadequate to meet the numerous cases that needed relief, it became the germ of that noble institution which redounds so greatly to the benefit and honour of the city of Montreal. The expenses of this miniature establishment enabled the managers of it to form a probable estimate of the sum requisite for an institution of such an extent as the wants of the poor required. They saw not, as yet, how to obtain it ; but from the spirit of active charity which had displayed itself, they were led to believe that, by a further appeal to the benevolent, through the medium of charity sermons, subscription lists sent round the city, and other means of raising donations, they would be enabled to establish and support a hospital on a more extended scale. The Protestant Clergymen of the city, in union with the most eminent medical practitioners and the Committee then existing, proceeded to hire a larger house in Craig Street. This was soon fitted up with the necessary articles of furniture, and an additional quantity of Barrack bedding was procured from the Governor. The building consisted of three wards, capable of receiving about twenty-four patients, and so arranged that a nearer approach to classification could be made than in the former confined building. A meeting of the citizens was called, a Committee was appointed, a house-keeper and other attendants engaged. A certain number of directors or visiting members were chosen, two of whom took the duty of visiting the hospital weekly in rotation. The medical department was placed under the direction of four professional gentlemen, who attended monthly in rotation, and one of them, as house surgeon, attended daily in case of accidents. On the first of May, 1819, such patients as were in the House of Recovery, together with the little property belonging to that establishment, were removed into the new institution, which now assumed the title of the MONTREAL GENERAL HOSPITAL, and for the more effectual management of which a code of rules was drawn up and brought into immediate operation.

This was a most important step in the progress of benevolent effort in behalf of the poor in the city. The regularity and good order in which the institution was kept, and the interest excited in its favour from the numbers concerned in its management, soon made it an object of public consideration. The quarterly reports evinced the benefits which resulted from it, and induced many to become subscribers, while the confidence excited by its judicious management prevailed upon its supporters to make greater exertions in its behalf. By many of them, indeed, it was considered only as an experiment, which, if it succeeded, might tend to something yet more permanent and effectual. About this time there was a piece of ground on sale, which belonged to Mr. Marshall, and was occupied by him as a nursery. With a liberality which deserves to be recorded to their honour, the Hon. John Richardson, the Hon. William M'Gillivray, and Samuel Gerrard, Esq., purchased this ground on their joint credit, and held it in trust for the purpose of erecting an hospital upon it. This purchase was made in August, 1820, and operated strongly as a stimulus to increased energy on the part of the inhabitants.

At a meeting afterwards held, Mr. Thomas Phillips submitted a plan, which was approved, and which was so constructed as to admit of enlargement, if necessary, without destroying the symmetry of the erection. The estimate for the centre building, with its appurtenances, was £2,200, of which £800 was immediately subscribed by individuals present at the meeting, and so much of the remainder was obtained by the beginning of the next year, that the Committee felt themselves justified in entering into contracts for the work in January, 1821. The Hon. John Richardson, the Rev. John Bethune, Dr. William Robertson, John Molson, Sen., David Ross, John Try, and Alexander Skakel, Esquires, were a Committee appointed for this duty. Mr. Phillips was chosen to superintend the building, as architect, for which £50 were allowed him, but he relinquished it as his subscription to the general fund. On the 6th day of June, 1821, the foundation stone was laid with Masonic ceremonies. In a cavity formed in the stone, a crystal tube was deposited, hermetically sealed, and containing two written pieces of parchment, and several coins.

First Parchment.

MONTREAL GENERAL HOSPITAL.

The centre part of this building, situate upon Dorchester Street, in the St. Lawrence Suburbs, of the city of Montreal, was erected in the year of our Lord Christ 1821, and in the 2d year of the Reign of our Sovereign Lord George the 4th, (under the administration in this Province of His Excellency the Right Honorable George Earl of Dalhousie, Governor in Chief of the British North American Provinces) by voluntary contributions, for the benevolent purpose of establishing an Hospital, to be called the *Montreal General Hospital*, for the reception and cure of diseased poor, and others who may not have the means or conveniency of being duly cared for when sick, at their own places of residence.

The only institution of this kind, hitherto, has been the Hotel Dieu Nunnery, which, although highly useful, yet the accommodations therein for the sick being very limited, and their rules excluding certain diseases, it is found to be now inadequate to the growing population of this City and Suburbs, which is now estimated at about twenty thousand souls.

An effort therefore to establish an Hospital upon a more extended and general plan as to residents, and embracing also the reception and cure of diseased poor emigrants from the mother country, on passing through Montreal, became indispensable, and happily has succeeded beyond expectation.

The present building is so constructed, as to be capable hereafter of a three-fold extension when needful, by adding thereto a wing at each end of equal capacity with the centre.

The contributors up to the 5th day of June, 1821, when the corner stone of the centre building was laid with masonic ceremony ; and the amount of their respective subscriptions to this praiseworthy undertaking, are as follows, viz. :

[*The List is here inserted, on the parchment.*]

The first Directors consist of George Auldjo, Robert Armour, Thomas Blackwood, William Blackwood, J. T. Barrett, I. Winslow Clarke, Joseph Chapman, Henry Corse, Jacob Dewitt, David David, Fredk. Wm. Ermatinger, John Fisher, senior, Samuel Gerrard, George Garden, Benaiah Gibb, sen., Robert Gillespie, William Gray, James Leslie, William Lunn, James Millar, John Molson, sen., the Honble. William M'Gillivray, Peter M'Gill,

John Molson, jun., Adam L. M'Nider, Henry M'Kenzie, Wm. M. Porter, Thomas Phillips, the Hon. John Richardson, David Ross, Alexander Skakel, Michael Scott, John Try, Thomas Torrance, Andrew White, and Kenneth Walker.

The Directors ex-officio are the Rev. John Bethune, Rector of the Parish of Montreal, the Rev. Mr. Somerville, Mr. Easton, Mr. Esson, Mr. Lusher.

The Committee for carrying on the building are the Hon. John Richardson, David Ross, John Molson, the Rev. Mr. Bethune, Alexander Skakel, John Try, and Dr. Wm. Robertson.

The Treasurer for the institution is Samuel Gerrard.

The contractors for the Masonry are John Redpath and William Riley.

The contractors for the Carpenter's and Joiner's work are Edward Barnett and Gordon Forbes.

And the professional superintendant of the work is Thomas Phillips, who contributes his services in that respect, in lieu of a pecuniary subscription—such services being considered and accepted as equivalent to fifty pounds.

Second Parchment.

At Montreal, in the Province of Lower Canada, in the year of our Lord Christ 1821, and of Masonry 5821,—being the second year of the reign of our Sovereign Lord George the Fourth of the United Kingdom of Great Britain and Ireland, King, Defender of the Faith, His Royal Highness Prince Augustus Frederick, Duke of Sussex, Most Worshipful Grand Master of the United Grand Lodge of Antient Free and Accepted Masons of England, and the Right Hon. George, Earl of Dalhousie, Governor General of British North America.

This Chief Corner Stone of the Montreal Hospital, was laid in due form by the Right Worshipful Sir John Johnston, Baronet, Past Provincial Grand Master of Canada, deputed by and acting as substitute for the Right Worshipful and Honorable Claude Dene-chaud, Present Provincial Grand Master under authority of the Grand Lodge aforesaid, attended and assisted by the officers of the Provincial Grand Lodge, and the Masters, Wardens, and Brethren of the three Lodges held in this city, being Nos. 8, 12, and 20 in the Registry of the said Province, and in the presence of several visiting Brethren of distinction in Free Masonry.

COINS DEPOSITED UNDER THE STONE.

A Half Crown of George IV.

A Guinea, Sovereign, a Half Sovereign, a Third of a Guinea, Two Shillings, a Sixpence, a Farthing, of George III.

A Shilling of Ann.

An Irish Halfpenny of William and Mary.

A Halfpenny of James II.

In less than a year the building was finished, and on the first of May, 1822, it was opened for the reception of patients, when the whole of the former establishment was removed into it. The number of patients admitted the first year was 421, and of out-patients 397, making a total of 818 indigent human beings, who in sickness were carefully attended to, and every thing in the power of medical skill done for their recovery. In the session of 1823 the Provincial Legislature, on the recommendation of Lord Dalhousie, Governor in Chief, granted the sum of £850 Currency to defray the annual expenses of the Hospital; and a further mark of favour and patronage was extended to it by granting it a Charter of Incorporation. The total cost of the central building and the land belonging to it, was £5856 8 0. The Secretary in his report at the end of the year, observes that " though the Hospital has cost much more than the estimate, it is to be remembered that many additions have been made to the original plan, which were not, at first, contemplated; and that that estimate was merely for the building itself, exclusive of any appendages. Those capable of judging, who have seen it, consider it to have been erected at a very cheap rate." Not half the amount was raised during the year, but the deficiency was advanced in equal shares by the three gentlemen who purchased the ground. Shortly afterwards, at a meeting of the directors, the Hon. John Richardson assured them that means had been found to cancel

the debt, amounting to £4099 6 10, but that he was not
at liberty to make any explanation as to the manner in
which this most liberal deed had been accomplished.
A legacy of £100 bequeathed by David David, Esq.,
enabled the directors to purchase a building adjacent to
the hospital grounds, by which the premises were rendered more complete, and an addition made to its
revenue. The first medical department consisted of Drs.
Caldwell, Robertson, Holmes, Leodel, and Stephenson,
the last of whom acted as House Surgeon. These, with
an Apothecary, Matron, three Nurses, and the necessary servants and attendants, constituted the effective force
of the establishment. In the year ending the 1st May,
1824, there had been received 254 Protestants and 216
Roman Catholics; out-patients 254 Protestants, and 110
Roman Catholics. Total number of cases from the
commencement, 933, shewing an increase of 115.

Within ten years from the first foundation of the
hospital, a most important addition was made to it, in
consequence of the following very interesting circumstances. On the demise of the Hon. John Richardson,
the first President of the institution, a voluntary subscription was entered into, for the purpose of erecting a
cenotaph to his memory in the Episcopal Church.
Large sums were obtained in this city, as well as in
Quebec, York, and London. As the amount collected
far exceeded what was required to carry this object into
effect, and the demands for admission into the hospital
exceeded its capacity, it was resolved to devote the
money thus acquired to the enlargement of the building,
by erecting a wing to be called the *Richardson Wing*,
as the best means of combining honour to the dead with
utility to the living. The corner stone was laid on the 16th
September, 1831. A glass tube, hermetically sealed,
and containing two parchments, was deposited in it.

Their contents were as follow :

First Parchment.

This edifice is intended, under the Divine blessing, to commemorate the public and private virtues of the late Honorable **John Richardson**, a Member of the Executive and Legislative Councils of Lower Canada, distinguished during a residence of near fifty years in this Province, by the rectitude and consistency of his conduct, by his spirit of enterprise in promoting improvement, and by the most extensive benevolence. He was born at Portsoy, in the County of Banff, North Britain, emigrated to the late British Colonies in 1774, and came into Canada in 1787, where he attained great eminence as a Merchant, and displayed in his long career of public service, the variety of talent with which he was endowed. He departed this life on the 18th day of May last, in the 77th year of his age.

The erection of a monument to this distinguished individual, was taken into immediate consideration by those who knew and justly appreciated his character ; and voluntary contributions were obtained for the purpose of placing a cenotaph to his memory in Christ Church of this city. Desirous, also, of handing down to posterity a just sense of the important share which this their first President had in founding, incorporating, and supporting the Montreal General Hospital, the members of the Corporation raised a contribution for the purpose of placing within its walls some memorial of so great a benefactor. This desire to honour the memory of one of the most distinguished of His Majesty's subjects in British North America, was not confined to Montreal, but extended wherever his name and character were known. Contributions for the same purpose were made in Quebec, in York, and in other parts of both Provinces. The amount thus collected having exceeded the most sanguine expectations, it has been deemed expedient by the contributors to both monuments, and considered most congenial to the character of the deceased, to unite the funds, and enlarge that asylum for afflicted humanity, which, as its President, he to his last moments cherished with pastoral care, by erecting this building to be called " The Richardson Wing of the Montreal General Hospital."

Second Parchment.

Names of Officers of Grand and Provincial Lodges of Free Masons.

The following Medals and Coins were enclosed in a box, and placed also in the corner stone:

A Medal commemorative of the Reign and Demise of his late Majesty George III.

A Medal commemorative of the Reign and Demise of his late Majesty, George IV.

A Sovereign of George IV.

A half do.   do.

A Crown   do.

A Shilling.

A Sixpence.

A Penny.

A Halfpenny and Farthing.

A Five Livre piece of Louis Phillipe I., King of France; coined 1831.

A Ten Cent piece } United States.
A Five do. do.

Another tin box contained a copy of the Charters and By-Laws of the Corporation, First Annual Report, lists of the original contributors to the central building, an Almanac for the year 1831, and the papers of the day.

This wing was opened for the reception of patients on the 7th of December, 1832. With this addition, the Hospital contains 19 wards, and 160 beds.

On a marble tablet, in the front of this wing, is the following inscription:

THE

RICHARDSON WING OF THE MONTREAL GENERAL HOSPITAL.

This Building was erected, A. D. 1832,

To commemorate the public and private virtues of the.

Hon. John Richardson,

A distinguished Merchant of this city, and
Member of the Executive and Legislative Councils of the Province.
He was the first President of this Hospital,
And a liberal Contributor to its Foundation and Support.
He was born at Portsoy, North Britain, and died 18th May, 1831,
Aged 76 years.

SCALE OF PATIENTS, FOR SEVERAL YEARS.

		In door.	Out door.
Year ending May 1,	1826	601	682
—	— 1827	591	381
—	— 1828	772	491
—	— 1829	556	?19
—	— 1830	451	440
—	— 1831	797	782
—	— 1832	1830	2452
—	— 1833	1909	1650
—	— 1834	1296	1072
—	— 1835	769	819
—	— 1836	1029	635
—	— 1837	1152	1528
To Oct. 1,	1838	561	377

PRESENT RULES OF THE INSTITUTION.

Every person who has contributed to the erection of the Hospital, or who shall hereafter contribute to its fund £25 Currency, and an Annual Subscription for life of £3 Currency, is constituted a Life Governor.   Annual Governors are eligible on contributing a sum under £25, and not less than £10, and an annual payment thereto of £2 or more.   There are at present forty-four Governors, including those annually elected: they meet every quarter for the transaction of business.   Two Governors are appointed weekly to visit the Hospital, and report upon its condition.

The Committee of Management, elected from among the Governors, meet weekly (on Friday) to audit, inspect, and approve of all accounts, in order to their liquidation, and report, through the Secretary of the Corporation, a statement of all their transactions, to each quarterly meeting of the Governors.   They have charge of the property of the Corporation, and are empowered to enforce all necessary attention to economy, cleanliness, &c.

The Medical Officers are eight in number, and visit the Hospital in rotation every two months;—under ordinary circumstances, once a day.   Their services are gratuitous.   The Medical Officers form a Board, called the "Medical Board of the Montreal General Hospital"   Its duty is to superintend the Medical Department, and examine and report upon the qualifications of individuals applying for the appointments of House Physician, House Surgeon, Apothecary, Clerks, Dressers, &c.

Every Governor and Medical Officer of the Hospital, and the Clergymen belonging to the congregations of this city, may recommend patients for admission into the Hospital, subject to the approval of the attending Physician or Surgeon. Such persons as are unable to pay for their maintenance are received as paupers. Such as can afford it, pay a sum not less than five shillings per week : the persons recommending patients under these circumstances, are responsible for the payment.

Women in advanced stages of pregnancy are inadmissible. Insane and incurable diseases are not admissible : all other complaints are.

The out-door patients receive medicines and advice without reference to the nature of their diseases.

Students can attend the practice of the Hospital on the payment of two Guineas for one year. For a further sum of two Guineas the ticket is made perpetual. No Student is eligible to a dressership unless he has studied for 18 months with some medical practitioner, and attended the Hospital six months at least. He will require to be approved of by the Medical Board, before he can be admitted to that office.

The Medical Board consists of—Wm. Robertson, M.D., A. F. Holmes, M.D., Physicians and Surgeons extraordinary ; J. Stephenson, M.D., T. Bruneau, M.D., A. Hall, M.D., G. W. Campbell, M.D., J. Crawford, M.D., and S. Sewell, M.D. Apothecary, J. R. Dick.

Two marble tablets, one to the memory of Dr. Caldwell, and the other to that of Mr. Leodel, are in the vestibule of the Hospital.

This building is one of the principal ornaments of the city. Seen from various points of view, it is a striking and elegant object, independently of the pleasing ideas which its design cannot fail to suggest to the benevolent mind. Its situation, too, is highly favourable ; and probably if all the ground in the vicinity had been vacant, a more eligible spot could not have been selected. Near enough to the crowded part of the city, to be easily accessible, it has yet the advantages of a rising ground, pure air, and pleasant prospects in every direction.

NATIONAL SCHOOL,

IN BONSECOURS STREET.

This institution is under the patronage of the Montreal District Committee of the *Society for Promoting Christian Knowledge.* It was founded in the year 1816, and consists of two departments, the male and the female. There are separate Committees for the respective departments. All who contribute 11s. 8d. annually to the funds of the District Committee are entitled to act as visitors. The building is plain, but neat and extensive, and well adapted to its purpose. In addition to the School and Committee rooms, there are apartments for the master and mistress : these offices are at present held by Mr. and Mrs. Rollet. The number of boys in the school is 36 French and 120 English—average attendance about 100 ; of girls 20 French and 84 English—average attendance about 70.

GREY NUNNERY

CONGREGATIONAL NUNNERY

CHAPEL OF THE HOTEL DIEU NUNNERY

CHAPTER X.

GREY NUNNERY;

Or GENERAL HOSPITAL of the CHARITABLE SISTERS.

When Louis the Fourteenth, in 1692, had granted,
by letters patent, to the Bishop of Quebec, the Governor, and their successors, power to establish General
Hospitals and other similar institutions, for the relief of
the sick and aged poor in different parts of the country,
several laymen, citizens of Montreal, at the head of
whom was M. Charron, a native of Normandy, determined to establish such an hospital in this city. They
accordingly signified their intention to the proper authorities, and under letters patent especially granted to
themselves in 1692, proceeded to found and endow a
General Hospital in Montreal, upon the same plan as
that which was then building in Quebec, and determined
to devote their time and fortunes to this benevolent
purpose. Their design was encouraged by the gentlemen of the Seminary, who made extensive donations
en fief et en rôture, and granted also, free of all charges,

rents, and seigniorial dues, that extensive lot near the
town gate on which the hospital now stands, with only
this proviso, that if, at any future time, the said hospital should cease to exist, the whole premises should
then revert to the Ecclesiastics of the Seminary of
Montreal. The citizens in general, whose circumstances enabled them to render aid, contributed liberally to
this purpose, and the hospital was soon erected and put
into operation.

The objects of this institution were to provide an
assylum for lame, superannuated, and infirm persons,
where they could be lodged and fed, and have all their
wants supplied, and likewise a refuge for orphan children who were left in destitute circumstances, where
they could be employed in work suitable to their ages,
put in the way of learning some trade, and receive such
an education as would enable them to become valuable
members of the community. The direction of the hospital and the management of its revenues were vested
in the founders and their successors, but under the
superintendance of the administrators in chief, who were
to have the right of selling and transferring any part of
the fixed property.

Under the wise and prudent direction of M. Charron,
the first superior, the institution made rapid progress in
prosperity and importance ; new powers were given to
the managers of the establishment, under the title of the
FRERES CHARRONS, particularly one to erect within
their precincts such manufactories as they might think
needful for the employment of the poor ; and several
purchases of real estate were made in the vicinity of
Montreal, among which may be mentioned that at Pointe
St. Charles, in 1693.

The revenues arising from the estates were, however,
at that time, very trifling, and the institution soon fell

into difficulties, and was obliged to restrict its admissions. After the death of M. Charron, his successor
proved to be a man ill qualified to direct the affairs of
the establishment, and many of the brotherhood withdrew from it, till only two or three friars were left. On
examination, it was found that the hospital was more
than two thousand pounds in debt. The whole was
transferred, therefore, into the hands of the seigniors
administrators, in 1747 ; and by them soon afterwards
committed to the care of a Society of Ladies, under the
superintendance of Madame Youville. This excellent
lady was the daughter of Christopher Duffort, Esq., a
native of Breton, and Captain of a troop of Cavalry in
that Colony, and of Miss Gauthier of Varennes. Miss
Duffort, who had married in early life a Canadian gentleman, M. François de Youville, was left a widow at
28 years of age. She retired from the world, and
devoted herself to acts of charity and other religious
duties. With a competent fortune from her patrimo-
nial estate, she possessed also a dignity of person, a
modesty of deportment, an accomplished taste, a lively
wit tempered with great solidity of judgment, which
gave her much influence among those who knew her,
and enabled her to gratify extensively her benevolent
desires. Meeting with some other ladies, whose minds
were congenial with her own, they agreed, in 1737, to
unite in works of charity, to live by their own industry,
and place their revenues in one common fund. They
procured a habitation in the city, where they all resided,
taking with them six aged and infirm persons for whom
they provided. Having adopted rules for their mutual
government, they bound themselves by vows as religious
recluses, and irrevocably devoted themselves to the
service of the poor, Madame Youville being recognised
as the Superior of the community.

On the surrender of the hospital by the Freres Charrons, M. Louis de Normand, Vicar-General of the diocese
of Quebec, Seignior of Montreal, and President of the
Seminary, pointed out Madame Youville and her associates as very proper persons to take charge of the
institution. The excellent conduct, and great benevolence of these ladies, had long been the theme of remark
and admiration. To them the Seigniors and principal
administrators of the hospital, had recourse, and immediately confided its management to their care. It was
most readily, and even joyfully, undertaken, in the
month of August, 1747, when they were only nine in
number. Having taken an inventory of all the property
belonging to the hospital, they took possession of it,
accompanied by nine poor persons who had formerly
been under their care, and four others whom they found
there.

The Freres, as has been stated, had left the hospital
in debt. This debt Madame Youville engaged to discharge, either from her own private funds, or from such
charitable donations as she might obtain, on condition
that she should be judicially appointed manager of the
institution. Her name, and those of her colleagues,
were inserted in the deed passed between her and the
administrators, and a copy of it transmitted to the Court
of France. The king, in council, confirmed and enlarged
these arrangements, by letters patent dated the 3d of
June, 1753. By these Madame Youville and her associates were duly installed, and legally authorized to
establish this community, with its internal regulations,
under the surveillance of the Bishop of Quebec.

It is not easy to conceive a situation more critical
than that in which these ladies were placed. They had
undertaken the charge of an institution almost destitute
of revenue—burdened with debts—and the building in

so ruinous a condition as to require immediate and extensive repairs.   But their zeal, industry, and rigid economy happily surmounted all these difficulties.   Assisted
by the generosity of the benevolent, who came liberally forward to aid them in this pious undertaking,
instead of twelve poor and infirm old persons whom
they had at first to support, the hospital was soon in a
condition to extend its benefits to persons of all ages
and stations of life.   Its doors were freely thrown open
for the reception of every unfortunate individual, and
its charity and assistance extended to all who applied
for them.   A place was fitted up for the use of the sick
and wounded.   In the course of a short time no fewer
than one hundred persons of these classes were receiving
assistance and support from this institution, while the
active benevolence of these excellent ladies made the
requisite provision for them.

In the year 1755 a farther extension was made in the
plan of the hospital.   One day in the preceding winter,
as Madame Youville was going into town on business
connected with the institution, she observed an infant in
the ice on the " Little River"—then uncovered.   It was
hard frozen, with a poignard sticking in its throat, and
one of its little hands raised through the ice, as if in the
attitude of demanding justice against the perpetrator of
so atrocious a crime.   Her benevolent feelings were
dreadfully shocked at witnessing so horrid a spectacle ;
and after consulting with her associates, who were all
deeply affected at such an event, they came to the
determination, notwithstanding the additional expense,
of extending their charity and protection to orphans and
foundlings.   In the year 1765, a fire happened in their
premises which consumed the greater part of the building.   By the fruits of their continued industry, aided
by donations from the charitable, these ladies soon

rebuilt the house upon a more extensive and commodious plan than before. A neat gateway has been recently erected in the wall in front of the chapel, bearing this inscription :

Hôpital Général des Sœurs Grises
FONDE EN 1755.
Mon Pére et ma mére m'ont abandonné, mais le
Seigneur m'a recueilli. Ps. 26.

A few years after the fire, Madame Youville purchased, from her own private funds, the small island of Chateauguay, which had at that time a farm upon it, as at present ; and a short time afterwards the whole seigniory of Chateauguay was likewise bought for the institution, partly by Madame Youville and one of the other ladies. But this and other property in the neighbourhood of Montreal did not, till recently, yield much revenue to the support of the hospital. Grants from the legislature have enabled the Society to extend its bounty to a greater number of lunatics and foundlings. Yet notwithstanding the aid they have received, it deserves to be recorded, to the honour of these benevolent ladies, that to their industry, economy, and good management, is to be ascribed the continued and increasing prosperity of an institution, which has been of incalculable benefit, and has relieved the Province from a number of necessitous and infirm individuals, who, without such a refuge, must have been a burden on society, while they dragged out their existence in a miserable condition.

A yearly allowance was made by the French Government to this hospital, which was paid for many years after the colony became British ; but at the revolution it ceased, until the restoration of the Bourbon family to the throne, when, on application to the Court, all arrears were paid, both principal and interest. From this and other sources a sum has been obtained, by means of which very material additions have recently been made to the buildings of the institution.

Of the scale on which this establishment is now conducted, some judgment may be formed from the fact, that at least one hundred and sixty individuals are resident within its walls, and maintained by its resources, besides servants and attendants whose wages amount to a considerable sum.

BLACK NUNNERY;

Or CONVENT OF LA CONGREGATION DE NOTRE DAME,

Was founded by the celebrated Marguerite Bourgeois, who commenced the undertaking in the year 1659, with some young ladies she had brought from France. The front of the Nunnery is in Notre Dame Street, where it extends 234 feet, and its depth along St. John Baptist Street, is 433 feet. Beside the principal edifice for the residence of the members and pupils, the Nunnery contains a chapel, numerous detached buildings, and a large garden. Recently, a high wall, which ran along Notre Dame Street, has been taken down, and a range of very elegant shops and houses, all of cut stone, and uniform design, has been erected. The Congregation is composed of a Superior and sixty sisters. The object of the institution is female instruction in its different branches ; and the greater part of the members are employed in the work of tuition and training. Boarders are taken into the house on moderate terms, and receive a careful education. From this establishment some of the sisters are sent as missionaries to different parts of the district, for the purpose of opening and conducting schools in parishes remote from the convent,

The pious and benevolent foundress of this institution was born at Troyes, in France, on the 15th of April, 1620, and was brought to this country in September, 1653, by M. Maison-neuve, the Governor of the Island of Montreal, who had been revisiting France. On her arrival in this city, she commenced those labours for the instruction of young females, both of Indian and French origin, which she continued with much success for many years, and which, amidst many difficulties, enabled her to establish the Nunnery of the Congregation. Her design was approved by the priest of the parish, and by the Governor, who gave her the choice of any ground that was then unoccupied. She selected the spot on which the Church of Bonsecours now stands, and laid there the foundation of a chapel, in the year 1658; but the Abbe Quelus, who had come out to establish the Seminary of the Sulpicians, not being acquainted with her excellencies, and looking upon her design as an interference with his department and plan, he forbade her to proceed. Yielding instant obedience to him as her superior, she desisted, and returned to France for the purpose of obtaining the direction and authority of the Government. In this object she succeeded, and met also with much encouragement from the congregation to which she belonged, and other individuals, in France. In the following year she returned to Ville Marie, bringing with her, for instruction in her proposed Seminary, several young females who had been entrusted to her care. Finding the timber and other materials which she had collected for the Chapel of Bonsecours, either removed or rendered useless, she sought for another spot on which to execute her design, now become more extensive from the encouragement she had received. An offer of some out-houses near the place where the Nunnery now stands, induced her to commence her establishment there; and in subsequent years, other grants, both of land and money, fresh arrivals of young females from France, the countenance of the authorities both there and in Canada, and lastly the issuing of Letters Patent from the King, placed the institution upon a solid basis, and secured at once both its permanency and its extension. The benevolent foundress had the pleasure, for many years, of witnessing its growing prosperity, and of contributing to that prosperity by her own unwearied exertions. At length, full of days and honours, she died on the 12th of January, 1700, in the 80th year of her age.

The black dress worn by the sisters of the Congregation has given to the establishment the colloquial title we have prefixed, while by many it is denominated the Congregational Nunnery, from the fact of its being conducted by the " sisters," for the benefit of the " daughters" of the CONGREGATION de Notre Dame.

THE HOTEL DIEU NUNNERY,

IN ST. JOSEPH, AND ST. PAUL STREETS.

This was the first of the Religious houses formed in Montreal, and was commenced within two years after the first occupation of the city by the Sulpicians. It was founded in 1644, by Madame de Bouillon, for the reception of the sick and diseased poor of both sexes. It extends, in St. Paul Street 324 feet in front, and 468 feet in depth in St. Joseph Street. It is conducted by a Superior and thirty-six Nuns. Under the French Government, it was formerly supplied with medicines and many other necessaries; the funds for maintaining the charity are principally derived from the rent of lands, assisted occasionally by grants from the Provincial Parliament. The establishment includes a hospital, a convent, and a church, with a large garden, a cattle-yard, out-buildings, and a cemetery. It has furnished for many years a refuge for the miserable, and help for the sick, to whose comfort the sisters devote themselves with most praiseworthy benevolence. There is an air of neatness and convenience about all the buildings belonging to this charitable institution. Before the establishment of the Montreal General Hospital, in 1822, this was the only place to which the afflicted poor of various descriptions could be sent for relief. The front of the church is in St. Paul Street : it is of stone, has four pilasters of the Tuscan order, surmounted by a triangular pediment and cross, as represented in the plate.

SEMINARY OF ST. SULPICE,

IN NOTRE DAME STREET.

This establishment is one of the oldest connected with the Roman Catholic Church in Montreal. It was founded about the year 1657, by the Abbé Quelus, who had recently arrived from France with a commission from the St. Sulpicians at Paris, to superintend the settlement and cultivation of the island, and especially to found an institution on a plan similar to their own. The Seminary is the dwelling-house of those members of the Sulpician family who are occupied in parochial duties. The houses of this order in France are all Ecclesiastical Seminaries ; so that when some of the members came out to Montreal, the establishment here received the same name. The Seminary is a large and commodious building, adjoining the Parish Church. It

COLLEGE

SEMINARY

BRITISH & CANADIAN SCHOOL

occupies three sides of a square, 132 feet long by 90 deep, with spacious gardens and ground attached, extending 342 feet in Notre Dame Street, and 444 along St. François Xavier Street. Connected with it is a school for junior pupils on the opposite side of Notre Dame Street, which is conducted by *Les Frères des écoles Chrétiennes*, and contains about 300 children. The Seminary has also established a number of schools in different parts of the parish for a similar purpose.

THE NEW COLLEGE,

Or PETIT SEMINAIRE.

This institution is situated in the Recollet Suburbs, not far from M'Gill Street, and very near what was called the Little River, but which is now almost entirely arched over. The building was erected a few years ago, by the Seminary of St. Sulpice, at an expense of more than £10,000, for the purpose of rendering their plan of education as extensive as possible. The College is a handsome and capacious edifice : the body of it is 210 feet in length, by 45 broad, having at each end a wing that runs at right angles 186 feet by nearly 45. The arrangements have been made with every attention to convenience, utility, and salubrity, consisting of residences for the principal, professors, and masters ; a chapel, airy dormitories, and apartments for the senior and junior classes, refectories, and every domestic office. The grounds attached to the College are ample, both for gardens and places of exercise ; and the whole is surrounded by a high wall, except the immediate front of the building, which is separated by palisades on a parapet from College Street. The director, M. Roque, and the chief professors, are distinguished for eminence in literature, and skill and activity in the art of instruction. A moderate annual stipend is paid with each of the pupils. The College was originally built for 120 resident pupils. Alterations were made about three years ago, which rendered it capable of receiving 160 pupils. The number of resident pupils now varies from 130 to 150, and of non-resident pupils from 100 to 130. They are received young; as early as ten or eleven years of age: the regular course of study lasts eight years. Besides the principal, there are in the College four professors and eight tutors.

THE

BRITISH AND CANADIAN SCHOOL,

IN LAGAUCHETIERE STREET.

The British and Canadian School Society was instituted on the 21st of September, 1822, for the purpose of promoting the education of the labouring classes of the people of every religious persuasion. Its objects were, first, to maintain a School on an extensive scale to educate children, and, secondly, to train up and qualify young persons of both sexes to supply well-instructed teachers to such of the inhabitants of Canada as shall be desirous of establishing Schools on the British system. The success which attended the early efforts of the Society, the number of pupils admitted and pressing for admission, and the inadequacy of the rooms then occupied to afford them suitable accommodation, induced the managers to adopt measures for erectir a commodious school-house. The funds were obtained partly from voluntary contributions, and partly from grants of the Provincial Legislature. The foundation-stone was laid on the 17th of October, 1826, and the

building finished the next year, at an expense of £1510
Currency. The plan was furnished gratuitously by
Mr. O'Donnell, the architect of the French Cathedral.
The building, which is very neat and substantial, is of
sufficient magnitude to contain 414 boys and 232 girls,
together with room for the residence of the teacher. In
the year 1826, the number of children in attendance was
as follows :

	Boys.	Girls.
Roman Catholics	97	38
Episcopal Church	27	9
Presbyterians	42	21
Methodists	30	11
	196	79
Total	275	

This number has been for several years pretty well
kept up ; but at present it is not so great, as, since the
troubles commenced, several of the Canadian children
have not continued to attend.

The contributions also, it is to be lamented, have in
some measure fallen off. It is most desirable that this
excellent institution should be encouraged, and enabled
to extend its beneficial influence among the rising generation. Mr. Minchall is the master of the boys', and
Mrs. Bendall the governess of the girls' School.

ST. ANN'S MARKET

Owes its origin to the public spirit of several of our
citizens owning property in the neighbourhood, who
have invested capital to the amount of nearly £15,000
in its erection.. Messrs. Wells and Thompson furnished
the plan.

It extends 342 feet in length, and is two stories high.

It is built entirely of cut stone, and is a very handsome edifice. In the centre, for about forty-six feet in length, the building is fifty-eight feet wide ; the remainder being only fifty feet. The stalls are arranged to the east and west of the centre building, with a passage direct from one end of the market to the other. Fifty feet are reserved at the eastern end for poultry and vegetables, and an equal space at the western end for fish. The remainder for butcher meat is divided into thirty-two commodious and distinct stalls. A fine large hall is in the second story, in the centre part of the building, forty-six feet in height, fifty-eight in width, and forty-six in length. Proper accommodation is afforded around the building to market gardeners and dealers in grain. The creek or " Little River," which runs under the market, exactly in the centre, has been tunnelled over ; and to the right and left of the tunnel, cellars have been constructed seven feet in height. The butchers' stalls, we may add, are twelve feet high, and are elevated above the level of the street a few feet, to which elegant flights of steps afford an easy ascent. Porticoes have been erected at each end of the building, thus maintaining the truly chaste and architectural character of the design.

RASCO'S HOTEL,

IN ST. PAUL STREET.

This is the largest Hotel in the city : it can accommodate 150 guests. On its site formerly stood the palace of Mons. Vaudreuil, Governor-General. The hotel is formed of two large separate buildings erected at the expense of £9840 : the furniture in them cost £3300. It was opened on the first of May, 1836. The

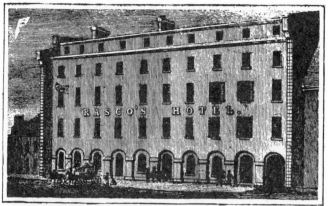

RASCO'S HOTEL.

NEWS ROOM

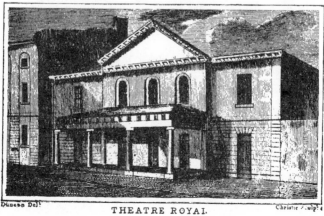

Duncan Del.   THEATRE ROYAL.   Christie Sculp.

enterprising conductor formerly occupied the splendid building next the Theatre Royal, known as the Masonic Hall, which was destroyed by fire on the 24th of April, 1833. The alarm was given while company were assembling for a *Soirée Musicale*, and in a few minutes the whole was in flames, producing a scene of awful grandeur and desolation scarcely paralleled in the history of Montreal. The celebrated Captain Back had been residing in the hotel, and had just sent forward the greater part of his baggage and scientific instruments, preparatory to his own removal to Lachine that evening, in his way to the Northern Regions ; so that, though most of the property in the house was consumed, he had chiefly to regret the loss of his only available barometer. The parts of the building that escaped the flames have remained a solitary ruin ever since.

EXCHANGE HOTEL,

IN ST. PAUL STREET,

Formerly Goodenough's, kept afterwards by Cady & Doolittle, has been established about forty years, and can furnish accommodation for seventy guests.

COMMERCIAL HOTEL,

IN ST. PAUL STREET,

Kept by Mr. Baker, has been established thirty-five years, and will accommodate seventy guests.

OTTAWA HOTEL,

IN M'GILL STREET,

Has been established about fifteen years, is conducted by Mr. Hall, and will accommodate forty guests.

ORR'S HOTEL,

IN NOTRE DAME STREET,

Has been established six years, in the house formerly the residence of the Hon. J. Richardson. It contains accommodations for forty guests.

There are several other hotels of a minor class, some of them very respectable, and well adapted for comfort. All of them are so constructed as to be able to accommodate a greater number of guests in cases of urgency.

NEWS ROOM

IN ST. JOSEPH STREET.

The News Room and Exchange was established A. D. 1821, in a neat stone building, originally erected for, and used as, the Methodist Chapel, in St. Joseph Street. The spacious room on the ground floor, well lighted and conveniently furnished for the purpose, is abundantly supplied with newspapers from the United Kingdom—its Colonies—these Provinces—the United States, &c. &c. By the merchants in particular and the public generally, it is well supported by annual subscriptions. Strangers are admitted on the recommendation of subscribers.

THEATRE ROYAL,

IN ST. PAUL STREET.

The Theatre, at the eastern extremity of this street, was built in 1825, by subscription, the late Hon. John Molson being the principal shareholder. The original cost was about £6000. The late Mr. Forbes was the

Duncan Del.

Christie Sculp.

NEW MARKET & NELSON'S MONUMENT.

architect. It has a neat front, with a portico of the Doric order. The whole is now the property of John Molson, Esq. Not only dramatic entertainments are performed here, but other public exhibitions are made when a large audience is expected.

NELSON'S MONUMENT,

IN NOTRE DAME STREET.

Intelligence of the death of this illustrious commander arrived in Montreal in the winter of 1805-6, and the inhabitants of the city, eager to testify their sense of his merit, immediately commenced a subscription for the erection of a monument to his memory. The required amount was speedily raised. A Committee of five was chosen among the subscribers, and these gentlemen, in conjunction with Sir Alexander M'Kenzie, Thomas Forsyth, and John Gillespie, Esqrs., then in London, proceeded without delay to carry the measure into effect. The Magistrates of the city having obtained from the Governor-in-Chief, Sir J. Craig, a piece of ground for general improvement, granted a portion of it at the upper end of the New Market-place, as a site for the intended column. The foundation stone was laid on the 17th of August, 1809. In the first cut stone at the east corner of the base, a plate of lead was deposited, bearing the following inscription :

" In memory of the Right Honourable Admiral Lord Viscount Nelson, Duke of Bronté, who terminated his career of naval glory in the memorable battle of Trafalgar, on the 21st of October, 1805, this Monumental Pillar was erected, by a subscription of the inhabitants of Montreal, whereof the Hon. Sir John Johnston, Knight and Baronet, the Hon. James Monk, Chief Justice of Montreal, John Richardson, John Ogilvie, and Louis Chaboillez, Esquires, were a

Committee appointed for carrying it into execution, and the same was erected under the direction of William Gilmore, stone-cutter and mason, from designs obtained from —— Mitchell, an architect in London.—17th August, 1809."

The monument is built of the best gray compact limestone, the Gemeiner Kalkstein of the German mineralogists, which is found in the neighbourhood, and possesses all the requisites for dressing well, and being exceedingly durable. The ornaments are of the artificial stone invented by Coade and Sealy of London, and were executed by them in a style most honourable to, their skill. The base or pedestal is square, about six and a half feet broad on each side, and about ten and a half feet in height from the ground. From the top of this a circular shaft or column rises fifty feet in height, and about five in diameter. It is of the Doric order, and finished with mouldings of the same description of stone. On the top of the pillar a square tablet is placed, and the whole is surmounted with a statue of the hero whose death it commemorates, eight feet in height, but appearing to a spectator on the ground of the ordinary size. The likeness is well preserved, and the attitude judiciously chosen. The face is directed towards the west, and looks as if intently watching the termination of some great event. His left arm (the other was lost in defence of his country) is resting upon the stump of a broken mast, surrounded by tackles, blocks, &c., as they appear to have fallen from the rigging. He is dressed in his full uniform, and decorated with the insignia of the various orders of nobility which had been so deservedly conferred upon him. In this attitude he stood at the moment he received the fatal shot which terminated his brilliant career in the action off Trafalgar. The statue is formed of the same artificial stone as the rest of the ornaments. As it lay in the manufactory, in

London, a sailor who served under his Lordship found his way in, and, struck with the likeness of the figure, embraced it with great enthusiasm, sending forth ejaculations expressive of the love he had for his gallant commander. Turning round, he exclaimed, " This is really a grand figure of the noble Admiral : I hope it is made of good stuff, and will be as lasting as the world." " I have nothing to fear on that score," replied the artist, " for his Lordship has been in a hot fire for a week without intermission." " Ah, Master !" said the tar, " I find you know something of the character of Lord Nelson, for there never was a British officer that could stand fire better than he."

The ornaments are emblematical of the principal events in the professional life of the hero. Round the top of the pedestal, there is a cornice of the figure termed by artists " eye and tongue ;" and encircling the base of the pillar, where it issues from its pedestal, is a cincture in the form of the coil of a cable or rope. The principal ornaments are in pannels on the four sides of the pedestal. On the pannel facing the north, is a sea-piece representing shipping engaged, intended to designate the battle of the Nile, as appears from the inscription :

" On the first and second days of August, 1798, Rear Admiral Sir Horatio Nelson, with a British fleet of 12 sail of the line and a ship of 50 guns, defeated in Aboukir Bay, a French fleet of 13 sail of the line and 4 frigates, without the loss of a British ship."

In the pannel on the east side, the figures represent the interview between Lord Nelson and the Prince Regent of Denmark, on the landing of the former after the engagement off Copenhagen. The inscription is :

" The Right Honourable Vice-Admiral Lord Viscount Nelson, Duke of Bronté, after having, on the 2nd of April, 1801, with 10 sail of the line and 2 ships of 50 guns, sunk, taken, and destroyed the Danish line, moored for the defence of Copenhagen, consisting of 6 sail of the line, 11 ship batteries, &c., supported by the Crown and other batteries, displayed equal precision and fortitude in the subsequent arrangements and negotiation with the Danish Government; whereby the effusion of human blood was spared, and the claims of his country established."

The south side of the pedestal represents another sea-fight, and is designed to commemorate the battle of Trafalgar, as appears from the inscription, which is as follows :

" On the 21st of October, 1805, the British fleet of 27 sail of the line, commanded by the Right Honourable Lord Viscount Nelson, Duke of Bronté, attacked, off Trafalgar, the combined fleets of France and Spain, of 33 sail of the line, commanded by Admirals Villeneuve and Gravina, when the latter were defeated, with the loss of 19 sail of the line captured or destroyed. In this memorable action, his country has to lament the loss of her greatest naval hero, but not a single ship."

On the front side which is toward the west, there is, on the plinth of the base, an elegant figure of a crocodile in bas-relief, emblematical of the battle of the Nile. The pannel on this side is peculiarly neat in the device, and workmanship. It is ornamented with cannon, anchors, and other appropriate naval trophies, with a circular laurel wreath, which surrounds the following inscription :

In Memory of
The Right Honourable Vice-Admiral Lord Viscount NELSON,
Duke of Bronté,
Who terminated his career of Naval glory in the memorable
Battle of Trafalgar,
On the 21st of October, 1805,
After inculcating by Signal
This Sentiment,
Never to be forgotten by his Country,
" ENGLAND EXPECTS EVERY MAN WILL DO HIS DUTY."
This Monumental Column was erected by the
Inhabitants of Montreal,
In the year 1808.

The eight pieces of cannon to support the iron chain which was originally placed around the whole, were furnished by Sir Gordon Drummond, then Commander of the Forces in Canada. Although the care taken to preserve the figures from mutilation. has succeeded to a great extent, as far as human agency was concerned, several of them have been injured by the climate.

The expense of this monument, when complete, was nearly £1300, of which the mason-work amounted to £523; the ornamental parts, £468 12; the design, estimates, and plans, £58 1; the iron railing, £66 18 11; and various contingencies the remainder of the sum.

CHAPTER XI.

THE COURT HOUSE,

IN NOTRE DAME STREET.

The Court House was built in the year 1800, under a Provincial Statute, passed the 3d of June, 1799, by which the sum of £5000 was appropriated for its erection. The ground upon which it stands was formerly the property of the late order of Jesuits, and was granted by the Government, into whose hands it had fallen, without any pecuniary indemnity. The Commissioners for building it, were Messrs. Davidson, Foucher, and Ross; Treasurer, Mr. Richardson; builder, Mr. François Xavier Davelin. The principal apartments in the Court House are the following : the Court Hall; the Quarter Sessions Hall; the Prothonotary's Office; the Offices of the Clerk of the Crown, and the Clerk of the Peace; the Judges' Chambers; the Grand Jury room, and one room for the Petty Jury; the Magistrates' room ; and the Law Library. Underneath are six vaults, where the notarials of deceased Notaries are deposited.

COURT HOUSE

NEW JAIL

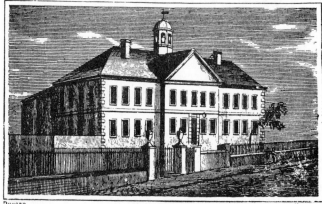

Duncan

Christie

OLD JAIL

THE ADVOCATES' LIBRARY

Was established in February, 1827, for the use of the gentlemen of the Bar, who, on becoming proprietors, have access to the books at all times for consultation, but are not at liberty to take them from the room. The members pay ten pounds for each share on becoming proprietors, and two pounds ten shillings per annum. The first or old members paid £30 each at the time of their admission.

THE OLD GAOL,

IN NOTRE DAME STREET.

This edifice, standing near the Court House, was also built on ground belonging to the Jesuits. The first Gaol, built on the same spot, was destroyed by fire in 1803. The present building was erected in the year 1806, in virtue of a Provincial Statute passed on the 25th of March, 1805, by which also a sum of £9000 was voted for the purpose. Mr. Joseph Courcelles dit Chevalier was the builder. After the New Gaol was erected, the old prison was occupied for one year as the House of Industry; and on the 12th of May, 1838, possession was relinquished, and it was immediately occupied by the Government as Barracks.

THE NEW GAOL,

IN THE QUEBEC SUBURBS,

On the road to Longue Point, was commenced in the year 1831, on ground purchased from the heirs of the late Sir John Johnston, but was not taken possession of by the Sheriff till 1836. The expenses were provided for by a vote of the House of Assembly. The plan was furnished by Mr. Blacklock, of Quebec, and approved by the House of Assembly in 1825. Some alterations, however, suggested by Mr. Wells, the architect who superintended the erection, were adopted as the building proceeded. The whole plan was not carried out for want of funds, which were not granted, in consequence of some difficulties and opposition then existing in the House. As far as the building has proceeded, the cost has been upwards of £26,000. The work was executed by Messrs. Lauder, Spier, & Co., Masons, and Mr. Robert Morton, Carpenter.

The length of the Gaol is 255 feet; the back wing extending at right angles from the centre of the building 82 feet. The basement story contains 32 cells for solitary confinement, each 12 feet by 8 inside; also two large cooking kitchens, washing and bath rooms, pantries, &c. The first story, which is raised five feet above the level of the yard, contains the entrance hall, guard and receiving rooms, Magistrates' or Grand Jury room, an instruction-room, and 64 cells, each 8 feet by 5 feet 6 inches. The second story contains the Gaoler's apartments, a living room and two bed-rooms; a large kitchen; the matron's living and bed-rooms; three day-rooms for prisoners, each 24 feet 6 inches by 18 feet 9 inches; and 50 cells the same size as those of the lower story. The cells in the back wings of each story are used for the female prisoners. All the cells and passages are arched with brick. The whole of the third story is occupied by the Debtors' bed-rooms and day-rooms—33 of the former, and 3 of the latter. The walls and ceilings of these rooms are all plastered, and the doors neatly panneled. The centre of the building is carried up a fourth story, which contains the chapel, the plan of which is so constructed, that five classes of prisoners can sit in view of the pulpit, and each class prevented from seeing the others : they enter by separate stairs. The garrets over each wing are floored, and used as drying rooms. At the extreme end of each is placed a cistern capable of holding 1077 gallons. From the three cisterns, which will contain 3231 gallons, every part of the Gaol is supplied with water. These cisterns can be filled in forty minutes by means of a forcing pump worked by ten of the prisoners, although fixed nearly 100 feet above the river. The pump is constructed on an improved principle, and was manufactured by the Montreal Water-works Company, under the direction of Mr. Wells. The building is surrounded by a high wall, at such a distance as to enclose about 4 arpents, or nearly $4\frac{3}{4}$ acres, of land. The Commissioners purchased twelve acres, from an idea that a Penitentiary might be established in addition to the prison.

There is no Chaplain attached to this Gaol, nor, we are sorry to learn, is there any provision made for the moral and religious instruction of the prisoners. Vice and immorality, we are informed, prevail to an alarming extent, and call loudly for the benevolent services of all who feel it important to check the prevalence of these enormous evils, and to reclaim the sinner " from the error of his way."

The present keeper of the Gaol is Mr. Charles Wand.

THE BARRACKS,

IN WATER STREET,

From their situation, are frequently distinguished as the Quebec Gate Barracks. The original building formerly belonged to a Nunnery, while the country was in possession of the French. Falling into the hands of Government when the English acquired Canada, they were afterwards converted into military barracks. They were considerably improved and enlarged about the year 1822, and are now capable of containing about 1000 troops. There are other, but not regular, barracks in different parts of the city and suburbs; besides the permanent barracks and store-house on the Island of St. Helen, and those in the Old Gaol.

THE GOVERNMENT HOUSE,

IN NOTRE DAME STREET.

This house was erected by a company of Fur Traders while the country was in possession of the French. It fell into private hands, and after the conquest was purchased by the Government for the occasional residence of the Governor. About fifteen years ago, the interior was repaired and modernized partially, so as to be made more convenient, but by no means sufficiently so for the residence of a Governor, who, besides apartments for himself and family, will require state rooms for public purposes. About the year 1830, the Provincial Legislature voted £1700 for further improvements, and appointed Messrs. Grant, De Rocheblave, and Try, Commissioners to carry the design into effect. But these gentlemen, finding the sum inadequate, asked for a larger amount, which was declined, and nothing was done, The house built by Mr. Bingham, at the corner of Notre Dame and Bonsecours streets, has been lately fitted up in a splendid manner for the residence of the Governor.

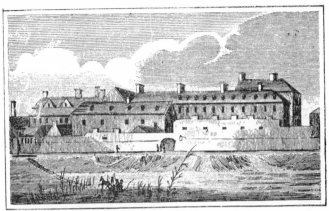

BARRACKS

GOVERNMENT HOUSE

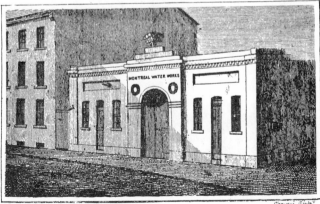

Duncan Del.

WATER WORKS.

WATER WORKS,

IN NOTRE DAME STREET.

The city of Montreal, and the parts thereto adjacent, are supplied with water under an act of Parliament of the year 1801. The old company under the management of Thomas Schiefelin and others, laid out a very large sum of money in order to supply the city by wooden pipes from a source in rear of the mountain, but owing to the scanty supply of water and the pipes bursting constantly, they could not proceed in their operations. In the year 1819, the company sold its charter to the late Thomas Porteous, Esq, and others, who took up all the wooden pipes, and relaid iron conduits of 4 inches bore, which lasted up to the year 1832. The works were then purchased by the present company of proprietors, who have laid out considerable sums of money in improving them. The main conduits now laid down through the principal parts of the city are of iron of 10 and 4 inches bore, and the other parts are laid down with lead and iron pipes of dimensions in proportion. There are now upwards of 11 miles of main conduits laid down. The water is forced by a steam engine of 14 horse power, from the river St. Lawrence up into two cisterns in a building in Notre Dame Street, containing a quarter of a million of gallons.

Montreal is better supplied with water than any other city on this continent, with the exception of Philadelphia.

From the commencement of these works up to the present time, the sum of nearly £70,000 has been expended by the several companies. M. J. Hays, Esq., is the manager of the works.

Those who have no wells, and are not supplied by the water-works, are served by water-carriers from the river.

THE CHAMP DE MARS

Was originally a small field not well adapted for military exercise, and very slightly entitled to the name that was given to it. Within a few years it has been made level, and very much extended, so as to form a space of 227 yards by 114. It is now an excellent parade, as well as an agreeable promenade for the inhabitants of the city. From this spot there is a fine view of the well-cultivated grounds, beautiful orchards, and country-houses towards the mountain. Our view is taken in a different direction from near the N. W. angle.

THE NEW MARKET.

The old market-place, where the Custom-house now stands, being found too small, a new site was rendered indispensable. The present market, occupying the ground on which stood the College founded by Sieur Charron, but destroyed by fire many years back, is 36 yards wide, and reaches from Notre Dame Street to St. Paul Street. In the middle of the space are ranges of stalls for butchers, covered in by a roof supported on wooden pillars. Great care is taken to enforce the regulations to insure cleanliness, and the good condition of the meat offered for sale. On the two principal market days—Tuesday and Friday—in each week, the market is well supplied with every necessary and almost every luxury for the table, in great abundance, both animal and vegetable. On other days, too, articles can be procured, though the supply is not equally abundant. The produce of the upper part of the district is almost wholly brought hither for sale, and some from the United States, especially fish from Boston in the

CHAMP DE MARS.

BANK OF MONTREAL.

CITY BANK.

CUSTOM HOUSE

winter.   At the upper end of this market is erected the monumental column in honour of Nelson, as described at page 153 ; and opposite to this is the military guard-room.   At the lower end, near the river, is the Fish Market.

BANK OF MONTREAL,

IN ST. JAMES STREET,

Was first chartered in 1817, with a capital of £250,000 ; and re-chartered in 1837, with a capital of £500,000. The building originally occupied by this company was destroyed by fire in 1820.   The present edifice was erected at an expense of more than eleven thousand pounds.   It is a large and elegant building of cut stone, ornamented in four compartments with emblematical devices of Agriculture, Manufactures, Arts, and Commerce, executed in bas-relief.   The portico is of the Doric order.   The Hon. Peter M'Gill is President, and the Hon. Joseph Masson, Vice-President of this Institution.   The days of discount are Tuesday and Friday.

CITY BANK,

ST. PAUL STREET.

This Bank was opened on the 1st of November, 1833, with a capital of £200,000, and chartered in April, 1838. It occupies a handsome building near the south-west end of the street.   A handsome portico, supported by fluted Tuscan pillars, has been added since our plate was engraved.   The President is John Frothingham, Esq. ; and the Vice-President, Alexander Millar, Esq. Days of discount Monday and Thursday.

PEOPLE'S BANK, *or* BANQUE DU PEUPLE,

IN ST. FRANCOIS XAVIER STREET,

Was opened on the 11th of July, 1835. The President is L. M. Viger, Esq.; and the Vice-President J. DeWitt, Esq. Days of discount, Tuesday and Friday.

BANK OF BRITISH NORTH AMERICA.

MONTREAL BRANCH,—IN ST. JAMES STREET.

This Bank was opened on the 8th of March, 1837, under the control of Austin Cuvillier, Albert Furniss, and James Ferrier, Esquires. Days of discount, Wednesday and Saturday.

BANK OF UPPER CANADA,

AGENCY OF, IN ST. JAMES STREET,

Commenced on the 1st of September, 1838. It is conducted by Joseph Wenham, Esq., as manager for the Upper Canada Bank.

CUSTOM HOUSE,

BETWEEN ST. PAUL STREET AND THE RIVER.

The business of the Customs was, till lately, transacted in a building situated in Capitol Street. This being found inconvenient, a new custom-house was erected on the site of the old market. It is of the Tuscan order, from a design by Mr. Ostell. The building was commenced in 1836, and opened for business in 1833. It has its

"Long Room," not yet occupied, excellent vaults, and every other requisite office, well fitted up, and adapted for a greater extent of business than the port at present supplies. Its size is 60 feet by 45, French; and the expense of its erection was £4500. It is one of the few buildings that have been completed without exceeding the estimate. The hall below is ornamented with fluted Doric pillars, which support the floor of the next story. The east front, next the river, has a handsome portico, supported by four stone pillars, and is rusticated to half its height. Both fronts are surmounted by triangular pediments. When the buildings which intercept the view from Commissioner Street are removed, the Custom House will appear to great advantage.

Some idea may be formed of the amount of business done here, in the Customs, from the following statement:—

Years.	Vessels.	Tonnage.	Provin. Duties. Currency.	Crown Duties. Sterling.
1831	80	19,085	£24,646 5 9	£4,492 19 3
1832	117	27,704	46,848 5 11	10,649 18 2

The amount of Duties will, of course, vary with circumstances each season: subsequent years have not been equally productive of revenue with 1832.

CHAPTER XII.

NATURAL HISTORY SOCIETY,

LITTLE ST. JAMES STREET.

The origin and object of this laudable Society, which
was founded in 1827, are thus clearly stated in the First
Annual Report, delivered by the Committee of Management, on the 26th of May, 1828:

" It is now only twelve months since a few gentlemen, casually
met together, proposed the establishment of this Society. They were
not unaware of the difficulties they would have to encounter. In all
communities, the persons who devote themselves to scientific pursuits, are few. In communities such as this, where wealth is comparatively little, where no opulent endowments take off the necessity
of attention to securing a livelihood, and where in consequence the
attention is directed into channels, very different from those of
scientific research, not many could be expected to join in assisting
the Society by their personal exertions, however pleased they might
be to see it arise. Anticipating, therefore, but a small list of members, and aware also that at different times, associations had been
formed for literary purposes, which had gradually been dissolved,
the founders of the Society saw the necessity of a bond of union
independent of the personal characters of the first members —a

visible sign of the existence and utility of the Institution, and around which the members might at all times rally. With a view, then, to afford this bond, to prevent the tendency to dissolution, the proposers of the *Natural History Society* resolved to found a Museum, an institution which experience has proved to have great power in calling the attention to scientific pursuits, and the want of which was forcibly felt by several members, who looked back upon the causes which in their younger days retarded their own improvement. But the mere collection of the productions of nature would leave the design of the Society imperfect without the possession of books, that treat of such objects. They are mutually dependent on each other. One without the other leaves the work half done, but both connected give the greatest facilities for instruction which can be afforded. In addition therefore to the possession of a Museum, it was one of the first objects of the Society to secure a library of books on Science in general. On these principles, and with these views, The *Natural History Society* was established."

Whatever serves innocently to occupy the mind is in itself a benefit, as it keeps the rational powers in healthy action, and may afford occasional relief from the severer pursuits of business or labour; but when researches like those of Natural History, which discover so many evidences of the wisdom and goodness of the Almighty, occupy the leisure of any considerable portion of the community, greater advantages still may be expected to result from such an employment of the faculties. A laudable curiosity is gratified, an elegant pursuit encouraged, useful knowledge increased, a habit of observation and arrangement promoted, the social principle exercised, and fresh motives presented to admire the Creator in his wonderful works. The design met with general approbation among those who were most able to support it. Numbers of gentlemen desirous of exciting a taste for scientific pursuits and of promoting the extension of knowledge, enrolled their names as members of the Society, which speedily assumed a form likely to render it both permanent and efficient. Its funds, derived originally from the subscriptions of the members, have been aided on several occasions by grants from the Legislature; and in the year 1832, an Act of Incorporation, passed by the two Houses of Parliament and sanctioned by the Royal assent, was granted to the Society, by which its permanence is secured upon a solid basis. The Museum and Library, by successive purchases, and donations from scientific friends in various parts of the world, have become very valuable depositories—the one of specimens of natural objects and the works of art, and the other of numerous important volumes on the subjects of Natural History and Philosophy. Its Mineralogical cabinet is extensive, and the specimens of the finest description. In that part of it containing the simple minerals, and not including those found in this country, the number in the catalogue amounts to upwards of 1600, exclusive of duplicates. In addition to these are the foreign and Canadian geological collections, and the simple minerals of Canada. In the Botanical department there is found a considerable collection of plants from Europe, from the United States, and from Canada. In Zoology, very considerable success has attended the efforts of the Society. Of Shells, a large number of fine specimens are exhibited in the Museum, and the Society possesses also numerous cases of Insects, natives of Canada, and of the East and West Indies; of Reptiles, the number is considerable; but of Quadrupeds there is a deficiency. The chief attraction is the large number of Birds, prepared in the best manner, and exhibiting a striking representation of life: in the Ornithological collection, indeed, are contained nearly all the birds found in this part of the world; also, a large number of the gorgeously decorated inhabitants of the torrid zone, both east and west,— and a large number of the birds of Britain.

In such a condition of society as that from which this country has not yet arisen, it cannot be expected that any great number of persons should take an active part in the pursuits of a Literary and Scientific Institution; and the Society has not yet been able to present to the public a criterion of its respectability or usefulness by any published transactions of its own. Several papers of value are in possession of the Society, but not yet sufficient to form a volume. Premiums are offered every year for the best contributions that may be sent to the Society, on the various subjects which its design embraces; but the judges of these compositions are empowered not only to ascertain the comparative merits of the pieces offered, but to determine whether any of them are worthy of the honorary medals of the Society: a judicious plan to secure to excellence the reward which otherwise mediocrity might claim.

So readily were the early efforts of the Society encouraged, that the rooms first occupied were soon found too small to allow of the proper arrangement or exhibition of the specimens, and when a more commodious situation had been occupied a few years, the same inconvenience ensued from the continued increase of the collections. The house at present belonging to the Society is well adapted to its purpose. It contains an excellent lecture room, well fitted up, in which the meetings of the Council are held, and lectures frequently delivered by the members during the winter half-year; and good accommodations for the Museum and Library.

In one of the late reports of this admirable institution it is judiciously remarked, that " the Society works more for posterity than for the present generation; and therefore it is that it pays so much attention to laying up materials for instruction, ready for use whenever the state of society in this country shall be such as to seek for facilities in acquiring more advanced knowledge than that which is generally sought after at present. When that period shall arrive, the Society, though now acting in a humble capacity, will be found to have performed a most important work in having collected the treasures of nature, and made them accessible to the studious and enquiring." Posterity, we doubt not, will confess the obligation.

MONTREAL LIBRARY,

LITTLE ST. JAMES STREET.

The Montreal Library was founded A. D. 1796. A joint stock association of 120 shares, at 50 dollars each, was formed to establish this Institution. It has never occupied a separate edifice. In May, 1837, the Library was removed from the old Methodist Chapel in St. Joseph Street (also partly occupied by the News-Room) to its present apartments, in the building of the Natural History Society. The collection contains about 2000 French and 6000 English works. The income, after paying current expenses, is laid out in the purchase of new and popular works. The recent additions are not equal in character and importance to those which constitute the basis of the Library. Upon that basis, by a judicious selection of the best works recently published in England, religious, historical, literary, and scientific, might be erected a noble repository of mental treasure, worthy of an enlightened community, gradually increasing in intelligence and wealth.

The Library is open every day, except Sunday, from eleven till four.

UNIVERSITY OF M'GILL COLLEGE.

In the year 1814, the Hon. James M'Gill, an opulent merchant of this city, bequeathed in trust to THE ROYAL INSTITUTION *for the Advancement of Learning in* LOWER CANADA, the valuable estate of Burnside, at the Mountain, together with the sum of ten thousand pounds, for the endowment of a College which should bear his name. The will was for several years contested, but was at length decided in favour of the Institution. In 1821 the College was incorporated in conformity with the intentions of the founder ; and the Governor and Lieutenant Governor of Lower Canada, the Lieutenant Governor of Upper Canada, the Chief Justices of Montreal and Upper Canada, the Lord Bishop of Quebec, were by the charter of incorporation, appointed Governors of the Institution. The following professors were appointed in 1823 : Principal and Professor of Divinity, the Rev. G. J. Mountain, D. D., of the University of Cambridge ; Professor of Moral Philosophy and learned languages, the Rev. J. L. Mills, D. D., of Oxford ; Professor of History and Civil Law, the Rev. J. Strachan, D. D., from Aberdeen ; Professor of Mathematics and Natural Philosophy, the Rev. G. J. Wilson, A. M., from Oxford ; Professor of Medicine, Thomas Fargues, M. D., from Edinburgh. It was not, however, till the 24th of June, 1828, that the corporation of M'Gill College obtained full possession of the property bequeathed to it. No religious tests are imposed, either upon the professors or the students, so that all the offices are freely open to both Protestants and Roman Catholics, while students of all denominations are permitted to attend. The practice has hitherto been to obtain the professors from the graduates of British Universities ; but a preference will hereafter be shown to those who shall have graduated in the Institution. The system of collegiate education will extend to all those branches which are embraced by similar establishments in Great Britain; and for the sake of advancing the medical department of the College, it is intended to engraft upon it the Montreal Medical Institution, which already stands high in public estimation. If wisely conducted, and well supported by the Imperial and Local Governments, and by the inhabitants of the Province, as may be reasonably expected, the newly established College will flourish, an honour and a blessing to the country, and an enduring monument of the liberality of its founder.

The first degree conferred by the College was that of M. D., on Mr. W. L. Logie, 24th May, 1833. Ten or twelve other gentlemen have since received their degree in the same. The only Professors at present connected with the Institution, are those in the Medical Department: they are as follow:—Dr. Holmes, of Chemistry, and Pharmacy: Dr. Robertson, of the Theory and Practice of Medicine; and Dr. Stephenson, of Anatomy and Phisiology. There are, besides, two Lecturers—Dr. George Campbell on Surgery, and Dr. Archibald Hall on Materia Medica.

Plans and estimates have been ordered for suitable buildings, and when these are erected the course of instruction intended by the College will commence, and the whole plan carried into efficient operation.

MR. M'TAVISH'S HOUSE.

On a well-chosen spot, most conspicuously situated beneath the abrupt part of the Mountain, the late Simon M'Tavish, Esq. erected a mansion, in a style of much

CITY OF MONTREAL FROM THE MOUNTAIN

Duncan Le¹

Christie Sculp

VIEW FROM THE HAYMARKET.

elegance. This gentleman had projected great improvements in the neighbourhood of the house thus intended for his residence ; and had he lived to complete them, the place would have been rendered an ornament to the island. His remains were deposited in a tomb placed at a short distance behind the house, surrounded by a shrubbery. On a rocky eminence above it, his friends have erected a monumental pillar as a tribute to his worth, and a memento of their regret. The house is a very prominent object, disclosing itself in almost every direction: the obelisk was formerly so, but is now much obscured by the growth of young trees. The inscription on the pedestal is as follows :

Sacred to the Memory of SIMON M'TAVISH, Esq.
Who died July 6, 1804,
Aged 54 years.

This Monument is erected by his Nephews,
WILLIAM and DUNCAN M'GILLIVRAY,
To commemorate their high sense of his manly virtues,
And as a grateful tribute
For his many acts of kindness shewn to them.

The unfinished building is already in a dilapidated state, and will, it is probable, shortly be taken down. The prospect from the house is very magnificent. At a short distance from it, towards the Priests' Farm, our " View FROM THE MOUNTAIN" was taken. The monument is shewn in the Vignette on the title-page.

VIEW FROM THE HAY MARKET.

This is taken from near the upper end on the north side of M'Gill Street, and shews a part of the Mountain, in front, with Beevor Hall near the centre, distinguished by its poplars, the Weigh-house, a little to the left, and on the extreme right a small portion of the American Presbyterian Church.

HOCHELAGA CHAPEL,

NEAR THE CROSS, OPPOSITE CURRENT ST. MARY;

Is a small but neat edifice connected with the Episcopal Church of this city. It was commenced in the year 1828, and finished in the spring of the following year. The cost was about £500, of which £80 was given by the Lord Bishop of Quebec from the church building fund, and the remainder raised by subscription. The style of architecture is the Gothic : height of the steeple 50 feet. The service of the English Church is conducted here, by the Rev. J. Ramsay, A. M.

ST. HELEN'S ISLAND,

IN THE ST. LAWRENCE RIVER,

Lies off the city of Montreal in an easterly direction. It formerly belonged to the Barons of Longueuil, and is now the property of the Crown, having been exchanged by the Hon. Charles Grant for the extensive ground and premises belonging to the monastery of the Recollets, in Notre Dame Street. Fortifications and buildings for stores, where great quantities are kept, have been erected on the Island, and a military garrison is established there. It is itself a beautiful spot, and affords a fine view of the city, from which it is distant about a mile. It rises gracefully from the shore, and the foliage of the trees which crown its more elevated parts, and are interspersed over the greater portion of it, gives it an attractive appearance from the town, and from

CITY OF MONTREAL FROM S? HELEN'S ISLAND.

various parts of the river. Our view of the city was taken from a spot near the Officers' Barracks, which appear a little to the right of the centre.

SHIP YARD,

CURRENT ST. MARY.

The first ships built in Montreal, were those constructed by Mr. David Munn, who commenced his operations about the year 1806. Two or three years afterward he entered into partnership with Mr. Robert Hunter: the vessels they built were generally from 200 to 350 tons burthen; one, the Earl of Buckinghamshire, was 600 tons. J. Storrow & Co. built two vessels in 1808 and 1809. James Dunlop, Esq. in the three following years built several, of 330 to 350 tons burthen each. Mr. James E. Campbell was engaged in the work for several years : the vessels he constructed were generally of the same burthen. Messrs. M'Kenzie & Bethune, and James Millar & Co., built a number of vessels. Mr. Gould states that there were built in the Province, in 1825, 61 vessels ... 22,636 tons.

in 1826, 59 –   ... 17,823 –

in 1827, 35 –   ... 7,540 –

in 1828, 30 – .... 7,272 –

decreasing till 1831, when only 9 were built. The Canada Ship Building Company from London began to build in 1828, but finished only two vessels.

In the year 1829, Messrs. Shay & Merritt took possession of the yard; and the following steamers and sailing vessels were built there under the superintendance of Mr. E. D. Merritt. The steamboat *British America*, 170 feet long, 30 feet beam, 10 feet high, for Messrs. John Torrance & Co., as a trader between

P

Montreal and Quebec. In 1830, the steamer *John Bull*, for Messrs. John Molson & Co., also as a trader between this city and Quebec: 182 feet long, 32 feet beam, 12 feet high; has two engines, each 85 horse power. In the same year the steamboat *St. George* was built for John Torrance & Co.; 160 feet long, 26 feet beam, and 11 feet high. The steamboat *Canada* was built in 1831, 175 feet in length, 26 feet beam, and 11 feet in the hold; also the steamboat *Eagle*, for Mr. James Greenfield, 140 feet long, 24 feet beam, 9½ feet hold; and the steamer *Canadian Patriot*, 130 feet long, 22 feet beam, and 8 feet hold, for a joint stock company. In 1833, the steamboat *Britannia*, for John Torrance & Co., 130 feet long, 24 beam, and 7½ hold; in the same year, the *Varennes*, for Rasco & Co., 140 feet long, 23 beam, 7½ hold; also the steamer *Montreal*, for Mr. James Wait, 96 feet long, 18 beam, 5 hold. In 1834, was built the ship *Toronto* of 345 tons, for Captain Collinson, running between this port and London; also the *Brilliant* and *Thalia*, each 472 tons, for James Millar & Co., sent home for the Baltic trade. The ship *Douglas*, 348 tons, was built in 1835 for Captain Douglas; the bark *Glasgow*, 347 tons, for Millar, Edmonstone & Co., sent home—and the bark *Thistle*, 260 tons, for the same firm, sent home for the West India Trade,—were built in 1836. In the following year, the *John Knox*, a bark of 347 tons, for the same company, sent home; and in 1838, were built the following—the ship *Gypsey*, 572 tons, also for Millar & Co.; the bark *Colborne*, 340 tons; and the brig *Wetherall*, 252 tons, both for Capt. Collinson.

The situation of this establishment is very favourable for the purposes of ship building of all descriptions, as the timber is hauled in at once from the St. Lawrence, and there is no reason to fear a deficiency of supply.

The length of the yard is 200 feet; and all conveniencies are at hand for facilitating and completing the work in the most perfect manner.

THE ROPE MANUFACTORY.

This establishment belongs to Mr. J. A. Converse, and has been several years in constant and successful operation. These works were established in 1825, on a smaller scale than that on which they are conducted at present. Every description of cordage is manufactured here, on a patent method, by appropriate machinery. The quantity of hemp consumed is from 150 to 250 tons annually, employing from thirty-six to fifty hands. The sale of the cordage manufactured, is generally in Quebec and the Upper Province. The walk is 1200 feet in length, the greater part (900 feet) two stories high, and another portion three stories. A new stone building has just been erected, to contain a steam-engine, giving motion to all the patent machinery for the manufacture of the different kinds of cordage, with additional apparatus for making ship blocks.

The hemp used in these works is Russian, imported from England. Various attempts have been made to introduce and encourage the growth of hemp in the Canadas, but hitherto without success. The soil and climate, in the opinion of good judges, appear to be well adapted to the cultivation of this article. The failure has been attributed to the mode in which encouragement has been offered. Every farmer who has raised any quantity of hemp, whether small or large, has been left to prepare it himself for the market, and as this is a process to which the growers were unaccustomed, it was scarcely ever performed well ; and so great a variety was found as to quality and dressing in the different parcels sold, that it was found impossible to work them together. It has been suggested, as a mode of overcoming this difficulty, that Government, or a company, should furnish seed to such of the farmers as would undertake to sow it, and, when raised, buy the hemp from them in the stalk ; that buildings should be erected in convenient places, to which the farmers might carry their produce, and in which the cleaning and dressing should be performed, so that the preparation should be uniform, and the article rendered fit for immediate manufacture in the Colony. The method formerly employed by Government was attended with great expense, and productive of small benefit ; and even that has ceased ; whereas the plan now proposed would not only ensure a saleable and uniform article, but would probably induce the farmer to devote a portion of his land every year to its cultivation. Mr. Bliss, in his work on the *Trade, Industry, and Resources of Canada*, observes, " it has been for sometime a subject of regret that attempts to introduce the culture of hemp in Canada, were not made or prosecuted with better success ;" and that by the repeal of a law by which Colonial hemp was admitted free into Britain, " a net revenue of many thousands was abandoned," while, " about one million yearly continues to be given to foreigners for what we might well begin to produce for ourselves."

THE POLICE FORCE.

This Force was organized in consequence of an ordinance issued during the administration of the Earl of Durham, on the 28th of June, 1838. It consists of

102 privates, four mounted patroles, six serjeants, and six corporals, under the command of four officers; viz., Capt. Alexander Comeau and Lieut. Worth, for division A, and Capt. William Brown and Lieut. William Suter, for division B. The superintendent is Mr. P. Leclere. The day duty commences at 7, A. M. and ends at 6, P. M. Every man is on duty every three hours in winter, and six hours in summer. Night duty commences at 6, P. M, and ends at 6, A. M. The time of relief in winter is governed by the weather, at the discretion of the officer on duty: in summer, every four hours duty relieves. The expense is borne by the Civil-Home Government, and amounts to at least six thousand pounds per annum. A book of admirable Regulations has been published for the guidance of the police, and all its operations are scrupulously conducted in accordance with them.

The jurisdiction of the police extends throughout the city, suburbs, harbour, and island of Montreal, together with the parishes of Laprairie de la Magdelaine, Longueuil, Boucherville, Varennes, Repentigny, Lachenaie, St. Vincent de Paul, St. Martin, and Isle Perrot.

The numerous apprehensions which the Police have effected shew the necessity of such a force, while it may be hoped that its future exercise, in conjunction with the efforts that are making to promote temperance and good morals, will contribute to the peace and good order of the city and its environs.

CHAPTER XIII.

ORPHAN ASYLUM — LADIES' BENEVOLENT SOCIETY —
BIBLE SOCIETY—TRACT SOCIETY—SUNDAY SCHOOL
UNION—TEMPERANCE SOCIETY—BAPTIST MISSION-
ARY SOCIETY——FRENCH CANADIAN MISSIONARY
SOCIETY—MECHANICS' INSTITUTION—GAS WORKS—
TRADE AND COMMERCE—LACHINE CANAL.

THE PROTESTANT
ORPHAN ASYLUM,
IN ST. ANTOINE STREET.

" Upon the dissolution of the Female Benevolent
Society, in February, 1822, the officers and members
of that institution consigned their orphan *proteges*, and
their flourishing little school, to the care and maintenance of the Protestant churches in this city. The
Rector of the English Episcopal, and the Ministers of
the two Presbyterian churches, accepted the charge."*
A house was taken in St. Louis Suburbs, and two rooms
in it fitted up as school rooms, that the boys and girls
might be taught separately. The officers of the Society
consist of a first and second Directress, a Treasurer,
Secretary, and Committee of management. Every

* From the Minute-Book of the Society.

lady who contributes annually £1 5s. is eligible to office. A meeting of the officers is held at the house of the institution on the first Monday in every month, to receive applications for admission, and attend to the general concerns of the establishment. Two members of the Committee in rotation take the monthly superintendance; they visit twice a week, and submit their report to the General Board of Directresses at each monthly meeting.

Children of all Protestant denominations are admitted into the asylum, but are afterwards brought up in the principles of the Church of England, uniformly attending the Episcopal place of worship and Sunday Schools. For ten years after its establishment, the wants of the community required that the asylum should receive both orphans and children whose surviving parent was unable to provide for them. But many disadvantages attended the arrangement; and upon the establishment of a *Ladies' Benevolent Society* for the support of widows and fatherless children, the directresses were happy to limit their inmates to orphans solely. They previously found that the good intentions of the Society were frustrated by the improper interference of the parents; and frequently after comfortable situations had been provided for the children, the ill-judging parents would insist on removing them, to the manifest injury of the Society who so placed them. At present each individual who selects a child from the asylum is required to sign a legal indenture in duplicate, by which he is bound to provide for the suitable maintenance, instruction, &c. of the child, to inform the directresses once every year of the condition and welfare of the child, and at the expiration of the term of service to provide him or her with a new and proper suit of clothes. A certificate is also required from the clergyman, or some

well-known individual, of the respectability and religious
character of the person to whom the child is to be entrusted. They are not suffered to leave the asylum
before the age of eight or nine years, except in cases
where they are to be adopted into respectable families,
which frequently happens. The superintendant and
matron instruct the orphans in the rudiments of a religious and *useful* English education ; and the girls, in
addition to plain needle work, are early taught to share
in all the domestic duties of the establishment. The
average income of the Society, derived from annual
subscriptions, donations, legacies, and Legislative grants,
is about £275. The expenditure, of course, will vary
with the number of children, and other circumstances.
The admissions for the first six years, viz. from 1822
to 1827 inclusive, were 110 ; in the following years, to
1838, they were, 3, 8, 17, 16, 42, 11, 26, 7, 14, 10,
respectively. The highest numbers belong to the years
of cholera—1832 and 1834.

In the Report for 1837, it is remarked that this
" charity has, by the munificence of the public,—yielded
the comforts of a humble, but happy home, to 264
children, of whom 238 have been provided for, the
greater proportion with respectable farmers in the country, from whence the ladies frequently have the satisfaction of receiving favourable accounts, both of their
spiritual and temporal welfare ; many are adopted into
religious families ; and several restored to their friends."

Officers of the institution—Mrs. Duncan Fisher, 1st
Directress ; Mrs. J. Macdonnell, 2d Directress ; Mrs.
Ross, Treasurer ; Mrs. M'Cord, Secretary ; Dr. Arnoldi,
jun., attending Physician.

There is something very consolatory and delightful
to a benevolent mind in the thought, that the exertions
of the Societies mentioned in this and the following

article have been so well supported by the inhabitants of Montreal, so wisely made and sustained by the Ladies engaged in the management, and so beneficial to the unfortunate objects for whose sake these "labours of love" were undertaken.

LADIES' BENEVOLENT SOCIETY.

This institution originated in the year 1832, after the first visitation of cholera in this city, and had for its object the relief of the widows and orphans left destitute by that awful pestilence.

The number of its inmates was increased by the return of that malady in 1834. Since that period destitute widows and orphans have been received from time to time, as its funds would permit. These funds are derived from voluntary contributions, annual subscriptions, and occasional Legislative votes.

The number of persons benefitted by this institution since its formation, up to the 2d of July, 1838, is as follows :—

Persons admitted	600
Assisted out of doors	320
Placed out	76
Restored to friends	208
Total	1204
Deaths	36

Great care is taken, and a judicious plan adopted, to place out the orphans when of sufficient age, as apprentices, with respectable farmers in the country, or with tradesmen in the towns. Their moral and religious training is a point never lost sight of in these engagements.   Many have thus been provided with comfortable homes, and the means of future settlement.

The average annual receipts, for six years, amount to £601 9 1¾; and the expenditure to £559 14 8.   Of the whole amount of the six years, viz., £3608 14 10½, the sum of £500 has been received from the Provincial Legislature, leaving a balance of £3108 14 10½, raised solely from the voluntary contributions of the charitable within the city of Montreal, to this object alone.   The Government, under the Earl of Durham, having caused enquiry to be made relative to this excellent charity, it may be hoped that further aid may be extended to it, to enable it, in coming years, to enlarge the sphere of its benevolent operations.   Our present kind-hearted Governor, we are persuaded, will not suffer this and other kindred institutions to languish for want of any support which he may have it in his power to render to them.

Of this Society, Mrs. Richardson is the 1st Directress ; Mrs. Ogden, the 2d ; Mrs. Stephenson, Treasurer ; Mrs. W. J. Coit, Secretary ; and Drs. Stephenson and Hall, attending Physicians.

MONTREAL BIBLE SOCIETY,

AUXILIARY TO THE BRITISH AND FOREIGN BIBLE SOCIETY.

Among the various benevolent institutions of the present day, those which are engaged in the circulation of the Bible " without note or comment," are among the most useful and unexceptionable.   Here is common ground, on which all Christians may unite to promote the honour of God and the highest happiness of man : the very idea of such a union is delightful.

The Montreal Society, Auxiliary to the Parent Society in London, was formed on the 28th day of August, in the year 1820, by a few zealous friends of the gospel. Its commencement, though not splendid, was encouraging ; and by perseverance in the good work its supporters had the pleasure of seeing it gradually increase in energy and usefulness. During the last year its issues and cash receipts have been greater than in any preceding period. After distributing the Scriptures, for many years, in the city, among the emigrants, in the immediate neighbourhood, and wherever application was made for them, the Committee resolved, " with reliance on God, and in co-operation with other Christians, as speedily as possible, to place a copy of the Bible, by sale or gift, in every family in the Province willing to purchase or receive it." This noble resolution was fully confirmed by the Society, and is now in the progress of accomplishment. Several Branch Societies and Associations are in connection with this Auxiliary.

RELIGIOUS TRACT SOCIETY,

AUXILIARY TO THE RELIGIOUS TRACT SOCIETY OF LONDON.

A Society for the same object, and with the same title, was formed in Montreal several years since ; but not being adequately supported, it became extinct. In the year 1836, a small number of friends to this mode of doing good, associated for the purpose of establishing a new one. The design succeeded ; and the Society thus formed has been doubling its issues every year since its formation. Much good has already resulted from its efforts, which have been materially aided and extended by the YOUNG MEN'S TRACT SOCIETY, a promising institution carried on with much zeal and prudence. The LOAN Tract Society, more recently established, has the same object in view, but, superadded to it, a systematic attempt to excite generally throughout the city, a greater attention to the concerns of religion.

SUNDAY SCHOOL UNION.

The objects of this association are to promote the establishment of Sabbath Schools, wherever it is deemed practicable throughout the Colony, and to encourage and strengthen those already in existence. The Society is composed of members of various denominations of Christians; and with a desire to promote union and fellowship among the followers of Christ, it is agreed that the Committee shall consist of the ministers and members from each of the Evangelical Protestant denominations of the city. A Society very similar to this was in being some years since; and during its existence was the cause of much good; but through various circumstances it expired. The new Society has been actively engaged in pursuance of its laudable design; an agent has been appointed who, after visiting various parts of the Province, went to the United States, and ultimately to England, from all which places he received encouraging aid. Many new schools have been opened in different settlements, and others have been enabled to extend their operations. Mr. James Court is the Treasurer of this Society; and Mr. Henry Lyman and Mr. J. C. Becket, the Secretaries.

TEMPERANCE SOCIETY.

The increasing prevalence of drunkenness, and the awful consequences thence arising, have induced a general desire among the sober and the virtuous part of the community, to stay the progress of so fearful an evil. Temperance Societies have been formed, with this express view, both in Europe and America; and have been productive of the happiest effects. Thousands of drunkards have been reclaimed from their destructive habits. A Society for the " Promotion of Temperance" was formed in this city on the 9th of June, 1828, at the suggestion of the Rev. J. S. Christmas : the declaration was against the use of distilled spirits only. The *Young Men's Temperance Society* was formed on the 29th November, 1831. The two were afterwards united. On the 27th of February, 1834, an executive Committee was appointed by a convention then held, which continued to act till the formation of the Montreal Society for the *Promotion of Temperance*, on the 22d of October, 1835. This Society had the two pledges of— abstinence from ardent spirits, and total abstinence from all intoxicating liquors. On the 1st of September, 1837, the Society was re-modelled on the total abstinence principle alone, under the name of the *Montreal Temperance Society.* The CANADA TEMPERANCE ADVOCATE was first published on the 1st of May, 1835, and is now in its 5th volume. It is issued monthly, at the low rate of 1s. ᵱ annum for each copy delivered in town, or 1s. 8d., if sent by mail into the country. It is edited with ability, and contains in its successive numbers much important matter relative to the great reformation which it is the object of the Society to accomplish. Public meetings for the purpose of hearing addresses in its favour are held at least monthly.

The Society has an Agent employed in circulating its publications ; calling attention to and explaining its object ; endeavouring to persuade those who are unhappily under the debilitating and demoralizing power of intemperate indulgence, to consider their danger, and renounce a habit so inconsistent with the dictates of reason, and so derogatory to the dignity of human nature ; and in any other way that may present itself to check the prevalence of so monstrous an evil as that against which the efforts of the Society are directed. The pledge subscribed by the members, is as follows :

" We, the undersigned, do agree, that we will not use intoxicating liquors as a beverage, nor traffic in them ; that we will not provide them as an article of entertainment, or for persons in our employment ; and that in all suitable ways we will discountenance their use throughout the community."

THE CANADA

BAPTIST MISSIONARY SOCIETY

Was formed to co-operate with a Society established in London in 1836, for the purpose of propagating the Gospel in the destitute parts of Canada.   It is well known to all who have paid attention to the religious state of this Colony, that a want of the means of spiritual instruction prevails in many places, to a lamentable degree.   To supply this want is the object of the Societies above mentioned : ministers and missionaries have been employed to as great an extent as the means of the Societies would allow ; and a Collegiate Institution has been commenced, under the able superintendence of the Rev. Dr. Davies.   Seven students have already entered, and are preparing for the work of the ministry in these Provinces.   There can be no doubt that these institutions, if well supported, may have an important bearing upon the future welfare of Canada ; and it is, therefore, most earnestly to be desired that such effective support as they need may be afforded to them.

The great success which has attended the efforts of

this denomination of Christians in the missions to the East and West Indies, and other parts of the world, gives encouragement to hope that similar efforts in this Colony will conduce equally to the spread of Christianity and civilization—and, in conjunction with those of other Christians, have a happy effect in raising the standard of moral feeling and action, as well as in answering the higher purposes for which the Gospel was revealed. The attention of the people generally appears to be increasingly alive to this interesting subject.

Every one knows how common it is to read of disturbances in Ireland, and it deserves to be known, that, " wherever our English missionaries have gone to preach the Gospel, and where Irish Scripture-readers have been employed, there has been no disturbance, when in other districts the soldiers have found great difficulty in quelling the riots." This simple fact, even in the absence of higher considerations, is more than sufficient to justify the utmost activity in disseminating Christian knowledge.

FRENCH

CANADIAN MISSIONARY SOCIETY.

From a conviction that the French Canadians are, at the present time, in a more favourable attitude for the reception of the Gospel than they have ever been, the founders and supporters of this Society have been desirous of taking advantage of this circumstance, for the purpose of making known the Gospel among them. It is ascertained that the desire of the French *habitans* for a liberal and Christian education is increasing daily, and that many of them are determined to secure the advantages of it for themselves and their families. The object of the Society, exclusively, is to provide means

Q 2

for preaching and otherwise disseminating the truths of
Christianity among the inhabitants of Canada using the
French language.   The plan embraces the employment
of Ministers, Teachers, Book-venders, and Scripture
readers, (whose native language is French)—the establishment and support of schools and places of worship
—and the distribution of the Holy Scriptures and other
suitable books. The Constitution of the Society is liberal
and truly catholic, embracing all classes of Evangelical
Christians, and excluding all sectarian peculiarities.

THE MECHANICS' INSTITUTION.

Associations of persons with a view to the benefit of
the working classes, have, in many parts of Britain, been
undertaken with spirit, and been productive of much
good. Under proper management, they are well adapted
to promote not only the mental improvement, but
the moral benefit of those in whose behalf they are
undertaken. By inducing those who would otherwise
spend their earnings at the tavern, to pay some attention
to the improvement of their minds, and by placing
within their reach the means of becoming acquainted
with the principles of their art, and of gaining otherwise
useful knowledge, a great advantage is conferred upon
them. The institute of this city was founded after the
model of those at home ; the greater part of its members being artizans, by whom its affairs were chiefly
conducted. It commenced in 1828, and for several years
was carried on with much harmony and success. An
interruption of its meetings occurred about three years
since, and was followed by the two winters of insurrection, which effectually precluded all other topics than
those which related to self-defence. In addition to the

ordinary exercises allotted to the hours of meeting, lectures on the principles of Mechanics, and Natural Philosophy, were occasionally delivered by Mr. Skakel, whose valuable collection of apparatus, and familiar knowledge of the subject, enabled him to render them highly interesting and instructive. It were to be wished that, on the establishment of tranquillity amongst us, the operations of this useful Society may be resumed, as it is capable, in many respects, of being made conducive to the improvement of a valuable class of our citizens in habits and intelligence. Apparatus and books, to the value of one hundred and fifty pounds, remain, ready for use, in the care of its officers.

THE GAS WORKS

Are situated at the Cross, about one mile from the city. They were begun in 1836, and some shops were lighted on the 23d of November, 1837. The cost of building, works, pipes, &c., is about £15,000. Mr. Armstrong was the projector. The stock is in a few hands only, E. A. Furniss, Esq., being the principal holder and manager. The proprietors were incorporated by an Act of the Provincial Legislature, in April, 1836. The service pipes and lamps have been ready for some time, and only wait for an advance of money from the city to put them into effectual operation.

TRADE AND COMMERCE.

We have more than once alluded to the favourable situation of this city for the purposes of Trade, both foreign and domestic. It is to this circumstance that its growth and prosperity must be traced ; for as it is not the permanent seat of Government, and has but few extensive manufactories to support it, its continued increase must depend upon the trade it can command. Placed at the head of the navigation of the St. Lawrence for sea-going vessels, it has ever been, and must continue, an important place of commerce. Even if the magnificent idea should eve be realized of forming a channel for ships up to Lake Huron, it must still secure a large share of commercial activity. There is an immense back country to be supplied with foreign productions through it, and should that territory, as is probable, become more thickly settled, and the state of agriculture be improved, an augmented demand of commodities will arise from that quarter, and greater supplies of home produce be conveyed to the city. Montreal was once the emporium of the fur trade, which is now carried on directly between Red River settlement, Hudson's Bay, and England. The delays and inconvenience of river navigation between this city and Quebec are now overcome by steamboats, which for the power of their engines, speed, and accommodations for passengers, as well as their utility in towing large vessels, are scarcely to be surpassed. Formerly much time was lost by vessels from sea, and it was no unusual thing for them to be detained for weeks at the foot of the Current St. Mary, by the want of a favourable wind to bring them up to the town. A serious bar to the increase of shipping continues to exist in the intricacy and shallowness of the ship channel in Lake St. Peter. Were this removed—and means have been recently taken to ascertain the practicability of it by a Commission of Survey—and were the " culling" of timber rendered easily practicable by some simple method, there can be no doubt that much of the timber trade of Quebec would be transferred to this port. Large quantities of timber pass down in rafts in front of the city, which could be more speedily, safely, and cheaply transported direct from this place in a ship's hold, if no impediment to navigation remained in the Lake.

The position of Montreal with regard to the United States is very favourable also to the extension of commerce in that quarter. The facilities of transport to Laprairie, and thence on the railroad to St. John's, and onward by water to New York, render the conveyance of goods both easy and expeditious, so that the produce of Canada may be disposed of in the States, and other articles needed here readily forwarded from that country Thus an intercourse, mutually profitable, may be preserved, and Montreal afford a convenient *depôt* of merchandise for both parties. The spirit and enterprise of the principal merchants, and of the trading community generally, if aided by the Local Government, cannot fail to render this an increasingly prosperous and flourishing city. It is not many years since a New York traveller, on landing from a batteau which brought him from Laprairie, thus expressed himself :—" The approach to Montreal conveyed no prepossessing idea of the enterprise of its municipality ; ships, brigs, and steamboats lay on the margin of the river at the foot of a hill ; no long line of wharves, built of the substantial free stone of which there is abundance in the neighbourhood, affording security to vessels and profit to owners ; the commercial haven looked as ragged and as muddy as the shores of *Nieu Nederlandt* when the *Guede Vrow* first made her appearance off the battery." Now, if he were to repeat his visit, he would be constrained to make a different report, and find himself able to step on shore without more trouble than in walking across a room.

The " island," then nearly useless, is now united by an isthmus to the shore, and forms a most convenient landing place.   The line of beautiful and substantial wharfs that now border the magnificent St. Lawrence in front of the town, was begun in 1832, when Montreal became a Port of Entry.   The funds were granted by the Provincial Parliament, and the works carried on under the direction of Commissioners appointed by Government, who rendered their services gratuitously in this and other measures for the improvement of the city.   After a few years' interruption, the works were resumed in the summer of last year, in consequence of additional grants by Government, and are now advancing towards the Lachine Canal, where they will terminate in that direction.   When they are completed, the harbour of Montreal will be one of the best, if it be not indeed superior to every other, in North America.

Commerce, then, in its various branches, has been, is, and must be, an object of primary attention to the inhabitants of this city ; and if the fostering care of the Home and Provincial Governments be extended to it, by the enactment of wholesome regulations, and the encouragement of useful public works, there will be every reason to expect a progressive advancement in the scale of importance and utility.

The increase of population in the city, as nearly as can now be ascertained, will be shewn by the following statement :

Population of the city in 1800   9000
      —   —   —   1825 22,000
      —   —   —   1831 27,297

To these numbers must be added the inhabitants of the parish without the city.   These, in 1831, amounted to   4486

Making the whole population 31,783

No census has been taken since the year last mentioned ; and that is thought not to have been made very correctly, being more probably under than above the actual number of residents in the city and parish. From a comparison of various accounts, and modes of estimating, it is probable that the number at present is about thirty-five thousand.

The state of commerce for some years back will appear from the following scale of Vessels and their Tonnage which arrived at Montreal :

In 1832 arrived 117 Vessels with a Tonnage of	27,713
1833	137	30,864
1834	89	20,105
1835	108	22,729
1836	93	22,133
1837	91	22,668
1838	63	15,750

Of these vessels and their cargoes, by far the greater part were from England and Scotland. A few arrive every year from Halifax in Nova Scotia, and other British ports in North America, and sometimes cargoes of grain, &c. from other ports in Europe.

A statement of the Imports in the year 1837, and of the Exports of the two preceding years, will give an idea of the nature and extent of the foreign commerce of this city :

DECLARED VALUE OF GOODS IMPORTED INTO THE PORT OF MONTREAL, DIRECT FROM SEA, IN THE YEAR ENDING THE 5TH OF JANUARY, 1837.

From the United Kingdom,

	£	s.	d.
Dry Goods, British manufacture and produce..	1,211,391	12	1
Refined Sugar	19,091	16	6
British Spirits	884	8	7
Playing Cards	636	1	0
Salt	20	0	0
Total value of British manufacture	£1,241,933	18	2

Total value of British manufacture £1,241,933 18 2

Value of Foreign Dry Goods 64,054 6 3

Value of Liquors, Sugar, Tea, and other Groceries, Foreign and Colonial 85,865 9 9

Total value of imports from the United Kingdom. £1,391,854 14 2

From British North American Colonies.

Dry Goods and Colonial produce, except Gro-
ceries £2,740 13 2

Liquors, Sugar, and other Groceries, &c.,
Foreign and Colonial production... ... ... 25,222 14 4

£27,963 7 6

From the United States of America.

Dry Goods £206 6 1

Tobacco, Sugar, Molasses, &c.. ... ... 5671 0 11

£5877 16 2

From other Foreign States.

Dry Goods and Grain £6530 5 8

Liquors, Tea, and other Groceries 14,023 10 2

£20,543 15 10

Total value of imports (Sterling).. ... ... £1,446,239 13 8

Statement of the Principal Articles exported by Sea at the Port of Montreal, in the years 1835 and 1836.

	1835.	1836.		1835.	1836.
Ashes—Pot, brls.	18,901	17,120	Lard, kegs	63	31
Do Pearl, do.	4,765	8,656	Beef, barrels..	693	389
Apples, do....	352	36	Do half do..	165	20
Biscuit, do....	223	201	Pork, barrels..	1,003	174
Do bags	104	6	Do half do..	26	—
Do cwt	15	—	Oil—Seal, casks... ..	79	387
Butter, kegs..	51	193	Onions, barrels	16	1
Do firkins	12	—	Oil Cake, pieces... ..	1,649	
Candles, boxes	239	42	Do. tons	18	84
Furs and Skins, pkgs..	56	25	Oars—Ash....	2,422	2,178
Flour, barrels	20,918	26,107	Staves, puncheon ..	248,997	237,141
Do half do	3	—	Do Standard ..	164,065	171,424
Peas, minots..	4,170	144	Do Barrel.	14,275	
Do casks	61	6	Do Ends..	9,360	—
Wheat, minots	55,255	49	Timber—Ash, tons..	139	52
Oats. do..	920	500	Do Birch, do..	4½	67

Statement of the Principal Articles exported by Sea at the Port of Montreal, in the years 1835 and 1836.—CONTINUED.

	1835.	1836.		1835.	1836.
Timber, Elm, tons.. ..	858	576	Starch, boxes., ...	100	—
Do Oak, do.. ..	792	569	Tobacco, Leaf, hhds ..	9	2
Do Pine, do.. ..	1,628	2,103	Wax, Bees', barrels ..	3	—
Do Butter Nut, do	5	1	Brandy, Canada manu-		
Do Maple, do	16	—	facture, pipes..	52	—
Do *Hickory, do	40	—	Do do hhds, ...	75	100
Boards, pieces	2,965	—	Do do quarter casks ..	12	—
Deals.	19,277	49,993	Geneva do hhds..	2	10
Do Ends	306	1,337	Whiskey, do. puns..	19	—
Do Planks....	4,126	—	Brandy, foreign, hhds..	6	—
Handspikes	7,034	5,737	Wine, pipes	47	—
Spars....	12	2	Do hhd	1	—
Soap, boxes	90	—	Do quarter casks ..	27	—
Do half do..	5	—	Do cases	24	—

By the Lachine Canal much business is done with Upper Canada, and some with the United States, as the following Table will shew :

Statement of the Principal Articles imported into Montreal, by the Lachine Canal, in the years 1834, 1835, and 1836.

	1834.		Total 1834.	1835.		Total 1835.	1836.		Total 1836.
	U. C.	U S.		U. C.	U. S.		U. C.	U. S.	
Ashes, barrels	9438	1731	11169	10004	4055	14059	11668	2579	14247
Beef, „	23	931	954	—	936	936	943	92	1035
Butter, kegs..	1446	191	1637	1235	82	1317	1894	14	1908
Biscuit, bags..	438	—	438	719	4	723	—	—	—
Do cwt..	38	—	38	—	—	—	—	—	—
Barley, bushel	1956	—	1956	686	—	686	12637	—	12637
Flour, barrels.	102017	20169	122186	97269	6807	104076	162726	7598	170324
Oats, bushels..	672	—	672	—	—	—	1550	—	1550
Pork, barrels.	755	22519	23274	931	1232	12163	11978	1710	13688
Peas, bushels..	14551	—	14551	370	—	370	14725	—	14725
Starch, boxes.	175	—	175	558	—	558	657	—	657
Tobacco, hhds	353	—	353	536	8	544	1059	—	1059
Wheat, bushel	291726	333	292059	31572	—	31572	51810	—	51810
Whisky, pipes	2	—	2	1	—	1	52	—	52
Do puns..	8	—	8	11	—	11	—	—	—
Do barrels	502	7	509	930	1	937	2153	—	2153
Do casks..	32	—	32	22	—	22	142	—	142
Do hhds..	2	—	2	1	—	1	63	—	63
Hams, tierces.	1	78	79	8	—	8	8	1	9
Do loose .	—	355	365	—	508	508	—	—	—
Live Hogs....	96	2852	2948	348	1377	1725	103	618	721
Indian Corn, bushels	793	659	1392	118	—	118	—	—	—
Lard, barrels.	—	491	491	1	62	63	69	—	69
Do kegs...	—	1691	1691	155	151	306	223	1	224

NOTE.—U. C. denotes that from Upper Canada, and U. S. from the United States.

Great quantities of merchandise are sent from Montreal to Upper Canada by the same Canal : the transport upwards amounted in the year 1835 to nearly 16,000 tons, and in 1836 to nearly 14,000.

The opening of the navigation in the spring is a circumstance of much importance here; and after the severity of the winter is over, is looked forward to with much interest. The following table exhibits a statement of the different periods, in the last ten years, at which the ice broke up in front of the city, at which the first steamboat arrived in the harbour, and at which the first vessel from sea came into port.

Years.	Ice broke opposite Montreal.	Steam-boat arrived in Harbour.	1st Vessel at Montreal from Sea.
1829	8th April ...	16th April..	15th May...
1830	1st April ...	8th April ...	11th May...
1831	30th March	10th April..	26th April..
1832	16th April..	28th April..	11th May...
1833	2d April	11th April..	13th May...
1834	30th March	10th April..	9th May....
1835	8th April ...	20th April..	13th May...
1836	23rd April..	2nd May ...	14th May...
1837	11th April..	23rd April..	4th May....
1838	9th April...	23rd April..	3rd May....
1839	9th April...	16th April..	10th May...

THE LACHINE CANAL.

So early were some of the intelligent inhabitants of the province convinced of the numerous advantages that would result to internal navigation and commerce from a Canal that should unite Montreal with Lachine, that it became an object of desire even before the passing of the Constitutional Act in 1791. In the first

Provincial Parliament under that act, which commenced its session in December, 1792, a bill to effect that object was proposed by one of the Members for Montreal. The bill did not pass, because the undertaking was then considered beyond the pecuniary means of the province. The matter, therefore, slept for some years. In 1815, during the war with the United States, the expense of conveying the Government stores brought the subject under the consideration of the Governor, who sent a message to the Assembly in favour of the measure, and the sum of £25,000 was voted to assist in its execution, with an Act of the Legislature to give it effect. Peace soon following, nothing more was done except taking a few levels. In 1819, a petition from several persons in Montreal desirous of undertaking the work at their own expense, was presented to the Legislature, requesting aid and authority for that purpose. A bill was accordingly passed in April, authorizing subscriptions to the extent of £150,000 currency, at the rate of £50 a share, and erecting the subscribers into a joint stock company. This plan was afterwards abandoned, and the work was undertaken by the Province, on the conditions that the subscribers should relinquish their rights on receiving back the money they had advanced on their shares, and that, on the contribution of £10,000 by the Government, all stores and effects belonging to His Majesty should pass through the canal free of toll. An act of the Legislature having passed to this effect in 1821, the work was commenced on the 17th of July in that year, and completed in 1825. The route originally proposed was along the beach of the St. Lawrence at Lachine till the commencement of the turnpike road, then by the foot of the Cote St. Paul, continuing till it arrived at a point between the St. Joseph and St. Antoine Suburbs, when the route was to

R

fork out and diverge, one branch to cross the St. Lawrence and Quebec Suburbs, and enter the river below the King's Naval Store at the foot of the Current St. Mary, while the other branch was to enter above the harbour near the Ship Yard. The former branch was for the present abandoned, from insufficiency of means; and the latter route, owing to some difficulties, was altered so as to bring its mouth near the windmills.

The Canal is 28 feet wide at the bottom, and 48 at the water line, with five feet depth of water throughout, and 18 inches from the water line to the level of the towing path   There are in the whole six locks, each one hundred feet in length, and twenty feet of opening, with an entire fall of forty-two feet, and a regulating lock at either end. The workmanship of these locks, and the various stone bridges along the route, are all of masonry of a superior and most substantial character, creditable to the builders, to the country, and to the whole undertaking : the bridges at the extremities are elegant as well as durable.   This Canal, at the time of its formation, was greater as to breadth, depth of water, and length and breadth of locks, than any similar work in Great Britain, with the exception of the Caledonian and the Forth and Clyde canals.   The stone of which the bridges and locks were built, was brought from the opposite shore, near the Indian village of Caughnawaga.   In addition to its excellent qualities, the cheapness of its carriage, being conveyed entirely by water, rendered it very eligible for the purpose. In forming the canal, the quantity of rock excavation was found very great, and presented an unexpected obstacle to the progress of the work ; but the increased labour, expense, and delay occasioned by it, were more than compensated by its durability : this part of the canal can never need repair. Beside the stone bridges, several others of wood are thrown over the canal at suitable distances.

The vast utility of this undertaking, obvious as it was at first sight, has been amply confirmed by the experience of several years. Forming a line of junction, in effect, between the Upper Province and the Lower, it has facilitated the passage of goods, particularly of the heavier kinds, not only from the former, but also from many parts of the latter, which would otherwise have scarcely reached the emporium, or have been brought hither at an expense which would have been all but a prohibition. The same may be remarked of goods going upward from Montreal. The Tolls collected on this canal amounted in the year 1834, to £6531 2 $10\frac{1}{2}$ Currency. The Provincial statute, authorizing their collection, expired on the 30th of April, 1835. To that time there had been collected for that year—

Downward... ... ...£39 12	$7\frac{1}{2}$
Upward... ... ... 41 3	1
£80 15	$8\frac{1}{2}$

Had the Statute continued in force, the receipt of Tolls would that year have been £5497 19.

CHAPTER XIV.

EDUCATION AND LITERATURE.

Whatever other circumstances are conducive to the prosperity and welfare of a people, there can be no doubt that Education is essential to the perfection and stability of the social state. Intelligence and virtue, founded on religious principle, are the strongest safeguard of individual character, and the best preservative of general utility. That much has been done in different parts of the Province for the advancement of education, it would be improper to deny; but that the system is defective, both in the nature and extent of the instruction it provides, will scarcely admit of a question. The state of education, throughout the Province, it is hoped will undergo a strict and rigorous investigation, and such measures be resorted to as will render its benefits absolutely universal, and counteract the ignorance which is so inimical to good feeling and rational exertion.

In the city of Montreal there appear to be means in existence for imparting instruction, of a slighter or more solid kind, to a great proportion of the young persons resident within it; but it is to be lamented that large numbers of children, especially those of Catholic parents, are suffered to grow up without availing themselves of its benefits. The British population are much more desirous of procuring instruction for their offspring, and hence they are in general more intelligent and enterprising than others. Not that there is a want of capacity among the Canadian youth, for where they have been placed in favourable circumstances they have exhibited abundant proof of the contrary; but the general insensibility of their parents to the value of education, and the almost total absence among them of any rational conception on the subject, render them indifferent to its advantages. Most ardently is it to be desired that means may be discovered to remove this grand obstacle to national improvement. Great numbers of children, however, in both communities, receive instruction in Montreal. In addition to the schools already noticed, there are several respectable academies in the City; as, the Royal Grammar School, in Little St. James Street, conducted by A. Skakel, Esq.; the Rev. Dr. Black's, adjoining St. Paul's Church; Rev. J. Ramsay's, Main Street, St. Lawrence Suburbs; Messrs. Howden & Taggart's, Craig Street; Mr. Workman's in Hospital Street; and Mr. Bruce's in M'Gill Street. There are also young ladies' schools in high reputation; as Miss Easton's, in Bonaventure Street,—Miss Felton's in St. Gabriel Street,—and Mrs. Fitzgerald's, in Notre Dame Street. The total number of schools, it would be difficult to assign. A few years since, two gentlemen of this city made personal enquiry throughout the place, with a view of determining the point: they found fifty-nine of different classes; but it is probable not only that some were overlooked, but that the number is greater now than it was then. There is also much private

tuition in the families of the more wealthy inhabitants.
It is no small consolation for persons about to settle
here, to know that they can readily obtain instruction
for their children in almost every department that they
may desire.

The ROYAL INSTITUTION *for the Advancement of
Learning* was projected about the year 1801, and an
act of the Legislature was passed in its favour. In
1818 it was incorporated by a Royal Charter. Its
object is distinctly announced in its title ; and, for the
purpose of attaining it, encouragement has been given
to the establishment of schools in different parts of the
Province, and support afforded in other instances to
schools already formed. The Principal of the institution
is the Lord Bishop of Quebec ; and the trustees consist
of several official persons in both Provinces, with other
gentlemen residing in the Lower. Grants have been
made to the Royal Grammar School, and the National
School in this city, and to the Royal Grammar School
at Quebec.

The Literature of a newly settled country is necessarily of slow growth, and generally very limited in extent.
The persons who form the community are induced to
colonize by motives not very congenial with a desire
for reading and study. Nor are the other circumstances
of a new or a rising colony often more favourable to
mental cultivation. The physical necessities of our
nature must first be supplied : Literature and refine-
ment come afterward. The column must be raised,
and probably be sometime in use, before the thought
occurs of placing an ornamented capital upon it. But
little temptation to authorship is presented in so rude a
state of society. It appears that the art of printing was
not known, at any rate not practised, in the colony, until
after it came into the hands of the British. It was

introduced in the year 1764, by William Brown and Thomas Gilmore, who issued the first number of the *Quebec Gazette* on the 21st of June. This paper was projected in Philadelphia the year before. Gilmore went to England to procure types, and Brown to Quebec, "with a Prospectus of the *Gazette*, to obtain subscribers, and make the necessary arrangements for commencing business in the spring. The subscription list then amounted to about 150, half of whom were Canadians. The tardy establishment of the press in Canada, and the quarter from whence it was first introduced, are facts than which none can be more strongly illustrative of the genius of the government and people of Canada, and of the then British Colonies in North America. Canada had been longer settled than any of them : its population was then probably nearly as numerous as that of Pennsylvania, yet the first printing establishment for Canada was projected and carried into effect from that Colony.*"

It has been observed that " the newspaper is the Literature of America†." The observation is nearly as true now as when it was first made ; since, whatever improvement in literary taste and the publication of books, may have taken place in the United States, this Colony can scarcely be said to have emerged from the condition implied in the remark. There have been at different times attempts made to establish periodicals of a more literary cast in this country, but none of them can be said to have completely succeeded. A very respectable monthly journal was commenced in 1823, under the title of *The Canadian Magazine :* it reached the twenty-fourth number, and was discontinued in 1825, for want of adequate support. Perhaps the plan was of

---

* Smith's Canada, Vol. II., pa. 8.　　† Ward's *Spring of Life.* 1834.

rather too ambitious a character for the then state of the
Province. Though some of the articles were trifling,
many were of a high order; the work was well edited,
and certainly *deserved* more support than it received.
The Canadian Review made its first appearance in
July, 1824, and continued to be published at intervals
till September 1826, when the fifth and last number
appeared. Both works contain much information relative
to Canada; and to both, especially the former, the editor
of this volume has been frequently indebted. Each
number of the Magazine contained about 96 pages; the
numbers of the Review were more than twice as large,
containing each 240 pages or more—a scale too extensive then for the wants of the reading public in Canada.
Other periodicals of a smaller size, and more moderate
pretensions, have since been attempted. The only
monthly publications now issuing from the Montreal
press, are *The Literary Garland*, in Royal 8vo, 48
pages—an agreeable *mélange* to the lovers of light
reading, very likely to remunerate the publisher;—the
Canada Baptist Magazine, a religious periodical of 24
pages each number;—and the *Temperance Advocate*.
The newspapers published in this city are, in general,
edited with ability, and maintain with considerable point
and pertinacity their distinguishing political views and
sentiments. The *Montreal Gazette* is issued three
times a week; and, being published by the Queen's
printer, may be considered as the Government paper.
It is distinguished by the copiousness of its intelligence,
particularly on local and domestic subjects; and is of a
more literary cast than the others, which are almost
exclusively devoted to business and politics. The
Montreal Herald, of tory politics, is published daily
from the 1st of May to the first of November; and
three times a week during the remainder of the year.

There is also an edition for the country, in which most of the advertisements are omitted, published twice a week; and a *Weekly Abstract* for Europe. The *Morning Courier* is also a daily paper to the same extent as the *Herald*, with an edition for the country, issued twice a week. It is the advocate of whig principles. *L'Ami du Peuple* appears in French, twice a week. The *Montreal Transcript* is published three times a week. Beside the periodicals, a few separate volumes have made their appearance in Montreal, chiefly on poetical subjects. Some, however, are on Theology; and several sermons and addresses have been printed within the last ten years. Two treatises on Agriculture, by Mr. Evans, of Cote St. Paul, contain many valuable observations, which, if reduced to practice by the *habitans* generally, would conduce to the improved cultivation of the Lower Province.

CONCLUDING REMARKS.

The number and variety of objects which present themselves successively before the mind, while taking an excursive survey of any considerable place, have a tendency to dissipate or weaken the power of attention, and render it necessary for the writer to pause awhile, and then to look back, and see what has been accomplished or attempted. In the course of enquiry undertaken for the compilation of this volume, it has happened that some topics have been brought to light which, had they been noticed sooner, would have had appropriate places assigned to them in the preceding chapters; and others have claimed a passing notice, while yet they could not be dealt with as matters requiring separate description. Of such miscellaneous remarks as subjects of this nature have suggested, the conclusion of this chapter will be composed.

The state of society, whether viewed in classes, or in the aggregate, or as composed of individuals, and whether it be considered in its social, its civil, or its moral characteristics, will always be regarded as worthy of serious attention. From the manner in which the country was at first settled, and in which the population of this city has since been formed, two things were naturally to be expected, first, that the majority of inhabitants would for a long time continue to be French and Roman Catholics, and in the second place, that the number of British would be continually increasing, so as gradually to bring the two races nearer to an equality. This is precisely the case at present, and is likely to be more so if such public measures be adopted as will call forth and reward the enterprise and energy ready to act and extend themselves wherever there is any promise of success. In every large community there must be a great diversity of talent and condition, restricting the intercourse, in a great degree, to particular classes, without much admixture with individuals of other classes. Whether the privileges of *caste* are more jealously maintained, and the lines of demarcation more distinctly drawn, in Montreal, than in other cities of equal magnitude, it may not be possible absolutely to determine, though suggestions have been made to the effect of shewing its probability. Certain it is, that the citizens of Montreal are distinguished by one feature which is highly honourable to them, standing out as it does in pleasing and strong relief—and that is, a habit of active benevolence. Perhaps there is no place where, in proportion to the number and wealth of the inhabitants, more has been done to relieve the wretched and support the weak by deeds of real charity, than in this city—and this, not by thoughtless and indiscriminate profusion, but in the exercise of calm, cautious, and pains-taking administration. Some illustrations of this fact the preceding pages will have exhibited; and it may be right to mention here (no opportunity having occurred before) on the authority of Nathaniel Gould, Esq. of London, a warm and steady friend to Canada, that " the Montreal Emigrant Society, during the last year (1832), forwarded to their destination, or otherwise relieved, 10,744 of these poor creatures, at an expense of £2,126 11 4. Too much praise cannot be bestowed on the exertions of those pure philanthropists, who, during a season of such distress and danger, gave up their time, money, and health to so worthy a purpose." *Sketch*, pa. 5. That the principle is neither dormant, nor diminished in vigour, more recent and continued acts of a similar character most satisfactorily prove. Long may it be ere it shall decline—or rather, may it never cease to distinguish the inhabitants of Montreal till there shall be no misery that benevolence can relieve.

From the testimony of those who knew the city fifteen or twenty years since, it appears that its moral condition has very much improved within that period : profaneness, intoxication, and disturbance, were much more prevalent in the former part of it than afterward. The amendment, however, has not been uninterruptedly progressive ; for in the last year or two an evident relaxation in the public morals has taken place ; a counteracting influence has been opposing the tendency to improvement. The passions drawn forth by the rebellion have disturbed the repose of many ; and military habits and pursuits have not only diverted them from their regular course of action, but have introduced a martial and unsettled spirit which has operated unfavourably upon a large portion of the community.

It is to be regretted that many of the regular troops are, from time to time, seen reeling in the streets, to the interruption of that good order, which their services in other respects are so efficient in promoting ; and that intemperance has increased among the volunteers since they have received pay.

Both in Quebec and Montreal the windows in many of the old stores and shops are small, not larger than those of ordinary dwelling-houses, very little calculated for display, and not giving indications of the extensive depositories of goods that may be found within. The modern shops, however, are much better furnished with windows, giving every facility for the exposure of articles intended for sale. A very great number of the recent shops are elegantly, and some of them splendidly, fitted up. Perhaps there is scarcely in any part of the commercial world, either in Europe or America, a more superb or exquisitely finished room, for its size, than the shop of Mr. M'Donald at the corner of Place d'Armes and Notre Dame Street. It forms the principal ornament in a block called Muir's Buildings, a recent erection, which is itself an ornament to the spot on which it stands, in one of the most public places of the city.

The iron shutters which were nearly universal when the houses were built of wood, and of which strangers were in the habit of complaining as giving to some parts of the city the gloom of a prison, have either been exchanged for wooden ones in the new stone houses, or succeeded by pannelled shutters of a lighter and more elegant construction than the primitive ones. Liberty has also been given to many of the puddles which used to tarry in the streets, to make their way through drains prepared for their escape to a distance where their noxious qualities are either neutralized, or rendered harmless to the inhabitants. It is pleasing to witness the progress of reform in these matters, though more tardy in general than the wants and wishes of the public would require. Notwithstanding the great and numerous improvements which have long been going on, and are now proceeding, there still remain some things calling for an alteration, and susceptible of it. Among the evils yet unremedied, stands foremost the state of the streets and roads, which in dry weather are covered with dust, and in rainy with mud, to an enormous and very inconvenient degree. When the roads are dusty, and the wind blows briskly,—no unusual occurrence—the effect is distressingly annoying. So much pulverized lime-stone as is then necessarily swallowed, cannot fail to produce some injury to the general health, and the mortar that is formed in the eyes by the union of their moisture with the powdered lime, must be pernicious to those delicate organs. The difficulty is, to find, and apply, a remedy. The general and frequent application of water by machines constructed for the purpose of sprinkling the roads, as is done in London and other great cities, would palliate or lessen the evil. But some change might be made in the materials of the roads themselves. The amount of traffic in every direction through the city and suburbs, will necessarily produce and raise up large quantities of dust, whatever may be the materials of which the roads are made. But it is evident that the harder and less friable these materials are, the greater will be the freedom from annoyance. It may be worthy of consideration, then, whether some improvement might not be effected in this particular. The lime-stone ordinarily used in making roads here, is easily broken and pulverized, and will endure but little wear before it becomes offensive. There is a harder species—perhaps more than one species—of granite, to be met with

in the neighbourhood of the city, which would probably
answer much better for roads than the substance now
employed.   It would require more labour in its preparation.   Yet with the successive application of heat and
cold water, the large stones might be split, and afterwards broken with hammers into pieces of a proper size ;
and the longer duration of the material when laid down,
by the removal in part of the pernicious evils which
now prevail, would more than repay the additional
labour and expense of preparing the harder stone.
Another method of improving the roads has been suggested—that of paving them with wood ; an experiment
which has been tried in some other places, and succeeded,
even on carriage roads.   The side walks which have
been made of this material in some of the streets, are a
decided improvement, and are hailed by the inhabitants
as a great addition to their accommodation.   Far
superior will they prove to the rough and uncomfortable
pavements, formed of stones of all sizes, shapes, and
positions, which stretch their " weary length" through
some parts of the suburbs, and even of the city.   Of
really *good* stone pavements, so agreeable to pedestrians,
the north side of Place d'Armes, and the walk in front
of the Catholic Cathedral, are excellent specimens.

If good pavements be essential to the convenience of
a city, illumination by night is not less so.   In this respect Montreal has, for the last three years, been
lamentably deficient.   Under the old system of lighting,
the oil lamps, though not very brilliant, did yet suffice
to shew the pathway to the observant traveller ; but
now on every dark night, the danger of collision and
of falling is imminent and perpetual.   This danger has
been increased by the very means which are intended
ultimately to remove it : the opening of the ground in
various places to lay down the mains and other pipes

connected with the Gas-works, has occasioned much unevenness where the places are filled in again ; and generally some parts or other are left open in the progress of the work. The shops here and there illuminated by gas, do something towards guiding the steps of the traveller by night ; but when they are closed, all is darkness. Through some cause or other, the funds of the city are at present inadequate to meet the demands of the Company for a general lighting. It cannot be supposed that *many* more dark winters will elapse before some means will be found to replenish the treasury, and give to the inhabitants of this city a benefit with which many towns of inferior consequence have long been familiar.

The hill on the west, in the rear of the city, though somewhat unaptly dignified with the title of The Mountain, is in reality a most interesting object. It is seen finely rising from the city, with its graceful and well defined outline. Its summit is almost entirely covered with trees, which, though not of large growth from the shallowness of the soil there, give a softened and cheerful appearance to the scene. The sides of it present numerous beautiful spots, several of which the wealthier citizens have selected as the sites of elegant and retired dwellings, from which the views of the city, and adjacent country on both sides the " mighty river," are exceedingly delightful ; while its base and more gentle risings are covered with farms, and gardens, and hundreds of acres of most productive orchards, abounding with trees which bear fruit of the finest quality. The eastern side of the mountain appears to be better adapted, both by soil and situation, for the growth and perfection of certain kinds of fruit than almost any other place in either Province. The apples, in particular, are of the

choicest sorts and richest flavour : among them may be
noticed, *Pomme de Neige, Pomme Gris, Bourrassa,*
and *Fameuse.*

The Geological character of the Province has not
been by any means adequately investigated ; but from
what is known, we may presume that a rich harvest of
discovery is in reserve, to reward the talent and industry
of some future explorer. For our knowledge of the
geology of the Island of Montreal, we are indebted to
Dr. Bigsby, of New York, from whose paper in the
Annals of the New York *Lyceum of Natural History,*
an abridged view is here presented. The environs of
Montreal abound in geological facts of great value. The
lowest rock is a trap, of a kind unique in the Canadas.
By its peculiar composition, which includes all the
ingredients of granite, and by its associations, it illus-
trates in a beautiful manner the affinity existing between
the formation of which it is a member, and the primitive
class in general. The nearest kindred rock is found in
the mountain of Chambly, sixteen miles distant. The
extended trappose ramifications which it has projected
into the superincumbent horizontal layers of lime-stone,
without injury or displacement accruing to them, are
very remarkable. The lime-stone and its organic remains, numerous and sometimes new and rare, are
unchanged, although in contact with, imbedded in, and
even impregnating the trap.

A very compound trap constitutes the largest part of
Montreal Hill, and appears in great quantity in the
plains on its south. The trap supports, and traverses
in direct contact, a conchiferous lime-stone, which
floors nearly the whole island : at a distance from the
hill it probably rests on quartzose conglomerate, or
sand-stone. The trap may be said to consist chiefly of
crystalline hornblende, largely mixed with quartz,

feldspar, mica, and augite. Except where it assumes the form of dykes or veins, as is common in the plain about the hill, it is massive and usually much weathered. On the summit of the hill, and sometimes elsewhere, it rises above the vegetation in naked flattish mounds, closely compacted, and seldom exceeding five yards in diameter. In the small ruinous ledges and cliffs, it is fissured perpendicularly, and rent by cold into large cuboid blocks.

The varieties are very numerous, but may all be derived from *four* principal forms, running into each other without apparent order, and occupying indiscriminately all levels. The *first* consists of promiscuously aggregated, shining, black prisms of hornblende, from half an inch to three inches long, sometimes pure ; and so mutually compressed as almost to disappear ; but more frequently white or ferruginous masses of glassy feldspar and quartz, mixed in various proportions, are interposed, so as to give the whole a strong resemblance to sienite. Cubic iron pyrites is common, and spicular iron ore in confused crystallization, as a coating. This form is met with on the summit of the east division of the hill, above M'Tavish's tomb, on the middle of its north and west flanks, and the greater part of Mount Trafalgar, especially the lower. On the north east declivity, near the west road to St. Catharine, the crystals of hornblende arrange themselves in continuous lines or bands, from a sixth to half an inch thick, and sometimes several feet long ; with occasional cross rents. They are parted by a mixture of quartz and feldspar, forming, of course, similar bands, but white. This curious structure is more remarkable as occurring among rocks otherwise disorderly ; and seems to indicate that the mass has consolidated during motion. The *second* form exists in most parts of the hill, and in the route of the Lachine Canal, and is well marked in the low cliff above M'Tavish's tomb. It is black, or brownish black, opaque, homogeneous, rather fine grained, with blunt edges. It yields a grey streak readily to steel. Its specific gravity is that of trap rocks generally. It is sometimes dotted with crystals of white glassy feldspar, which having increased to a good size, in one case converted the mass into a porphyry. The *third* kind very much resembles the black trap of the Sabine country near Rome, containing solitary crystals of augite. Among other localities this form occurs on the declivity overlooking the race course, and in greater quantity near the seat of Edward Gregory, Esq. It may be described as a confused assemblage of short needle-shaped black crystals, cemented together by a fine mixture of pink feldspar and white quartz. The *fourth* form abounds most near the lime-stone at the sides of the eastern divisions of the hill. It is much like the sienite of Peek Island, in Lake Superior; and is a mixture, occasionally fine, of white or transparent feldspar, white crystalline quartz, and a little copper-coloured mica. This form, by an augmentation of its hornblende, passes into perfect trap, or, on the other hand, loses its crystals. The white cement often contains carbonate of lime; and when the black and white ingredients are distributed with some uniformity, and in equal quantity their strongly contrasting shades give great beauty. These four forms of trap, together with their numerous gradations, occur in the veins or dykes which form so singular a feature in the geology of the environs of Montreal. The second or homogeneous kind is most abundant. Near the north end of a lime-stone quarry, a few hundred yards north of the Race-course, there is a dyke of a composition not observed on the hill. It consists of a soft cement, passing into powder, white and green (each colour predominating in patches), which contains numerous finely marked crystals of basaltic hornblende, distributed confusedly, but equally, and not often confluent. The cement is principally calcareous ; the remainder being green earth, which frequently coats the crystals.

The lime-stone overlying the trap, and receiving its ramifications, is a portion of the great basin of secondary rocks of North America. The particular form occurring in Montreal Island, and overspreading nearly the whole of it, extends into Lake Champlain and the Richelieu on the south, and downwards as far as Cape Tourment, thirty miles below Quebec. The lime-stone of Montreal hill is blueish black, or blueish brown, without lustre, fine grained passing into compact, easily scratched by steel, and of conchoidal fracture when free from shells. When exposed to the weather, it is divided into horizontal layers, from six to twenty-four inches thick, some of them containing silica, and others chertz. This form of the lime-stone is well seen at M'Tavish's tomb, and on the north of the hill at the base, every where full of the organic remains of the level country. The lime-stone varies in different parts of the island. The accidental minerals occurring in it, are in small quantity, and few in number—purple fluor, yellow blende, and iron and copper pyrites. The alluvial ridge which surrounds two-thirds of the island, may be considered as an ancient embankment, in one of those vast bodies of water which were left by the last deluge, and which in the lapse of ages have undergone repeated subsidences, until they have assumed their present shapes and number. This deposite is universal along the St. Lawrence—in some places broken into as many as seven terraces—and continued downwards from Montreal towards the Atlantic in one or more of these platforms.

In the immediate vicinity of the city, the deposite, including the ridge and the marshy flat at its base, is composed of different ingredients in different places— sand, clay, gravel, bowlders of primitive rocks, limestone, decayed vegetables, and fresh water shells. At St. Henry it consists of beds of sand resting upon clay.

The quarries of excellent stone found near the Mountain, render it not less an object of interest to the citizens of Montreal for the purposes of building, than the facilities it offers for the investigation of its geology do to the naturalist for the purposes of study.

The business of Montreal, though much of it is conducted as systematically as that of London, is more variable at different seasons of the year than is customary at home. In the winter, but little is doing, except by retail trading. At the opening of the river in the spring, vessels come in from Europe, and with their arrival, which is hailed with delight, commences the bustle and activity of the season. The merchants' stores are replenished; and both inhabitants of the town, and traders from a distance, make their purchases with avidity. This continues a few months, till all the spring cargoes have arrived, and been mostly disposed of, when another, though partial stagnation takes place, till the second arrival, in the " fall," gives again animation to the scene, to subside in like manner, after its brief, but busy, existence.

The state of Agriculture, throughout the island generally, is far from what it ought to be, and might be. Some few cases there certainly are of successful cultivation; but those are exceptions. There was, for many years, an Agricultural Society holding its meetings here; but that exists no longer. There are others, however, in different parts of the District; but there seems to be needed a more lively impulse to bring the state of tillage to that point of excellence which the soil now requires, and which it would well repay. For the purpose of improving the cultivation of flowers, fruits, and culinary vegetables, a Horticultural Society was established here, and conducted some time with much harmony and advantage; but that also has been some years extinct. Those of the inhabitants who possess no gardens, are in the habit of supplying the want by keeping plants in their windows, both winter and summer; and this is done to an extent which imparts much liveliness to the streets at all seasons of the year. Many have succeeded to admiration, and shewn, by their ardour in the rearing of their favourites, with what zest *they* enjoy

" A peep at nature, when they can no more."

The following account of the CEMETERIES, from not having the materials then at hand, could not be prepared in time to be inserted in its proper place. It may, however, not unaptly terminate this series of miscellaneous remarks.

The original Burial Ground was attached to the first French Church in Ville Marie, and occupied the space where the Cathedral now stands, and other parts of the Place d'Armes. Afterwards the Fabrique appropriated to this purpose the ground at the end of Cemeterie Street, in St. Antoine Suburbs.

The Protestant inhabitants of this city, feeling the want of a place to " bury their dead," according to rites of their own preference, purchased a piece of land in Dorchester Street, in 1799. At a meeting held at the Court House on the 21st of June in that year, Messrs.

Edward W. Gray, Isaac W. Clarke, Arthur Davidson, John Russell, and William Hunter, were chosen Trustees " to receive a deed of the burying ground in trust for the Protestant inhabitants of Montreal and vicinity; and during their lives to make rules and regulations for the good order thereof; and in a vacancy of the Trustees, the remaining members to elect others." The original cost of the ground was £550, with interest until the same was liquidated, which was done by instalments created as the lots were taken up.

In 1824, a considerable addition was made to the Cemetery by the purchase of the ground in the street along its whole length, which is the part at present used. The cost was £1000 with interest : it is not yet paid off.

The New Burial Ground was purchased in 1816, at the cost of £500. This amount has been paid off; and the revenue derived from it at present is appropriated to the liquidation of the debt on the Old ground. The Trustees are the same for both.

May every reader be prepared to descend with calmness to the tomb, and die with a hope " FULL OF IMMORTALITY."

APPENDIX

BRIEF ACCOUNT OF THE TWO REBELLIONS IN LOWER CANADA, 1837 AND 1838.

To trace the recent insurrections to their source, and to explore the means and steps by which they gradually attained their fearful character, would be foreign from the design of this work, and greatly exceed its limits. It may be sufficient to observe, that discontent and opposition to the Government on the part of many of the French inhabitants of this Province, and particularly of those who were, or assumed to be, political leaders, had been displaying themselves, in various forms, for many years ; and, growing more intense and bitter, at length broke out into actual rebellion.

In the summer, and towards the fall of the year 1837, public meetings were held in almost every parish and county in the Province, especially in the District of Montreal. At these meetings the people were harangued, by the leading members of the Assembly, in the most inflammatory language, and resolutions were passed repudiating the authority of Parliament, denying the obligations of the laws, and enforcing a scheme of general organization and terrorism, which were evidently the preliminary symptoms of insurrection and revolt.

About this time the tri-coloured flag was displayed for several days at St. Hyacinthe, and in the neighbourhood of St. Charles and St. Denis; and at a meeting held in the latter village, an influential person present warned the people to be ready to arm themselves; and some of the tavern-keepers substituted an eagle in place of their usual signs. Associations were formed, with a design of overthrowing the Government; and the " Central Committee of Montreal" were active in forwarding it. " The Sons of Liberty," as some of the associates called themselves, published in October an " Address to the Young Men of the North American Colonies," avowing sentiments of the most dangerous tendency. Every method was employed to circulate these sentiments, drilling took place in open day on Sundays and other holidays: armed bands paraded the streets of this city in the night time, the tri-coloured flag was hoisted, and the peaceable inhabitants felt themselves insecure if they ventured out unarmed, after the day had closed.

A grand meeting of the " Confederation of the Six Counties" took place at St. Charles, on the 23rd of October, when a fuller and unreserved avowal of treasonable designs was made. The Cap of Liberty was raised, and a solemn oath taken under it, to be faithful to the revolutionary principles of which it was emblematical. All allegiance, and every pretence to it, were at once discarded, and a determination evinced to take the management of affairs into their own hands. This meeting was attended by the Speaker (L. J. Papineau) and twelve Members of the House of Assembly, and no time was lost in carrying the treasonable part of the resolutions into effect. Bands of armed ruffians marched forth, spreading fear and consternation among the peaceable inhabitants of the country, threatening them with the loss of life and property if they did not immediately acquiesce in their views and projects. Justices of the Peace and Officers of Militia, were compelled to resign their commissions, and many took refuge in Montreal.

On the same day a meeting of the loyal and constitutional inhabitants took place in this city, for the " maintenance of good order, the protection of life and property, and the connection now happily existing between this Colony and the United Kindom, at present put in jeopardy by the machinations of a disorganizing and revolutionary faction within this Province." Troops were sent for from Nova Scotia and from Upper Canada. The Attorney General arrived from Quebec for the purpose of directing measures, and for dealing according to law with certain foreign military officers who had been introduced into the Province for the purpose of giving aid to the insurgents.

The Magistrates of Montreal having received information, on the 5th of November, that numerous bodies of men, of different parties, intended on the following day to parade the streets of the city, immediately issued a proclamation to prohibit such a measure. On Monday, the 6th, persons were anxiously enquiring as to the motions and intentions of the two parties; and about two o'clock it was known that a considerable number of the " Sons of Liberty" had assembled in an enclosed yard near St. James Street, although some of their leaders had pledged themselves to the Magistrates that no procession should take place. About three hundred of them sallied forth, armed with bludgeons, pistols, and other weapons, and made a furious and indiscriminate attack on all that fell in their way. For a time they had full possession of the street, breaking windows, and threatening other mischief. But the Constitutionalists were soon aroused, and dispersed the riotous assemblage,

T

but were far from satisfied with this success. About six o'clock the Riot Act was read, and the military were called out. A party of the Constitutionalists were encountered by the Royal Regiment in front of Papineau's house; but instead of offering any resistance, they heartily cheered the gallant regiment, and accompanied it to the *Champ de Mars*, where it was ordered to take post. A company of the Royals was posted near the Bishop's Church: the officer in command received from the Loyalists a seven-barrelled gun, two other guns, a sword, and a banner of the " Sons of Liberty," which had been taken from a house in Dorchester Street, where they were in the habit of meeting for drill. After this, all became quiet, and the Magistrates ordered the troops to their barracks. In proceeding thither, the Royals found a party attempting some injury to Papineau's house; but they desisted the moment the troops came upon them. In the course of the evening the office of the *Vindicator*, a seditious newspaper, was destroyed by some of the more zealous of the British party. The military patrolled the streets till day-light. No further violence was committed, no lives were lost, and no opposition offered to the soldiers.

On the 10th of November, Sir John Colborne, as Commander of the Forces, removed his head quarters from Sorel-to Montreal; and on the same day, in consequence of intelligence from St. John's, a detachment of the Montreal Volunteer Cavalry proceeded thither, as a corps of observation, under the command of Capt. Glasgow of the Royal Artillery. He found a large body of armed *habitans* posted on the opposite bank of the Richelieu River. Attended by two of his men, he approached this party, and demanded the cause of their being met together at that place. They answered that, if he did not immediately retire, they would fire upon him. The Cavalry were then ordered to take possession of the bridge, to prevent this armed body from crossing over to St. John's, and carrying on, as they said they were resolved to do, their treasonable practices of intimidation and coercion. The state of affairs throughout the district now became truly alarming; and it was evident that a spirit of disaffection and contempt of the laws had spread itself far and wide among the people.

On the 16th of November, warrants were issued, and rewards offered, for the apprehension of twenty-six individuals charged with High Treason, of whom all were of French origin, except one; eight were Members of the Provincial Parliament, and the greater part of the whole number were in the higher classes of society. Eight of them were committed to prison at the time; but all the others who resided in town made their escape. Two of them resided at St. John's, and one at St. Athanase, and the warrants for their apprehension were entrusted to a peace officer, who, accompanied by a body of the Royal Montreal Cavalry, proceeded to execute them, by way of Longueuil and Chambly. Demaray and Davignon were arrested at St. John's, and the party were returning to Montreal with them by the same route. When within about two miles of Longueuil, the Cavalry and peace officer in charge of the prisoners, were intercepted by a large body of armed peasantry, who fired upon them from their houses, from behind the fences, and from a barn which bordered the road, and compelled them to abandon their prisoners. Several of the Cavalry were wounded, and their horses injured, by the fire of the insurgents.

These partial successes infused fresh vigour into the rebels, and led them to suppose that no force could withstand them. Notice of the rescue having been conveyed to Montreal, it was deemed advisable to

re-inforce the garrison at Chambly.   Colonel Wetherall
was, therefore, ordered with his battalion to that place,
by way of Longueuil, accompanied by Major Jackson
of the Artillery with two six pounders, a detachment
of the Montreal Cavalry under Captain David, and
civil officers to re-capture the prisoners.   At Longueuil
they found all the houses closed, but the inhabitants at
home ; and for several miles beyond the case was the
same.   Several armed bands were met by Captain
David and his party, but they fled on a nearer approach.
Six individuals were apprehended with arms in their
hands.   About 300 men took a position about a mile
from Chambly for the purpose of resisting the Cavalry ;
but at the approach of the advanced guard of the Royals,
they fled in all directions, and the Cavalry succeeded in
capturing some of them.   The whole country appeared
to be in arms.

On the 20th of November, intelligence was received
that T. S. Brown had collected a large force at the
village of St. Charles on the river Richelieu, which he
was proceeding to fortify, and that Papineau, O'Cal-
laghan, and Wolfred Nelson were concerned in these
measures.   Warrants had been issued for their apprehension ; and the civil authorities applied to the
Commander of the Forces for aid in securing them.   On
the 23d a body of troops under Colonel Gore embarked
on board the steamer St. George for Sorel, where they
landed in the evening.   At ten o'clock they marched
towards St. Denis, intending to attack the force at that
place, and then move on rapidly to assist Colonel
Wetherall of the Royal Regiment in his attack upon
St. Charles.   The march was a terrible one, in consequence of a heavy rain, and the muddiness of the roads.
They did not reach St. Denis till after day-light.   An
attack was commenced ; several rebels were killed ; but

finding it impossible to dislodge some of the rebels from a large stone house from which they were firing, and his men being exhausted by the fatigues of the preceding night and day, the Colonel retreated upon Sorel, where, after much suffering, the party arrived on the morning of the 24th. Strong bodies of armed peasantry were seen in various places along the line of march.

Colonel Wetherall had received orders to attack St. Charles at the same time that the other forces were to be engaged at St. Denis. For this purpose he left Chambly on the 22d, but the roads were so bad, that his troops were not able to reach the place till noon of the 25th. The houses along the route were deserted, the bridges broken down, barricades erected, and every precaution taken against an attack. Halting to reconnoitre, Colonel Wetherall observed that two guns commanded the road, and he therefore resolved to attack by deploying to the right. The troops were saluted with a loud cheer from the stockade, and a constant fire was kept up by the rebels from the opposite bank of the river. When he had approached within two hundred and fifty yards from the works, he took up a position with the hope that a display of his force would induce some change among the infatuated people. They, however, opened a heavy fire, which was returned. He then advanced nearer to the works, but finding the defenders obstinate, he stormed and carried them, burning every building within the stockade, except Mr. Debartzch's house which was extinguished, and occupied, by the troops. The affair occupied about an hour. The slaughter was great on the side of the rebels, but slight on that of the troops. Several prisoners were taken, from one of whom Colonel Wetherall learned that Brown had assumed the rank of General, and actually commanded, for a short time; but that soon after the firing began, he galloped to the rear under pretence of bringing up re-inforcements, but was no more seen. Papineau, Drolet, and others crossed the river to St. Marc, on the arrival of the troops before St. Charles. On the whole, the means and preparations of the rebels were more formidable than many persons had supposed ; and had not the rebellion been checked at this point, the consequences to the country would have been dreadful. Having thus captured St. Charles, and dispersed the insurgents, who are said to have amounted at this place to fifteen hundred fighting men, the Colonel determined to attack a considerable body of the rebels collected for the purpose of cutting off his retreat to Chambly ; and on the morning of the 28th, he discovered them in a well-chosen position, and under the protection of an abattis. They fled, however, as soon as he had formed to attack, leaving their two guns behind them. On the 30th of November, Colonel Wetherall, and the whole of the troops under his command, landed from the steamboat *Victoria* from Laprairie, bringing with them twenty-five prisoners taken on the march to Chambly and at St. Charles, together with the pole and cap of liberty, which had been raised at the latter place. The troops, upon landing, were heartily and enthusiastically cheered by the people on the wharf, who escorted them to their quarters with shouts of applause. During these operations on the Richelieu, and before authentic intelligence arrived respecting them, the state of the public mind in this city was such as cannot easily be described. Every heart was anxious, and every countenance betrayed the emotion. The ordinary concerns of life were, now, minor considerations, and gave way to the all-engrossing topic. When the news arrived, on the afternoon of Sunday·26th of November, the joy with which it was welcomed, was extreme : there is no

doubt that the lives and fortunes of thousands of the
loyal inhabitants depended, in a great measure, on the
success or failure of this solitary expedition.   Happily,
the result was favourable, and the rebellion in that
quarter was so far crushed, as to set the minds of the
loyal at rest for the present, and excite their hopes for
the future.

While these operations were going on, a laudable
spirit of loyalty and zeal was displayed by many of the
citizens of Quebec and Montreal, as well as by the
inhabitants of the Townships and other parts of the
Province, in the formation of volunteer corps, of various
descriptions, for the purpose of putting down rebellious
attempts to overturn the Government.   At Montreal,
three Brigades were formed and thoroughly organized.
The first consists of the Royal Montreal Cavalry, having
two troops within the city, and one at Lachine, a
company of Artillery, and three (now five) companies
of Rifles   the second of the three Battalions of Ward
Associations , and the third, of the Montreal Light
Infantry, and the Queen's troop of Light Dragoons ;
amounting in all to about four thousand, rank and file.
In other parts of the district, and in that of St. Francis,
upwards of fifty corps of various descriptions were
formed.

Colonel Gore was ordered a second time to Sorel
with a view of proceeding to another attack on St.
Denis.   Having reached that place, he entered it without opposition, the occupants having fled.   An iron gun
and a considerable quantity of arms and ammunition,
were found in the place, and destroyed, as were the
fortified houses, and all the defences which had been
raised by the rebels.   Marching on to St. Charles, the
Colonel received information that some of the chiefs
were probably at St. Hyacinthe.   Thither he proceeded,

but found them not. After enduring great hardships
in their flight, most of them succeeded in reaching the
United States. Colonel Gore leaving part of his force
at St. Charles, and another part at St. Denis, returned
to Montreal; and thus that portion of the country was
quieted for a time.

Previously to these latter movements, a most tragical
event had taken place, the particulars of which were
not known till some time after the horrible deed had
been perpetrated. We allude to the murder of Lieut.
Weir. This deserving and lamented young officer
had been sent overland, on the 22d of November to
Sorel, with a despatch to the officer in command there,
directing him to prepare a force to accompany Colonel
Gore, who was to leave Montreal in the afternoon by
steamboat. The roads were so bad that he did not
reach Sorel till half an hour after Colonel Gore and his
division had marched on the route to St Denis.
Taking a fresh caleche, he hastened to join the troops;
but mistaking the road, he passed the troops, and arrived
at St. Denis before them. Here he was made a prisoner,
closely pinioned, sent forward to St. Charles, and on
the road was barbarously murdered by his brutal
guardians. The fact, and the cruel circumstances ac-
companying it, were fully ascertained on the second
expedition to St. Denis. The body, which was found
in the Richelieu, was brought to Montreal for interment.
The funeral took place on the 8th of December, with
military honours; and it may be said that Montreal
never before witnessed so solemn and imposing a
spectacle. A vast body of civilians of all ranks, and of
military, both regulars and volunteers, attended on the
occasion. The sympathy that was felt for the unfortunate sufferer, and the indignation excited against his
cruel murderers, were strongly expressed by the

assembled multitudes. So great was the concourse, that the road from the Quebec Suburbs to the burying ground, which is half a mile in length and of considerable breadth, was occupied by one living mass of men ; and no one could get admittance to the ground, except those who immediately followed the hearse.

On the 29th of November, the Governor-in-Chief issued a monitory Proclamation to the insurgents, inviting them to return to their allegiance, and promising them forgetfulness and immunity for the past, and a continuance of paternal protection and favour ; at the same time offering rewards for the apprehension of the leaders. Martial law was proclaimed in the district of Montreal on the 5th of December, and Sir John Colborne invested with authority to execute it.

Many of the insurgents who had fled took refuge in the United States, and, as some had expected, met with considerable support from a part of the inhabitants. A number of refugee rebels entered the Province from the State of Vermont ; but were met in the county of Mississquoi, by the loyal population of that county and the Shefford Volunteers. The number on each side was about two hundred ; the rebels were completely routed, and made a precipitate retreat into the United States, with great loss in prisoners, arms, and munitions, before they had penetrated a mile into the township of St. Armand. This brilliant affair took place near the residence of Mr. Hiram Moore, on a point popularly called Moore's corner. This exploit enabled Sir John Colborne to withdraw several companies from St. John's, and to make arrangements for suppressing the rebellion in other directions.

While these movements were taking place on the South side of the St. Lawrence, preparations almost as extensive, and perhaps more vigorous, were making by the rebel party on the North, particularly in the county of the Lake of the Two Mountains, at St. Eustache, St. Benoit, and St. Scholastique. In that neighbourhood, also, Magistrates and Officers of Militia were compelled to surrender their commissions, and many of the loyal and peaceable inhabitants were forced to take refuge in this city and other places, for the preservation of their lives, leaving their property of every description at the mercy of the insurgents. Bands of nocturnal marauders paraded the country, armed and disguised, threatening the lives and property of all who did not join them, with destruction; firing into the houses of those who were obnoxious to them; burning their barns and other out-houses; maiming and disfiguring their cattle; and finally carrying away, by force and violence, whatever they deemed essential to success in their treasonable projects. Here the insurgents were more fully prepared for resistance than in any other part of the district. They fortified themselves in various places, and were commanded by Girod, Chenier, Girouard and Dumouchelle,—supposed to have been the most active and able leaders of the revolt. Their strong holds were, St. Eustache, and St. Benoit or Grand Brulé. Accounts were frequently arriving in the city, sometimes perhaps exaggerated, but upon the whole sufficiently well attested, of the formidable aspect of affairs in this quarter; and produced an eager, and almost impatient, desire that troops might be sent immediately to disperse the rebel forces, and put an end to a state of things so truly painful and alarming.

For the purpose of rendering Montreal as secure as possible against any sudden attacks of the disaffected, the principal entrances into the city were fortified by strong timber and heavy gates, with loop-holes on the sides to command the outer roads; the subordinate streets were also strongly barricaded; so that we had all the appearance of a town in expectation of a siege.

Our excellent commander was by no means deficient in vigilance, but waited, with all the cool determination of an experienced soldier, for the most proper hour to commence his operations. As soon as a sufficient force was at his disposal, he lost no time in advancing to the scene of action. On the morning of Wednesday the 13th of December, the whole of the forces destined for this service marched out of Montreal, escorted by an immense number of the loyal inhabitants, cheering them in the most enthusiastic manner, and warmly wishing them success and safety. They formed two brigades, the first being under the command of Colonel Maitland of the 32d regiment, and consisting of that regiment commanded by Major Reid, and the 83d regiment commanded by Lieut. Colonel the Hon. Henry Dundas. The second brigade was under the command of Lieut. Colonel Wetherall, of the Royal Regiment, and consisted of the second battalion of that regiment and the Montreal Volunteer Rifles; Globenski's volunteers having joined this brigade at St. Martins, where they had been stationed some days, with Captain Birtwhistle's company of the 32d regiment, Captain Tunstall's company of the Montreal Volunteer Militia, and a detachment of Volunteer Cavalry under Captain Ermatinger, to protect Lachapelle's bridge, and to maintain a communication with head quarters. The Artillery, consisting of six field pieces, was under the command of Major Jackson. About 2 o'clock of the same day the Commander of the Forces also took his departure from head quarters, with his staff, escorted by the Royal Montreal Cavalry and the Queen's Light Dragoons. The whole party halted during the night at St. Martin, a village in the middle of Isle Jesus, on the direct route to St. Eustache, and about twelve miles from Montreal.   Instructions had been forwarded to Major Townshend, to march on the following day from Carrillon, on the Ottawa, with a detachment of the 24th Regiment, and the Volunteers of St. Andrews, towards St. Benoit.

On the following morning, Thursday the 14th of December, the forces marched forward to the scene of action, which they reached about noon, the greater part, with the Commander, crossing the northern branch of the Ottawa River, on the ice, about three miles below St. Eustache, while Captain Globensky's company (mostly composed of loyalists driven from their home by the rebels) marched in the direct route to the village. The attack was completely successful, though necessarily attended with much destruction, both of life and property on the part of the rebels.   The church, which was their strong hold, not yielding to the fire in front, was entered by the rear, and its occupants dislodged, many of them killed, and a still greater number secured as prisoners. That handsome edifice was then set on fire, as was the presbytere, and about sixty of the principal houses in the village.   The loss on the part of the forces was very small, only one or two men being killed, and a few wounded; that of the rebels is supposed to have been very great, and that nearly two hundred of them fell victims to their folly from the fire and charges of the troops, or were suffocated in the flames of the buildings destroyed.   The blaze was distinctly seen on high ground in the neighbourhood of Montreal, a distance of twenty-one miles.   Dr. Chenier, one of the leaders, was killed near the church; and Girod, Peltier, and others, are reported to have made their escape immediately after the first fire from the troops, on pretence of going to the rear to bring up reinforcements.

On the morning of the 15th, the main part of the forces marched forward to St. Benoit, twelve miles distant, where they arrived about noon. During the march, His Excellency was met by delegates, bearing a flag of truce from the rebels, and stating that they were prepared to lay down their arms unconditionally. On the line of march, similar tokens were exhibited in rags of something white from almost every house, and none of the inhabitants were at all molested. On arriving, the Commander fixed his head quarters at the house of Girouard, one of the insurgent chiefs, and opposite to it he found about two hundred and fifty of the rebels drawn up in line, suing for pardon, and stating that their leaders had deserted them. Their request was complied with, and they were dismissed to their homes and occupations. The intrenchments of the rebels at St. Benoit were destroyed, and several houses. Afterwards the church, the Priest's dwelling, and almost every house in the place were fired by the unrestrainable zeal of the volunteers in the neighbourhood. The purpose of the expedition having been accomplished in the dispersion or submission of the rebel forces, the troops prepared to return to Montreal, except that the 32d Regiment, two field pieces, and a detachment of the Queen's Light Dragoons, were sent forward to St. Scholastique to re-establish order in that quarter. On Saturday the 16th, His Excellency the Commander of the Forces, escorted by the Montreal Cavalry and the Light Dragoons, returned to the city, as did the Montreal Rifles. The next day the Royals, under Colonel Wetherall, marched in amidst the acclamations of the citizens, bringing with them 105 prisoners, among whom were three of their leaders. The Royal Artillery and 83rd Regiment also returned the same day, and were greeted with the cheers of the inhabitants, who went out to meet

U

their brave countrymen, for their services in putting
down a rebellion which had done much mischief and
threatened more.   His Excellency Sir John Colborne,
as Commander of the Forces, by his prudent foresight,
his prompt sagacity on the one hand when danger surrounded us, and his clemency on the other, when
submission allowed it, together with his readiness to
make known important intelligence to the community,
has entitled himself to the lasting esteem and gratitude
of every loyal inhabitant of Canada.

But not alone were the troops above mentioned
engaged in the duties of this eventful season.   During
the absence of the expedition, the garrison duty of
Montreal was entrusted to the companies of the 24th
Regiment remaining in town, and the different volunteer
corps of the city.   Their courage and loyalty were soon
put to the test.   About ten o'clock on the night of the
13th December, intelligence had reached the city that a
large body of rebels were marching upon Lachine, for
the purpose, it was supposed, of seizing the arms which
had a short time previously been deposited there for the
Beauharnois Volunteers, and then proceeding with them
to attack Montreal in the absence of the regular troops.
The report gaining ground, an alarm was sounded
through the city, and in an incredibly short space of time,
the whole volunteer force mustered in arms, and proceeded to meet the rebels in the direction in which they
were expected—Colonel Maitland's battalion marching
to the Tanneries, three miles out of town—every man
being resolved to do his duty.   The alarm proved to
be a false one, as far as regarded Montreal ; those rebels
who had collected about Lachine having been disappointed of their object by the removal of the arms on
board some batteaux in the river, and by the timely
appearance of the Lachine Cavalry.   The volunteers,

therefore, after being under arms most of the night, retired to their quarters. Their conduct, however, was such as to reflect the greatest credit both upon officers and men, all of whom evinced the best possible disposition, and by their zeal, courage, and activity, afforded ample evidence that the city had been safe in their keeping.

With the return of the troops from the County of the Lake of the Two Mountains, the military operations connected with the first rebellion in Lower Canada may be said to have terminated, except so far as it was necessary to keep different parties in motion to guard against surprise, and to check irruptions which were sometimes threatened, and at others attempted, from the United States, of refugee rebels and those who were inclined to join them. During the remainder of the winter, and the spring of 1838, various prisoners of greater or less distinction, who had been engaged in the insurrection, were from time to time apprehended and brought to Montreal. The transactions which took place in Upper Canada, during the period of which we have been treating, though of an equally important character, do not properly belong to our narrative.

In the course of the summer and autumn of 1838, rumours were circulated, and surmises formed, that another rising of the disaffected was in progress, or at least in agitation. An unusual run upon the banks, in the demand for cash on the part of the *habitans* who had notes in their possession, with various murmurings and other symptoms, gave sign that all was not at rest. The "sympathy," as it was termed, shewn to

the insurgents by many of the inhabitants of the border
States, kept alive the expectation. Early in October,
if not before, many facts were in the knowledge of the
Governor-in-Chief and the Commander of the Forces,
which called for increasing vigilance, and justified active
preparation. The lenient measures which had been
adopted with regard to several of those who had been
apprehended for their share in the first rebellion, instead
of being followed by a grateful return of allegiance,
were, in many instances, construed into fear, and abused
to the purposes of renewed aggression and tumult.
These seditious movements were, for the most part, confined to the south side of the St. Lawrence ; the country
above St. Eustache and its neighbourhood remaining
perfectly quiet, whatever might have been the hints or
threats of individuals.

On Friday the 2d of November information was
received of a preliminary meeting of a few of the leading rebels and refugees, to be held that evening at the
residence of Gagnon, about six miles from St. John's.
A party of soldiers, with a magistrate, were sent to
apprehend them. Seven were taken, and among them
the son of Gagnon, but the father was not to be found.
They were all armed. A few other arrests were made
at St. John's ; and all the prisoners afterwards brought
to Montreal. On Saturday the 3d, at La Tortu, about
eight miles above Laprairie, a number of rebels attacked
the scattered loyalists in that quarter, and two respectable farmers, named Walker and Vitrey, were so
cruelly treated, that the former died of his wounds, and
the other with difficulty survived. As many of the loyal
inhabitants as were able made their escape to the city.
A party of Hussars went off from Laprairie to attack
the insurgents, who fled at their approach. The same
day, a strong party mustered at St. Charles, with an

intention to join with others lower down the Richelieu, in an attempt upon Sorel, which, however, was not made. In Beauharnois a more extensive rising took place on the same evening, when a large party succeeded in surprising the loyalists of the village, and made prisoners of Messrs. Ellice (son of the Seignieur), Brown, Ross, Norman, and Dr. Surveyor. During the day the steamer took over four pieces of Artillery to Laprairie, for St. John's. At night an attempt was made to burn the boat, by conveying combustibles into the berths; but no material damage was done. The detaining of the Artillery was probably the means of saving the boat, if not the village, as an attack was meditated.

While the inhabitants of the Indian village of Caughnawaga were at worship on Sunday morning, the 4th, a party of rebels surrounded the church, upon which the Indians immediately turned out, and the Chief, setting an example promptly followed by all, raised the *war-whoop*, seized the rebel next him and wrested from him his musket. The others, being panic-struck, were made prisoners to the number of 64, and brought into Montreal. Just after the conclusion of the morning service, the alarm became general throughout the city; at least 2000 of the volunteers rushed to arms, though they had not met since the spring, and were so stationed as to guard all the passes into the town, none being allowed to proceed without giving a satisfactory answer to the challenge. On the same day a proclamation of martial law was made by the Administrator of the Government; and so intent upon mischief did the various bodies of insurgents appear, that it was deemed advisable, for several weeks, to keep the city in the best possible state of defence, and to burn lights in the windows after the day had closed. Several persons residing in the city, who were suspected of treasonable or rebellious designs

were taken up and imprisoned ; and for several days
in succession many were apprehended in different parts
of the district.

The rebels appear to have congregated in the greatest
number at the villages of Napierville and Chateauguay.
In the former place some thousands had collected,
imprisoned the loyal inhabitants, quartered themselves
at their houses, and made free with every thing they
could find.   In Chateauguay they indulged themselves
freely in eating and drinking ; but the report of the
war-whoop, and the expectation of the Indians from
Caughnawaga, had very much disconcerted them.
Colonel Cathcart with his dragoons, scoured the country
to a considerable distance round Chambly, and cleared
it of rebel forces : several villages were deserted, and
the houses of the most noted rebels reduced to ashes.
The country began to put on a most desolate appearance,
through the folly of those who in wickedness had con-
ceived a plan which in weakness they had undertaken
to execute.

The steamer *Henry Brougham*, on arriving at the
wharf at Beauharnois, on the morning of the 4th, was
taken possession of by the rebels, and all the passengers,
twenty-one in number, secured.   They were confined
in the house of Mr. Quintal, the Curé, who was also a
prisoner.   The following Saturday, a force of regulars
and volunteers arriving, they were set at liberty.   The
mail bag was on board the boat, but, by the good
management of Captain Whipple, was kept out of sight,
until the boat was regained for its owners.   In the
course of the week Sir John Colborne, with a sufficient
body of forces, crossed the river to proceed to Napierville, for the purpose of dislodging the rebels, and
delivering their captives ; but on entering the village
on Saturday they found that the rebels, to the number

of two thousand, had evacuated the place about two hours before, and that about the same number had previously gone off, many of them having thrown away their arms. A few days before this, Dr. Cote, with about 400 men, made an attack upon some loyalists at Lacolle Old Steam Mill, which ended in the complete route of the assailants, who lost their only six pounder, 250 stand of arms, eight prisoners, eleven killed and several wounded. The object of Cote was to open a communication between the Lines and Napierville. Dr. Nelson, with a force of one thousand men, advanced upon Odelltown, where he attacked about 200 of the volunteers under the command of Colonel Taylor. This small force, from Odelltown church, and with the aid of the gun taken at Lacolle, kept up such a fire upon the rebels, that, after an action of about two hours and a half, they were obliged to retreat, leaving fifty dead, and carrying off several wounded. This gallant behaviour of the volunteers obtained the highest praise from the Commanding Officer.

On the 10th of November, part of the 71st Regiment, with upwards of one thousand Glengary men, took Beauharnois, and rescued all the prisoners, with the exception of those who had been removed, On Sunday the 11th, a pleasing sensation was created in town by the arrival of Mr. Ellice, and various other gentlemen who had been seized by the rebels. It appears that, after their capture at Beauharnois, they were, as was supposed here, conveyed to Chateauguay, where they were confined in a room, from which day-light was excluded, but they were allowed to have candles burning. They were well treated by the Curé and the nuns, who were allowed to send them what they needed. On Saturday, they were placed in carts, for the purpose, as they believed, of being conveyed to Napierville, and had reached La Pigeonniere, in the Seigniory of St. George, when their escort, hearing of the evacuation of Napierville, left them and fled. They were allowed to proceed in the same carts to Laprairie, and were even advised which road to take, as the safest. They reached Laprairie about two o'clock in the morning, and Montreal about ten.

This new rebellion being thus promptly suppressed in the short space of ten days, attention was now engaged with the numerous prisoners that were secured at the different posts of disturbance, and with vigilantly looking after suspected persons and places. Ninety-one prisoners taken at Napierville were brought in on the 13th, and on the same day twenty others from Lachine, having been taken in arms at Chateauguay—some of them persons in respectable life. Forty others were brought in from the direction of Laprairie, on the 15th. Meantime volunteers, in various quarters, were on the alert to detect the least suspicious movement in their respective neighbourhoods, and, in conjunction with the regulars, to maintain the peace thus far restored. Intelligence having been received of a descent upon Prescott in Upper Canada, by a party of about four hundred men from the States, Colonel Wetherall left town on the 14th, with a sufficient force to resist the unprovoked aggression.

Among the prisoners taken at Odelltown, was a French officer, named Charles Hindenlang. This man, after his apprehension, put forth a document, in which he attemped to vindicate himself, and to cast imputations upon those who employed him. In some measure his statement was credited, and for a time divided the opinions of many as to the plans, and strength, and intentions of the rebels ; but his trial and subsequent conduct placed his character and professions in their true light.

A General Court Martial was appointed for the trial of the rebel prisoners. It met for the first time on Monday the 19th of November, in the Court House. The following Officers composed the Court:

Major General JOHN CLITHEROW, President.
Lieut.-Col. Sir JOHN R. EUSTACE, 2d Batt. Grenadier Guards.
Lieut.-Col. HENRY W. BARNARD,　　do.　　　　　do.
Lieut.-Col. WILLIAM GRIERSON, 15th Regiment.
Lieut.-Col. JAMES CRAUFORD, 2d Batt. Grenadier Guards.
Major SAMUEL DILMAN PRITCHARD, Major of Brigade.
Major HENRY TOWNSEND, 24th Regiment.
Major ARTHUR W. BIGGS, 7th Hussars,
Captain WILLIAM THORNTON, 2d Batt. Grenadier Guards.
Captain WILLIAM B. SMITH, 15th Regiment.
Captain ROBERT MARCH, 24th Regiment.
Captain HENRY A. KERR, 2d Battalion, Royal Regiment.
Captain AUGUSTUS COX, 2d Battalion, Grenadier Guards.
Captain the Hon. GEORGE CADOGAN, Grenadier Guards.
Captain Hugh A. R. MITCHELL,　　　　do.　　do.

" All of whom, or the said Major General John Clitherow, President, together with any twelve or more of the said last mentioned persons and officers, may constitute the said General Court Martial."

Captain Muller, of the Royal Regiment, was appointed Deputy Judge Advocate, to be assisted by Professional Gentlemen.

The Court Martial, thus constituted and appointed, immediately entered upon its arduous and responsible duties. The public expectation, however, from the ill effects of last year's clemency, out-ran the proceedings of the court, and, after waiting awhile, the people began to be suspicious that nothing effectual would be done against those who had occasioned so much misery, and who would probably, if no severe check were given, repeat their deeds of violence.

On the 20th of November orders were issued that, instead of burning lights in the windows, as had been done since the first alarm on the 4th, " every housekeeper in the town and suburbs, shall keep two candles ready to be lighted at the first signal of the sound of a drum or bell." Meantime the ardour of the British inhabitants increased, for the maintenance of their loyalty and the preservation of their lives and privileges—the volunteer corps were augmented—and the whole of this force put upon full pay, and rendered as effective as possible, so that, notwithstanding the occasional drafts from among the regulars to repress the incursions from the United States into the Upper Province, the city, after the first moment of alarm, was felt to be in a complete state of defence. Large quantities of arms and ammunition, either taken from the rebels, or found secreted for their use, were brought in from time to time ; and there can be no doubt that these were obtained either by purchase from the neighbouring States, or by donation from persons residing there, ill-affected to the interests of Canada. On the 29th and 30th of November nearly a hundred rebels from Napierville and Beauharnois were brought in as prisoners.

The Hon. D. Mondelet, and Charles D. Day, Esq., having been appointed Judge Advocates in conjunction with Captain Muller, the Court Martial commenced the trial of the twelve following prisoners on Wednesday the 28th of November :—Joseph Narcisse Cardinal, Joseph Duquette, Joseph L'Ecuyer, Jean Louis Thibert, Jean Marie Thibert, Léandre Ducharme, Joseph Guimond, Louis Guerin, Edouard Thérien, Antoine Côté, Maurice Lepailleur, Louis Lesiége. After a patient and impartial investigation, in which the prisoners had the benefit of able advocates, two of them, Edouard Therien and Louis Lesiége, were acquitted, the other ten were found guilty, and condemned to death, and two of them, J. N. Cardinal and J. Duquette were executed on Friday the 21st of December. They were both implicated in the rebellion of last year, and derived but little wisdom from the lenity then shewn to them.

The discontented inhabitants of Canada were not the only persons who disturbed its peace. Certain restless spirits beyond the lines, affecting to " sympathize" with those who enjoyed as much liberty as themselves, but really bent upon cruelty or plunder, made incursions at their pleasure, but sometimes to their disappointment and sorrow. We have already referred to one invasion of this sort, chiefly, indeed, under Canadian leaders, and to others commanded by Americans : the following occurred on Sunday, Dec. 30th, at Beech Ridge on the Province line, Rouville. About two o'clock in the morning a band of American ruffians from Alburg, to the number of fifteen or twenty, armed with muskets and swords, came across the line about half a mile, and broke open the house of a loyalist of the name of Gibson. The terrified family awoke from their sleep, and saw the glare of their barn on fire. Gibson leaped from a window, and fled, without putting on his clothes. The wife, and family of five children, the oldest not thirteen and the youngest an infant, were ordered to depart. The poor woman prayed for time to throw some clothes on the children and herself ; but they were driven out with imprecations, and the house fired. The night had been tempestuous, and the thermometer ranged between ten and eighteen degrees below zero. The mother with her babe in her arms and her shivering little ones by her side, all without shoes and nearly without clothes, was compelled to drag herself through the snow, drifted as it was, three quarters of a mile before she could find a shelter. The unfeeling wretches then proceeded to the next house, occupied by Isaac Johnson, a loyalist, with two daughters, ordered the inmates to leave it, and

then set fire to it and the barns. They visited some
other places which they served in like manner, and then
made good their retreat to Vermont.   The barns which
contained the whole grain produce of the farmers, and
all the other buildings, were a heap of smouldering ruins
before sun-rise.   In the course of the winter and spring
other similar incursions were made upon the border by
unprincipled men, so that a residence there became
both precarious and painful, though not always attended
with circumstances of so horrible a description.

The trials still proceeded ; and on the 18th of January
five other rebels were executed over the front gateway
at the New Gaol ; viz. P. J. Decoigne, engaged at
Napierville, and Jacques Robert, two brothers of the
name of Sanguinet, and P. Hamelin, concerned in the
murder of Mr. Walker, at La Tortu.   The gallows
had been removed to a more public situation to convince
the *habitans* of the reality of the executions, for on that
point they appear to have been previously incredulous.
Decoigne, who was a Notary, delivered an address on
the scaffold before he suffered, to the effect that they
wére all convinced of the enormity of their crimes, the
justice of their fate, and the folly of neglecting " the
good instructions that had been given them."

Last year several persons suspected of being engaged
in the murder of Narcisse Chartrand, underwent their
trial in the Criminal Court ; but, although the evidence
against them was most clear and decisive, they were
acquitted, in the face of it, by a Canadian jury.   Two of
them, Francois Nicolas and Amable Daunais, profited
so little by their former escape as to engage in the
second rebellion, and, being brought to trial and convicted, were, with three others, executed at Montreal,
on the 5th of February.   The first of these three,
Charles Hindenlang, was a native of France, and had

been an officer in the French service. He was taken in
the fight at Odelltown, where he had exercised command over a part of the insurgents. After his committal,
he made a confession tending to vindicate himself and
criminate his associates, but to which he gave the lie in
his speech on the scaffold. In his affidavit he had
declared that the cause in which he had embarked was
a bad one, and the men with whom he had been associated, villains ; adding that, if he were liberated, he
would use every exertion to uphold the Government,
and to bring under its power those with whom he had
acted. Yet now, with his dying breath, he applauds
the very revolt he had pretended to condemn—and says
it was a good cause. He denied the right of the
Government to put him to death, and concluded by
exclaiming " VIVE LA LIBERTE !" using the words in
a sense which his previous remarks made but too evident.
Nicolas, on the other hand, deprecated the cause in
which he had been engaged, confessed that it was begun
and maintained by the ardour of young men, to whom
their parents had neglected to give instruction, or who,
perhaps, had it not in their power to instruct them.
He admitted that he had led a bad life, and had deserved
long ago to die—declared the error of his ways, and
exhorted his countrymen to avoid his end. In a written
document, drawn up by himself in French, he says,—" I
recommend to all who have been blinded like me, either
by promises or by hopes of gain, to look more closely
to it, and to consider well that we have been the instruments of ambitious persons who had not the fear of God
before their eyes. I entreat all to take warning from
me. Although certainly I cannot do otherwise than
say that we need reform in this country, yet must you
wait until God lends his aid, and points out with his
all-powerful finger, to those who are to accomplish

v

them, the time and the means. I have seen the time when I was proud to be a British subject, and I had great reason—and it is only since fanatic spirits have represented to me things in a different point of view that I have become disaffected towards my Government. Fathers and mothers, who bring up children...extinguish in their young hearts any possible animosity that may there exist against persons of a different country, or of a different creed." Happy indeed would it be if such prudent counsel were universally received and acted upon by our deluded fellow-subjects. The other two who suffered on this occasion, Chevalier de Lorimier, and Pierre Remi Narbonne, were deeply engaged in the rebellion.

These were the last executions that have taken place under the recent convictions; our humane Governor having deemed it safe to gratify the kindness of his heart in tempering judgment with mercy, and to commute the sentences of death in other instances for punishments less severe. The sudden and violent extinction of human life, even for purposes of justice, and the conservation of the public peace, is a matter of such awful import, that every benevolent person will rejoice whenever it can safely be dispensed with. The danger in the present case is, that the act of clemency may be misunderstod and abused by those in whose favour it is exerted. Ignorant and uninstructed as the great mass of the French people unquestionably are, they are easily misled by designing men, and as easily persuaded to ascribe the exercise of mercy to motives just the opposite of those in which it originated. From the experience of the preceding year, it would seem that persons engaged in rebellion, possess not any very nice sense of honour, gratitude, or moral obligation in any shape. Some instances of the contrary may have appeared; and had they been more numerous, and formed the rule instead of the exception, we should have contemplated with more unmingled satisfaction, the amnesty already indulged in, and even the extension of it to a much greater number.

A deed of cruelty, as horrid as any that took place during the rebellion, was perpetrated on the night of Saturday the 2d of February. A party of about twenty came in from the American side, with blackened faces, and armed. They proceeded to the third concession in Caldwell's Manor, which is a considerable distance from the boundary line, to the house of a man living there in peace with his family. They stabbed him through and through with a bayonet, and used such violence with the weapon, after the wounds were inflicted, that they wrenched the bayonet from off the musket to which it was attached. They also inflicted three bayonet wounds on the son, a fine young man, one through his thigh, one through his leg, and another through his body and shoulder blade. The father soon died of his wounds, and the son suffered dreadfully. The villains then deliberately packed up the man's furniture upon their sleighs, set fire to the buildings, and absconded. On first entering the house, they locked up all the females of the family in a room by themselves; and, after setting fire to the house, left them there to be burned to death. They were unable to release themselves, and it was not till the arrival of neighbours that they were rescued, and the fire extinguished. This border warfare is the most annoying, and, under all the circumstances, the most unjustifiable, of all the modes which the insurrection has assumed, or been connected with.

On the 6th of May Benjamin Mott, of Alburgh, Vermont, was found guilty of Treason at Lacolle by the Court Martial, and sentenced to death. With this

trial the Court finished its labours, after a session of five
months and a half, during which one hundred and ten
prisoners had been tried ;—twelve executed, nine acquitted, and the remainder, now in gaol, under sentence
of death.   These eighty-nine will probably not suffer
the extreme penalty of the law.

As a relief to the painful details above given, it is
matter of consolation to record that the case of the wives
and families of those brave men who fell at Odelltown,
Lacolle, and other places, in defence of their country,
drew forth the sympathy of their companions in arms ;
and numerous contributions were made, both among
the regulars and the volunteers, to relieve their necessities, and private individuals were also forward to
mitigate, as far as possible, the sorrows of those whose
friends had suffered in the common cause.

Thus far have we been enabled to trace the progress
and defeat of the second attempt to change the Government, and overturn the Constitution of this land, by
means as unjustifiable as they were uncalled for.   That
grievances existed need not be denied ; but there were
other and far better modes of removing them than the
criminal ones which were resorted to.   Whatever may
in justice and equity be granted as to the ground of
complaint, there is much truth in the following remarks
of an American writer.   They were written and published several years ago ; and though the language of
rebellion was not then distinctly uttered, the author saw
that the elements of discord were in motion :—" The Canadians," said he, " by the original treaty of Quebec, and
by subsequent laws, have secured to themselves greater
privileges than the people of the United States possess,
even in the government of their own creation and
adoption ; and yet there is always a settled opposition
to certain acts of the Government affecting local objects,

There is always a jealousy, a suspicion, and distrust of the Mother Country. Hence the judicious projects of the British Government for the benefit of Canada, meet opposition from the Colonial Legislature; and such is the apprehension that their religion, language, laws, and ancient customs may be abrogated by the gradual encroachments of British influence, that they are content to retrograde in civilization and the arts, rather than yield one atom of custom or power." What has transpired, we have painfully witnessed. What the future will disclose, who can tell, or conjecture?

When the Earl of Durham, soon after his arrival last year, with powers more ample than were ever granted to any previous Governor, issued his declaration of impartiality, and announced his intention to regard all classes without distinction, and adjust as far as possible their respective claims, many persons thought, at least they hoped, that rebellion and discontent would cease. Nor was this an unreasonable expectation; but it was disappointed. The resignation and departure of his Lordship might have had some effect upon the malcontents, as well as others; but it must have been slight in relation to the former; as the second outbreak had commenced before he could have proceeded many miles down the river—and must have been planned and arranged before he had thought of leaving Canada. The conclusion suggested by experience is, that, as honesty is the best policy, and the most direct way is generally the best, it will be no longer safe or wise to hide from ourselves the necessity, now more than ever imperative, that Canada must not only be, but appear to be, a decidedly British Colony. As it belongs to Britain, British influence must predominate; but it must be exercised justly and kindly for the encouragement and benefit of all.

Should it please Providence to restore harmony to
this long agitated country, and endow our " Senators
with wisdom" to enact such laws as are suited to its
state, and place its various interests on a good foundation, we shall have every reason to look for not only
a continuance, but an increase of prosperity. The
amazing natural advantages of the country, if duly
improved, would yield an ample return; and furnish
not only to its present inhabitants, but to millions more,
a comfortable home and subsistence; and contribute
largely to the diffusion of happiness through the empire.
The parent state, kindly and wisely cherishing this part
of her colonial family, would meet not only with a return
of warm affection, but a large accession to her strength,
dignity, and importance. Amid this general improvement, of which it is rational to indulge the hope, the
city of Montreal will have its full share of benefit. Its
admirable location, the spirit and enterprise of its inhabitants, the increase among them of intelligence and moral
worth, unite in cherishing the expectation that Montreal
may attain a yet higher station among the cities of the
western world.

AMERICAN ANTIQUITIES.

Under this or similar titles the attention of the public
has of late been frequently called to the consideration of
various objects, in different parts of this continent, which
seem to indicate that it has been occupied by a race very
different from any which are now known to inhabit it.

In the opinion of some who have examined these
matters, the tribes of Indians which were found here by
Columbus and subsequent travellers, were preceded by
a people far more advanced in civilization and science,

the remains of whose power and skill have from time
to time been brought to light. The ruins of forts and
cities, under the present surface of the country, mounds
and tumuli above it, together with utensils and curiosities of various kinds which have been dug up at different
places, are supposed to shew that the arts were practised
here, to a great extent, at periods antecedent to the
generally supposed origin of American history. The
idea has been plausibly supported that some parts, at
least, of this continent were known to certain inhabitants
of Europe, more particularly the Norwegians and the
Danes, before they were discovered by the great navigator to whom the honour has for ages been assigned;
not, however, to the disparagement of Columbus, for it
is admitted that, whatever might have been known
formerly, in his time the knowledge was lost, and the
western hemisphere was again absolutely a *terra
incognita.*

Whatever portion of truth there may be in any or all
of these conjectures, and whatever share fancy may have
had in their formation, the enquiry has at length assumed
a shape which entitles it, at least, to respectful consideration.

About six years since a volume appeared in the State
of New York, with the following title—" AMERICAN
ANTIQUITIES, and *Discoveries in the West:* being an
Exhibition of the Evidence that an ancient population
of partially civilized nations, differing entirely from
those of the present Indians, peopled America many
centuries before its discovery by Columbus; and enquiries into their origin; with a copious description of
many of their stupendous works, now in ruins, with
conjectures concerning what may have become of them.
Compiled from Travels, authentic sources, and the
researches of Antiquarian Societies. By JOSIAH

PRIEST." The compiler has collected a multitude of papers, testimonies, and descriptions, which had been written at different places, through a series of years, both in the new and the old world, and has given many observations of his own ; though without much attention to order and method.   Among a number of strange and fanciful conjectures, there are some statements which will be read with astonishment, if not with incredulity, by those who have never ventured to think it possble that a civilized being had ever set his foot upon this continent till nearly the close of the fifteenth century. In Mexico, in Peru, in some parts of Canada, in Ohio, Pennsylvania, Carolina, and others of the United States, monuments of antiquity appear to have been discovered, which have excited much attention among naturalists and historians.   Drawings are given in the volume, of the most singular or important of these curiosities.

Some years ago the Society of Geography in Paris offered a large premium for a voyage to Guatemala, and for a new survey of the antiquities of Yucatan and Chiapa.   The ruins of a large stone-built city have been discovered, worthy of being compared to the Thebes of ancient Egypt.   The following is M. C. F. Rafinesque's account :

From Palenque, the last town northward in the province of *Ciudad Real de Chiapa*, taking a south-westerly direction, and ascending a ridge of high land that divides the kingdom of Guatemala from Yucatan, at the distance of six miles is the little river *Micol*, whose waters flow in a westerly direction, and unite with the great river *Tulija*, which bends its course towards the province of *Tabasco*.   Having passed Micol, the ascent begins ; and at half a league, or a mile and a half, the traveller crosses a little stream called OTOLUM ; from this point heaps of stone ruins are discovered, which render the roads very difficult for another half league, when you gain the height whereon the stone houses are situated, being still fourteen in number in one place, some more dilapidated than others, yet still having many of their apartments perfectly discernible.

A rectangular area, three hundred yards in breadth by four hundred and fifty in length, which is a fraction over fifty-six rods wide, and eighty-four rods long, being, in the whole circuit, two hundred and eighty rods, which is three-fourths of a mile, and a trifle over. This area presents a plain at the base of the highest mountain forming the ridge. In the centre of this plain is situated the largest of the structures which has been as yet discovered among these ruins. It stands on a mound or pyramid twenty yards high, which is sixty feet, or nearly four rods in perpendicular altitude, which gives it a lofty and beautiful majesty, as if it were a temple suspended in the sky. This is surrounded by other edifices, namely, five to the northward, four to the southward, one to the southwest, and three to the eastward—fourteen in all. In all directions, the fragments of other fallen buildings are seen extending along the mountain that stretches east and west either way from these buildings, as if they were the great temple of worship, or their government house, around which they built their city, and where dwelt their kings and officers of state. At this place was found a subterranean stone acqueduct, of great solidity and durability, which in its course passes beneath the largest building.

Let it be understood, this city of Otolum, the ruins of which are so immense, is in North, not South, America, in the same latitude with the island of Jamaica, which is about 18 degrees north of the equator, being on the highest ground between the northern end of the Caribbean sea and the Pacific Ocean, where the continent narrows towards the isthmus of Darien, and is about 800 miles south of New Orleans.

The discovery of these ruins, and also of many others, equally wonderful, in the same country, are just commencing to arouse the attention of the schools of Europe, who hitherto have denied that America could boast of her antiquities.

The neighbourhood of Brownville, or Redstone, in Pennsylvania, abounds with monuments of Antiquity. A fortified camp, of a very complete and curious kind, on the ramparts of which is timber of five feet in diameter, is found near the town of Brownville. This camp contains about thirteen acres, enclosed in a circle, the elevation of which is seven feet above the adjoining ground; this was a Herculean work. Within the circle a pentagon is accurately described; having its sides four feet high, and its angles uniformly three feet from the outside of the circle, thus leaving an unbroken communication all around. A pentagon is a figure, having five angles or sides. Each side of the pentagon has a postern or small gateway, opening into the passage between it and the circle; but the circle itself has only one grand gateway outward. Exactly in the centre stands a mound about thirty feet high, supposed to have been a place of observation. At a small distance from this place, was found a stone, eight feet by five, on which was accurately engraved a representation of the whole work, with the mound in the centre; whereon was the likeness of a human head, which signified that the chief who presided there lay buried beneath it. The engraving on this stone, is evidence of the knowledge of stone cutting, as it was executed with a considerable degree of accuracy.

On comparing the description of this circular monument with a description of works of a similar character, found in Denmark, Sweden, and Iceland, the conclusion is drawn, that at some era of time the authors of this kind of monumental works, in either of those countries have been the same." pp. 87—88.

" There are no parts of the kingdoms or countries of the old world, but have celebrated in poetry and sober history, the mighty relics and antiquities of ancient empires, as Rome, Babylon, Greece, Egypt, Hindostan, Tartary, Africa, China, Persia, Europe, Russia, and many of the islands of the sea. It yet remains for America to awake her story from its oblivious sleep, and tell the tale of her antiquities—the traits of nations, coeval, perhaps, with the eldest works of man this side the flood.

This curious subject, although it is obscured beneath the gloom of past ages, of which but small record remains ; beside that which is written in the dust, in the form of mighty mounds, tumuli, strange skeletons, and aboriginal fortifications ; and in some few instances, the bodies of preserved persons, as sometimes found in the nitrous caves of Kentucky, and the west, yet affords abundant premises to prompt investigation and rational conjecture. The mounds and tumuli of the west, are to be ranked among the most wonderful antiquities of the world, on the account of their number, magnitude, and obscurity of origin.

They generally are found on fertile bottoms and near the rivers. Several hundreds have been discovered along the valley of the Mississippi ; the largest of which stands not far from Wheeling, on the Ohio. This mound is fifty rods in circumference, and ninety feet in perpendicular height.'

This is found filled with thousands of human skeletons, and was doubtless a place of general deposite of the dead for ages ; which must have been contiguous to some large city, where the dead were placed in gradation, one layer above another, till it reached a natural climax, agreeing with the slope commenced at its base or foundation.

It is not credible, that this mound was made by the ancestors of the modern Indians. Its magnitude, and the vast numbers of dead deposited there, denote a population too great to have been supported by mere fishing and hunting, as the manner of Indians has always been. A population sufficient to raise such a mound as this, of earth, by the gradual interment of the deceased inhabitants, would necessarily be too far spread, to make it convenient for the living to transport their dead to *one single* place of repository. The modern Indians have ever been known, since the acquaintance of white men with them, to live only in *small* towns; which refutes the idea of its having been made by any other people than such as differed exceedingly from the improvident and indolent native; and must, therefore, have been erected by a people *more* ancient than the Indian aborigines, or wandering tribes.

Some of these mounds have been opened, when, not only vast quantities of human bones have been found, but also instruments of warfare, broken earthen vases, and trinkets. From the trees growing on them, it is supposed they have already existed at least six hundred years; and whether these trees were the first, second, or third crop, is unknown; if the second only, which, from the old and decayed timber, partly buried in the vegetable mould and leaves, seems to favour; then it is all of twelve hundred years since they were abandoned, if not more.

Foreign travellers complain, that America presents nothing like *ruins* within her boundaries; no ivy mantled towers, nor moss covered turrets, as in the other quarters of the earth. Old Fort Warren, on the Hudson, rearing its lofty decayed sides high above West Point; and the venerable remains of two wars, at Ticonderoga, upon Lake Champlain, they say, afford something of the kind. But what are mouldering castles, falling turrets, or crumbling abbeys, in comparison with those ancient and artificial aboriginal hills, which have outlived generations, and even all tradition; the workmanship of altogether unknown hands?

Place these monuments and secret repositories of the dead, together with the innumerable mounds and monstrous fortifications, which are scattered over America, in England, and on the continent of Europe, how would their virtuosi examine, and their antiquarians fill volumes with their probable histories. How would their fame be conveyed from learned bodies, and through literary volumes, inquiring who were the builders, of what age of the world, whence came they, and their descendants; if any, what has become of them; these would be the themes of constant speculation and inquiry.

At Marietta, a place not only celebrated as being the first settlement on the Ohio, but has also acquired much celebrity, from the existence of those extensive and supposed fortifications, which are situated near the town. They consist of walls and mounds of earth, running in straight lines, from six to ten feet high, and nearly forty broad at their base; but originally must have been much higher. There is also, at this place, one fort of this ancient description, which encloses nearly fifty acres of land.

There are openings in *this* fortification, which are supposed to have been, when thronged with its own busy multitude, ' used as gateways, with a passage from one of them, formed by two parallel walls of earth, leading towards the river.'

W

This contrivance was undoubtedly for a defence against surprise by an enemy, while the inhabitants dwelling within should fetch water from the river, or descend thither to wash, as in the Ganges, among the Hindoos. Also the greatness of this fort is evidence, not only of the power of its builders, but also of those they feared. Who can tell but that they have, by intestine feuds and wars, exterminated themselves? Such instances are not unfrequent among petty tribes of the earth. Witness the war between Benjamin and his brother tribes, when but a mere handful of their number remained to redeem them from complete annihilation. Many nations, on account of whom as once existing, is found on the page of history, now have not a trace left behind. More than sixty tribes which once traversed the woods of the west, and who were known to the first settlers of the New England states, are now extinct.

The French of the Mississippi have an account, that an exterminating battle was fought in the beginning of the seventeenth century, about two hundred and thirty years ago, on the ground where Fort Harrison *now* stands; between the Indians living on the Mississippi, and those of the Wabash. The bone of contention was, the lands lying between those rivers, which both parties claimed. There were about 1000 warriors on each side. The condition of the fight was, that the victors should possess the lands in dispute. The grandeur of the prize was peculiarly calculated to inflame the ardour of savage minds. The contest commenced about sunrise. Both parties fought desperately. The Wabash warriors came off conquerors, having *seven* men left alive at sunset, and their adversaries, the Mississippians, but *five*. This battle was fought nearly fifty years before their acquaintance with white men."—*Webster's Gazetteer*, 1817, p. 69.

Also the ancient *Eries*, once inhabiting about Lake Erie, and gave name to that body of water, were exterminated by their enemies, another tribe of Indians —so far as that but *one* member of that nation, a warrior, remained.

It is possible, whoever the authors of these great works were, or however long they may have lived on the continent, that they may have, in the same way, by intestine feuds and wars, weakened themselves, so that when the Tartars, Scythians, and descendants of the *ten* lost tribes, came across the straits of Bhering, that they fell an easy prey to those fierce and savage northern hordes.

It is not likely that the vast warlike preparations which extend over the whole continent, south of certain places in Canada, were thrown up all of a sudden, on a *first* discovery of a *strange* enemy; for it might be inquired, how should they know such a mode of defence, unless they had acquired it in the course of ages, arising from necessity, and were constructed to defend against the invasions of each other ?—being of various origin and separate interests, as was much the situation of the ancient nations, in every part of the world.

Petty tribes of the same origin, over the whole earth, have been found to wage perpetual war against each other, from motives of avarice, power, or hatred. In the most *ancient* eras of the history of man, little *walled* towns, which were raised for the security of a few families, under a chief, king, or patriarch, are known to have existed; which is evidence of the disjointed and unharmonious state of human society; out of which wars, rapine, and plunder arose. Such may have been the state of man in America, before the Indians found their way here; the evidence of which is the innumerable fortifications, found every where in the western regions.

Within this fort, of which we have been speaking, found at Marietta, are elevated *squares*, situated at the corners, one hundred and eighty feet long, by one hundred and thirty broad, nine feet high, and level on the top. On these squares, erected at the corners of *this* great enclosure, were doubtless placed some modes of annoyance to a besieging enemy; such as engines to sling stones with, or to throw the dart and spear, or whatever might have been their modes of defence.

Outside of this fort, is a mound, differing in form from their general configuration: its shape is that of a sugar loaf, the base of which is more than a hundred feet in circumference; its height thirty, encompassed by a ditch, and defended by a parapet, or wall beyond the ditch, about breast high, through which is a way toward the main fort. Human bones have been taken from many of these mounds, and *charcoal*, with fragments of pottery; in one place, a skeleton of a man, buried *east* and *west*, after the manner of enlightened nations, was found, as if they understood the cardinal points of the compass. On the breast of *this* skeleton was found a quantity of isinglass, a substance considered sacred by the Mexicans, and adored as a deity." pp. 40—44.

In Washington Irving's *Life of Columbus*, there is a reference to the supposed knowledge of this continent by Northern Islanders—" The most plausible or credible account respecting those discoveries is given by Snoro Sturleson, or Sturloins, in his *Saga*, or *Chronicle of King Olaus*. According to this writer, one *Biorn*, of Iceland, voyaging to Greenland in search of his father, from whom he had been separated by a storm, was driven by tempestuous 'weather far to the southwest, until he came in sight of a low country, covered with woods, with an island in its vicinity. The weather becoming favourable, he turned to the northeast, without landing, and arrived safe at Greenland. His account of the country he had seen, it is said, excited the enterprise of Lief, son of Eric Rauda, (or red head,) the first settler of Greenland. A vessel was fitted out, and *Lief* and *Biorn* departed together in quest of this unknown land. They found a rocky and sterile island, to which they gave the name of Helluland; also a low sandy country, covered with wood, to which they gave the name of Markland; and two days afterwards they observed a continuance of the coast, with an island to the north of it. This last they described as fertile, well wooded, producing agreeable fruits, and particularly grapes; a fruit with which they were not acquainted; but on being informed by one of their companions, à German, of its qualities and name, they called the country from it, *Vinland.* They ascended a river well stored with fish, particularly salmon, and came to a lake from which the river took its origin, where they passed the winter. It is very probable that this river was the St. Lawrence, as it abounded with salmon, and was the outlet of a lake, which it is likely, was Ontario. There is no other river capable of being navigated, very far from its mouth, with a sea vessel, and which comes from a lake, and empties into the sea, on that side of the coast, but the St. Lawrence. The climate appeared to them mild and pleasant, in comparison, being accustomed to the more rigorous seasons of the north. On the shortest day in the winter the sun was but eight hours above the horizon; hence it has been concluded, that the country was about the 49th degree of north latitude, and was either Newfoundland, or some part of the coast of North America, about the Gulf of St. Lawrence. It is said in those Chronicles of Sturloins, that the relatives of Lief made several voyages to Vinland; that they traded with the natives for peltry and furs; and that in 1121, 714

years ago, a bishop named Eric, went from **Greenland to**
Vinland, to convert the inhabitants to Christianity. A
knowledge of Christianity among the savage **Britons,**
Caledonians, and the **Welch,** was introduced, as is
supposed, by St. Paul, or some of his disciples, as early
as A. D. 63, more than 1700 years since. ' From this
time, about 1121, we know nothing of Vinland,' says
Forrester, in his book of northern voyages, vol. 3, p. 36,
as quoted by Irving. ' There is every appearance that
the tribe which still exists in the interior of Newfoundland, and who are so different from the other savages
of North America, both in their appearance and mode of
living, and as they are always in a state of warfare with
the Indians of the northern coast, are deemed descendants of the ancient Normans, Scandinavians, or Danes.'
In the chronicles of these northern nations, there is also
an account of the voyages of four boat crews in the year
1354, which corroborates the foregoing relations. This
little squadron of fishing boats being overtaken by a
mighty tempest, were driven about the sea for many
days, until a boat containing seven persons, was cast
upon an island call Estotiland, about 1000 miles from
Friesland. They were taken by the inhabitants and
carried to a fair and populous city, where the king sent
for many interpreters to converse with them, but none
that could understand, until a man was found who
likewise had been cast upon that coast some time before.
They remained several days upon the island, which was
rich and fruitful. The inhabitants were intelligent and
acquainted with the mechanical arts of Europe. They
cultivated grain, made beer, and lived in houses built of
stone. There were Latin books in the king's library,
though the inhabitants had no knowledge of that
language, and in manuscript, as the art of printing was
not yet discovered. They had many towns and castles,

and carried on a trade with Greenland for pitch, sulphur, and peltry. Though much given to navigation, they were ignorant of the use of the compass, and finding the Frieslanders acquainted with it, held them in great esteem, and the king sent them, with twelve barks, to visit a country to the south called Drogeo. Drogeo is, most likely, a Norman name ; as we find *Drogo* was a leader of the Normans against the ancient baronies of Italy, about A. D. 787. Drogeo is supposed to have been the continent of America. This voyage of the fishing squadron, it appears, was in 1354, more than fifty years after the discovery of the magnetic needle, which was in 1300, A. D.

They had nearly perished in this storm, but were cast away upon the coast of Drogeo. They found the people cannibals, and were upon the point of being killed and devoured (these were our Indians), but were spared on account of their great skill in fishing. Drogeo they found to be a country of vast extent, or rather a *new world ;* that the inhabitants were naked and barbarous, but that far to the southwest there was a more civilized region and temperate climate, where the inhabitants had a knowledge of gold and silver, lived in cities, erected splendid temples to idols, and sacrificed human victims to them. The same, it is likely, the ruins of which have been recently discovered and are now being explored, an account of which we shall give in another part of this work.

After the fisherman, who relates this account, had resided many years on the continent of Drogeo, during which time he had passed from the service of one chieftain to another, and traversed various parts of it, certain boats of Estotiland (now supposed to be Newfoundland) arrived on the coast of Drogeo. The fisherman got on board of them, and acted as interpreter, and followed the trade between the main land of Drogeo and the island of Estotiland, for some time, until he became very rich. He then fitted out a barque of his own, and with the assistance of some of the people of the island, made his way back across the intervening distance between Drogeo and his native country, Friesland, in Germany.

The account he gave of this country determined Zichmni, the Prince of Friesland, to send an expedition thither; and Antonio Zeno, a Venetian, was to command it. Just before starting, the fisherman, who was to have acted as pilot, died; but certain mariners who accompanied him from Estotiland were taken in his place. The expedition sailed under command of Zichmni—the Venetian, Zeno, merely accompanied it. It was unsuccessful. After having discovered an island called *Icaria*, where they met with a rough reception from the inhabitants, and were obliged to withdraw; the ships were driven by storm to Greenland. No record remains of any farther prosecution of the enterprise. The countries mentioned in the account written by this Zeno, were laid down on a map originally on wood. The island Estotiland has been supposed by M. Malte-Brun to be Newfoundland. Its partially civilized inhabitants, the descendants of the Scandinavian colonists of Vinland, and the Latin books in manuscript, found in the king's library, to have belonged to the remains of the library of the Greenland bishop who emigrated thither in 1121, 922 years ago. Drogeo, according to the same conjecture, was Nova Scotia and New England. The civilized people to the southwest, who sacrificed human beings in rich temples, he supposes to have been the Mexicans, or some ancient nations of Florida or Louisiana.

A distinguished writer of Copenhagen was not long

since engaged in the composition of a work on the early
voyages of discovery to this continent, as undertaken by
the inhabitants of the north of Europe, more than eight
hundred and thirty years ago. He has in his hands
genuine ancient documents, the examination of which
leads to curious and surprising results. They furnish
various and unquestionable evidence, not only that the
coast of North America was discovered soon after the
discovery of Greenland by northern explorers, a part of
whom remained there, and that it was again visited in the
11th, 12th, and 13th centuries, but also that Christianity
was introduced among the Indians of America. The
documents of this writer furnished even a map, cut in
wood, of the northern coast of America, and also an
account of the sea coast south, as far down as the
Carolinas, and that a principal station of these adventurers was the mouth of the river St. Lawrence. He
says that it was in the year 985 that America was *first*
discovered by Baiske Her Juefser, but that he did not
land ; and that in the year 1000 the coast was visited
by a man named Lief, a son of Eric the *Red*, who
colonized Greenland."

The celebrated traveller Humboldt observes :—
" Amidst the extensive plains of Upper Canada, in
Florida, near the Gulf of Mexico, and in the deserts
bordered by the Orinoco, in Colombia, dykes of a considerable length, weapons of brass, and sculptured stones,
are found, which are the indications that those countries
were formerly inhabited by industrious nations, which
are now traversed only by tribes of savage hunters."

On the subject of these and similar remains, Mr.
Keating very appositely remarks—" The country about
the Muskingum [river] appears to have been at a former
period the seat of a very extensive aboriginal population.
Every where do we observe in this valley, remains of

works which attest, at the same time, the number, the genius, and the perseverence of those departed nations. Their works have survived the lapse of ages; but the spirit which prompted them has disappeared. We wander over the face of the country; wherever we go, we mark the monuments which they have erected; we would interrogate them as to the authors of these mighty works, but no voice replies to ours, save that of the echo. The mind seeks in vain for some clew to assist it in unravelling the mystery. Was their industry stimulated by the desire of protecting themselves against the inroads of invaders, or were they themselves the trespassers? Did they emigrate to this spot? And if so, whence came they? Who were they? Whither went they? And wherefore came they here? Their works have been torn open; they have been searched into; but all in vain. The mound is now levelled with the sod of the valley; the accumulated earth, which was perhaps collected from a distance into one immense mass, to erect a monument deemed indestructible, over the remains of some western Pharoah, is now scattered over the ground, that its concealed treasure may be brought to light. Every bone is accurately examined, every piece of metal or fragment of broken pottery is curiously studied,—still no light has as yet been thrown upon the name and date of the once populous nation which formerly flourished on the banks of the numerous tributary streams of the Ohio."—*Narrative of an Expedition to the Source of St. Peter's River, &c.* 1823. Vol. I. pp. 39—40.

More recently still, there has appeared a work in the capital of Denmark, which casts some light upon this matter. As the "Northmen" have been supposed to have known something of America from a very early period, it is most fitting that their records should be inspected, and such of them as illustrate the history given to the public. Such a service has been performed by M. Rafn, and the Royal Society of Northern Antiquarians, of which he is the Secretary. First, we are presented with *Antiquitates Americanæ ; sive Scriptores, Septentrionales rerum ante-Columbianarum in America ; i. e.* " American Antiquities ; or Accounts from Northern Writers respecting America before the time of Columbus." Copenhagen. 1837. And, secondly, *Sawling af de i Nordens Oldscrifter indeholte Efterretninger om de gamle Nordboers Opdagelsesriser til America, fra det 10de til det 14de Aarhundrede ; i. e.* " Collection of the Evidence contained in Old Writings respecting the Voyages of Discovery made to America by the Ancient Inhabitants of the North, from the 10th to the 14th Century." Copenhagen. 1837. An epitome of contents in the English language is prefixed by M. Rafn ; and the Foreign Quarterly Review, in exhibiting specimens and results of the evidence, has the following observations :

" The early discovery of America by the Northmen is not now made known for the first time ; but the evidence on which it rests has never hitherto been published in an ample and satisfactory manner. As early as 1570, Ortelius claimed for them the merit of being the first discoverers of the New World.

A correct account of the early discoveries of the Scandinavians in the west, was given by Torfæus, in his ' Historia Vinlandiæ Antiquæ,' published in 1705, and in his ' Grönlandia Antiqua,' which appeared in the following year. But these works soon became too scarce to forward the ends of their publication, and have been long reckoned, even in the North, among the choicest bibliographical rarities. The writings of Suhm and Schöning, Lindeborg and Schröder, in which similar information is to be obtained, being in the northern languages, and in many instances only to be found in periodical publications, never enjoyed an extensive European circulation. John Reinhold Foster, in his History of Voyages and Discoveries in the North, and some other writers chiefly following in his steps and familiar to the English reader, have asserted the Discovery of America by the Northmen, but without entering into any statement of circumstances or of evidence; and their unexplained opinions consequently appear to be the offspring of predilection. The only mode of convincing the literary world of a fact, is to publish the documents which prove it. This task was undertaken in the present instance by M. Rafn alone, and he had advanced half way towards the completion of his work, when the Royal Society of Northern Antiquaries, of which he is the secretary, resolved to take the publication of it off his hands. We have here the original Icelandic text, with the various readings or even the different versions of the MSS., accompanied by translations in Danish and Latin; in this part of his task the editor has had the invaluable assistance of the learned Icelanders, Finn Magnusen and Sweinbiorn Egilsson. He has himself added copious notes, with geographical and historical disquisitions.

The learning and critical sagacity of Rafn, Finn Magnusen, and the other eminent scholars who have lent their aid in preparing this volume, of American Antiquities for the press, appear to us to have effectually prevented any objections that might be raised against the genuineness of the pieces entering into the collection; and to confine the question respecting the early discovery of America simply to the discussion of the meaning and intrinsic merits of the evidence.

Erik the Red, with whom our narrative begins,

appears to have been conspicuous even among Northmen
for turbulence of spirit and love of adventure. He was
twice obliged to change his residence in Iceland owing
to feuds with his neighbours, in which he committed
homicide. In his new abode on the western shores of
the island he was equally unfortunate, and became involved in disputes with a powerful individual named
Thorgest; in consequence of which, being arraigned
before the Thing, or Assembly, convened at Thorsness,
and knowing probably that his enemy's adherents out-
numbered his own, he felt that he had no chance of
escape but in quitting the island. He lay some time in
concealment, while his foes sought him on all the rocks
along the shore, and, his preparations being completed,
he embarked (in 983) with a few resolute followers,
and stood out to sea from the Snæfellsyökel, a towering
promontory pointing directly to the west. His friends
Thorbiorn, Eyolf, and Styr, accompanied him beyond
the rocks. In taking leave of them he announced his
intention of looking for Gunbiorn's rocks, as some islets
were called which had been discovered in the western
seas a short time before, and the situation of which
geographers have never been able to conjecture: it is
not improbable that they were the islands near the
southern extremity of Greenland. The conspicuous
feature of the first land made by him, was a glacier
(Snæfellsyökel) to which he gave the name of Blaserk,
or Blackrock: he then sailed southwards, until he at
length arrived at a habitable shore where he spent the
winter. During two summers he explored the newly
discovered country, to which he gave the flattering name
of Greenland, in order that its designation might encourage men to settle in it; and in the course of the
third summer he returned to Iceland according to
promise, to acquaint his friends with his success. He

x

remained there but one winter, during which time, after
a renewal of his quarrel with Thorgest, a reconciliation
was effected between them ; and in the following summer he returned to settle in Greenland.   Of five and
thirty vessels which set sail with him from Iceland, only
fourteen reached their destination ; of the remainder
some were lost, and others driven back by the winds.

One of the companions of Erik was Heriulf, whose
son, Biarne, at the time of the migration to Greenland,
was absent on a trading voyage to Norway.   Surprised,
on his return to Iceland, to find his family all gone, he
determined at once to follow them, and, as he expressed
it, to spend his winter, as he had been always used to
do, at his father's fire-side.   In this he uttered the
characteristic sentiments of the north, where the length
and severity of winter give double value to the comforts
of home and social intimacy, and where domestic
attachments seem to gain strength from the rigour of
the season.   He set sail accordingly, though unacquainted
with the Greenland sea, and for many days was driven
by tempestuous north winds, accompanied by thick fogs,
he knew not whither.   At length, when the weather
cleared up, he saw a land moderately elevated and
overgrown with wood.   As this did not correspond
with the description he had received of Greenland, he
left it to larboard ; and standing out to sea, in two days
more again descried land lower than the former, but
like it covered with wood.   He then continued his
course with a south-west wind, and after three days
descried an island, the lofty shores of which were beset by
icebergs, or, as it should perhaps be understood, covered
with glaciers.   Bearing away from this island, and sailing
for four days with fresh gales, he arrived at Heriulfsnes
in Greenland, where his father was settled.   There is
no reason to doubt that the well-wooded land first

descried by Biarne was some, we shall not at present
venture to describe what, part of the American continent, which thus appears to have been discovered by the
Northmen as early as 986. The discovery of the
continent was, in fact, by a natural accident, made con-
temporaneously with the colonization of Greenland.

A few years later, when Erik, Earl of Norway, heard
Biarne relate the incidents of his voyage, he expressed
his surprise and dissatisfaction at the absence of any
endeavour to examine the newly discovered country.
The earl's comments, when carried to Greenland, did
not fail to operate at once on the adventurous spirit of
the colonists. Lief, the son of Erik the Red, bought
Biarne's vessel, and in the year 1000 proceeded on a
voyage of discovery towards the south-west. He first
came to the island of snow-clad mountains, formerly
seen by Biarne, and went on shore with some of his
companions to examine. There was no herbage of any
kind upon it, but a bare and rugged plain of slate *(hella)*
extended from the feet of the glaciers down to the sea-
side. Hence they gave to this country the name of
Helluland. Continuing their voyage, they next arrived
at a low coast thickly covered with wood, and having
hillocks or banks of white sand near the shore. This
country they called *Markland,* or Woodland.

They then stood out to sea and sailed for two days
before they again made land, when, passing between an
island and the main, which here stretched out eastwards
so as to form a long peninsula, they held their course
westward along the shores of the latter, where they
observed that a great extent of ground was left dry at
ebb-tide. They explored in their small boat a river
which issued from a lake, and being pleased with the
appearance of the country, they brought their vessel up
into the lake when the tide rose, and moored her in it.

They proceeded forthwith to erect themselves some temporary log-huts, which, as soon as they had made up their minds to winter in the place, they enlarged into comfortable houses, and called them Liefs-booths; a name which recurs frequently in the Scandinavian history of the discovery of America.

It happened one day that they missed one of their companions, a Suderman, that is, a Southern or German, named Tyrker, an old servant and favourite of Liefs. A party was immediately despatched into the woods in quest of him. After some time spent in search, he was seen staggering towards his friends with an air of extravagant joy, and having first accosted them in German, much to their surprise, he at length went on to acquaint them in staggering accents with the fact that he had been feasting on grapes. It must be confessed that the northern historian, in describing a German inebriated by eating wild grapes, drew too much on his imagination; yet the amount of fiction in this instance does not exceed what may be allowed for as the inevitable colouring of facts preserved by tradition; and indeed the anecdote regarding Tyrker, if closely examined, will be found to furnish strong evidence of the genuineness of the narrative. The circumstance so carefully related, that the finder of the grapes was a Southern, in whose native country the vine abounded, and who was consequently well acquainted with that fruit, cannot fail to suggest to the reader how unlikely it is that such exotic productions should have presented themselves to the imagination of Icelanders in the twelfth century, or that grapes and vines should adorn regions in the fancy of that people who voluntarily settled on the frozen shores of Greenland. To the country in which the vines were discovered Lief gave the name of *Vinland*, and freighting his vessel with grapes and timber he returned homeward in the following spring. When near the coast of Greenland he saw a party of shipwrecked people on a rock: they were fifteen in all, including Thorer, the chief, and his wife, Gudrida. Lief took them on board and conveyed them to Greenland, and from this circumstance he obtained the appellation of the Lucky or Fortunate.

The account which Lief gave of his winter's sojourn in Vinland was calculated to incite others to visit that country; and his brother Thorwald borrowed his vessel for this purpose, under the engagement that he would first convey to Greenland the property which Thorer, when shipwrecked, had left upon the rock. This being effected, he sailed for Vinland, and arrived without accident at Liefs-booths. He spent the first winter in fishing. The following spring (1003) he sent a party southwards, to examine the coasts; they were absent for some months, and reported on their return, that the country explored by them was everywhere extremely beautiful, the woods extending down to within a short distance of the fine sandy beach which formed the shore. They saw no signs of human beings, except a wooden shed (literally in the language of the Icelandic historians, a corn-shed or granary) on one of the numerous islands near the coast. In the following year (1004) Thorwald sailed eastward from Liefs-booths, and then went northward past a remarkable headland which enclosed a bay, and was opposite to another headland. Here, driven by a tempest into shoal water, the vessel struck and injured her keel; the damage was soon repaired, and Thorwald ordered the broken keel to be erected on the headland, which he named from the circumstance *Kialarnes,* or Keel-Point. They came soon after to a promontory covered with wood, where, for the first time, they saw some of the natives. There were three

canoes drawn up on the shore, near each of which were
three Skrællings, as the northern writers call the
Esquimaux. Of the nine natives they murdered eight,
but found themselves in a short time surrounded by a
great multitude, hastening from all sides to avenge the
death of their fellows. The Northmen beat them off,
but Thorwald received a mortal wound in the combat.
His admiration of the woody promontory where he had
expressed a wish to abide, then seemed to him prophetic;
and as he expired he told his companions to bury him
on the shore of the headland, and planting a cross over
his grave, to call the place Krossanes, or Cross Point.
They returned to Greenland in 1005.

In the spring of the following year, Thorstein, third
son of Erik, accompanied by his wife Gudrida, set sail
with the intention of bringing home his brother Thorwald's body; but after being tossed about the whole
summer by adverse winds, he regained Greenland at the
beginning of winter, without having even seen Vinland,
and died soon after. The circumstances of Thorstein's
death are related by the Icelandic historians at ample
length, and with much simplicity and pathos.

The year 1006 was rendered memorable in Greenland by the arrival of two vessels from Iceland, one of
which was commanded by Thorfinn, better known by
the auspicious designation of Karlsefne; that is to say,
having the materials of a man, or, promising great
things. The chief person in the other vessel was
Biarne, the son of Grimolf. Karlsefne was a rich and
powerful man, of a distinguished family, and traced his
descent from some who were in those days called kings,
but must not be ranged in the same line with the
crowned heads of modern times.

We do not think there are many who will feel inclined to dispute the truth of the history. It has

throughout the substance and the colour of reality. Nothing can be more plain, natural, or vivid; and it is even, in some respects, remarkably circumstantial.

Lief's voyage offers us no nautical details. He went in search of the countries described by Biarne; and retracing the course of the latter, he, as well as all those who followed him, found three lands which he named Helluland, Markland, and Vinland. The fact that those three lands, of slate, of wood, and of the vine, always occurred in succession to the explorers from Greenland who commenced their voyage in a southward course, leave us, we repeat, no room to doubt that the regions so designated were respectively the projecting lands of Newfoundland, Nova Scotia, and New England about Massachusetts. The nature and aspect of these countries are in perfect accordance with the descriptions of those discovered by the Northmen. In Newfoundland we find the bare rocks and ice of Helluland; and in the depressed, well-wooded shores of Nova Scotia, we have no difficulty in recognising the Markland of the Northmen. As to Vinland we are not called upon to acknowledge its identity with the coast of Massachusetts merely on the evidence of such general resemblance. The narrative of Thorwald's voyage furnishes us with some particulars respecting it of a very unequivocal and cogent kind. His explorations of the coast from Liefs-booths appear to have been directed towards the east and west. He himself sailed eastwards, we are told, along the coast, and then turned northwards (at point Malabar) round the land which proved to be a peninsula (Nauset), enclosing a bay (Cape Cod Bay). Within this bay he anchored at the mouth of a river flowing from east to west (Pamot River). The point (Cape Cod) terminating the peninsula, and named by him Kialarnes, was opposite to another head-

land on the main (Gurnet Point), which was covered
with trees, and appeared to him eminently beautiful; a
description that suits well with the peninsula at Ply-
mouth, as may be collected from the names of the places
on its coast, High-Pines Ledge and Green-Harbour.
The details of Thorwald's voyage along the coast, eastwards and then northwards till he rounded a headland
enclosing a bay and found a river running westwards,
all square exactly with the coast of Cape Cod Peninsula,
and with no other spot in the New World on which
conjecture can plausibly fasten. In the same region
also we find the Furthurstrand, that is, the Marvellous
or Portentous Strand.   How appositely this designation
might be applied to the sandy plains near Cape Cod,
will be evident from the descriptions of them by a
modern writer, Hitchcock, on the Geology of Massachusetts.

We must not be supposed to undervalue the Collection of Northern Antiquities because we find in it some
manifestations of an excessive antiquarian zeal. It
contains enough to *prove* that the American continent
was known to the Northmen at the beginning of the
eleventh century; and we frankly avow that it appears
to us to contain much also, which, whatever be its
pretensions, proves nothing at all.

The discovery of Vinland, however, was not made
in an obscure age. It may have been preceded by
many remarkable voyages in the west, and we do not
venture to deny positively that the stories of the Limerick
merchants respecting the Northmen carried to Great
Ireland and the Whiteman's Land, may have had their
foundation in some very early transatlantic discoveries.

Still further it must be observed that the discovery
of Vinland was not a transient event, no sooner past
than forgotten. As it was thought likely to prove

advantageous, the family of Erik the Red with whom it commenced, persevered in promoting it for some years. They had a share in all the voyages made to Vinland from the year 1000 to 1013, which must, therefore, be considered as one series.

The general verisimilitude of the Icelandic histories which relate to Vinland is extremely remarkable.

The discovery of Vinland was immediately made known in Norway; and in the latter half of the eleventh century Adam of Bremen heard of it from Swein king of Denmark. " This discovery," he emphatically observes, " is not a fable, but we know of it from the certain information of the Danes."

Columbus visited Iceland in 1567; and from his general appetence of knowledge it cannot be doubted that he heard of the early voyages of the Northmen and their discovery of Vinland. It has been urged, however, that the voyage to Vinland, made in a few days from Greenland, a country at that time supposed to be joined to Europe, had little in common with the speculations of Columbus, or calculated to encourage his bold thought of launching across the Atlantic in a tropical latitude. But what could be more to his purpose or better adapted to his views, than the fact that the Northmen, the boldest of navigators, had knowledge of a land in the west which they supposed to extend far southwards till it met Africa? Or could not the intelligent Genoese find some suggestion in the following more accurate statement of an Icelandic geoprapher? " *On the west of the great sea of Spain*, which some call Ginyungagap, and leaning somewhat towards the north, the first land which occurs is the good Vinland." It would add little to the merit of Columbus, to maintain that he was incapable of benefiting by so good a hint.

We dare say that there are many who will learn with no less chagrin than surprise, that the discovery of America was made five centuries before Columbus. The fame of a hero is held so sacred by the bulk of mankind, that but little popularity can be expected to attend the historical justice which threatens in anywise to obscure it. It manifests, however, a very imperfect comprehension of the merits of that great navigator to suppose that they are likely to be effaced in the slightest degree by the authentic proof and general acknowledgment of the prior discoveries of the Northmen. The soul and spirit which launched Columbus across the Atlantic were never in the remotest manner prefigured by the motives which actuated the roving Scandinavians. A broad distinction is thus established at once between the merits of their respective discoveries, by the different characters of the speculations and incidents which led to them. The voyages of the Northmen are replete with the ordinary interest of human events, in which the most important consequences are often seen to arise unexpectedly : yet the series of lucky accidents which led those rovers in the course of years, from land to land, through a sea in which groups of islands at convenient distances encourage the mariner and tempt him onward in his first essays, till they at length reached the coast of America ; cannot emulate, but rather serves by comparison to exalt the achievement of Columbus, who with long premeditation, succeeded in realizing so far the dreams of an enthusiastic imagination ; and apparently verified his predictions by a discovery which must ever be reckoned the most extraordinary on record. The discoveries of the Northmen, made without aim or object, awakened no zeal, and easily fell into oblivion ; that of Columbus kindled an ardour which continued to operate on society for ages."—*No.* xli. *April,* 1838.

NOTES AND CORRECTIONS.

Page 12, line 13, *read* Voyage
—   23   29   Cartier was induced
—   41   12   Quelus,
—   75   27   character,
—   100   10   Mr. O'Donald ;
—   174   22   Physiology.

— 92. *View of the City in* 1803. On the right is shewn the artificial hill which was thrown up for the defence of the city. It is distinguished by barracks and a flag. Its position was the open space in front of Dalhousie Square; and it remained several years after the view was taken.

— 97. The *Bonsecours Church* was not *originally* built for public accommodation, though afterwards allotted to it. The history of its erection will be found on pp. 108, 9.

— 153. *Nelson's Monument.* The wooden building behind the Pedestal has been removed since the plate was engraved.

— 176. *View from the Haymarket.* A wooden paling has been run across from the market to the rear of the Chapel since the view was taken.

— 173. *Ship Yard.* The vessels enumerated in this article were not all built in the same yard, but in several. Mr. Munn's yard was on the south of the city toward the mouth of the Lachine Canal; the ground is now occupied by warehouses and stores. Beyond the lower end of the city, near the Current St. Mary, there are three ship yards. The nearest is that belonging to Hart. Logan, Esq., of London, and occupied by Mr. Johnson; and from which the steamer *Lady Colborne* was recently launched. The second is known as Young's Ship Yard. It belongs to Forsyth & Co., and is occupied by Millar & Co. This is the yard of which Shay & Merritt "took possession" in

1829, and in which Mr. M. built the vessels described in the paragraph. The third yard is still lower down the river, and was formerly occupied by Mr. Farringdou : it belongs to various individuals, being composed of the points of several farms which meet at that place. There is also a yard on the other side of the Lachine Canal, where barges and other small craft are built for the forwarders; and one farther up the Canal, on this side, at Whipple & Co.'s store, for the same purpose.

Page 216, 10. Dr. Bigsby, an English gentleman, was attached to the British Commission for determining the boundary between the United States and the British possessions, in 1824.

— 223, etc. In drawing up the Sketch of the First Rebellion, recourse was had to the summary which appeared originally in the *Montreal Gazette*.

— 215. *The River.* A striking feature in this majestic stream, independently of its magnitude, has always been the theme of just admiration. The Ottawa joins the St. Lawrence at the Cascades, by the Isle Perrot, and henceforward they unite their streams. But though they flow in company, each preserves its independence, as though it scorned to merge its characteristic qualities in those of its companion. This distinction is maintained as low down as Three Rivers, ninety miles beyond Montreal. The line of distinction is very clearly marked throughout nearly the whole distance. At Lake St. Peter it becomes somewhat obscure, and is lost in the tide waters that approach the town of Three Rivers. At any of the openings from Notre Dame Street in this city, or from any elevated part of the shore, the spectator may discern the beautiful green tinge of the St. Lawrence on the farther side, and the purpleish brown of the Ottawa on the half of the river nearest to him.

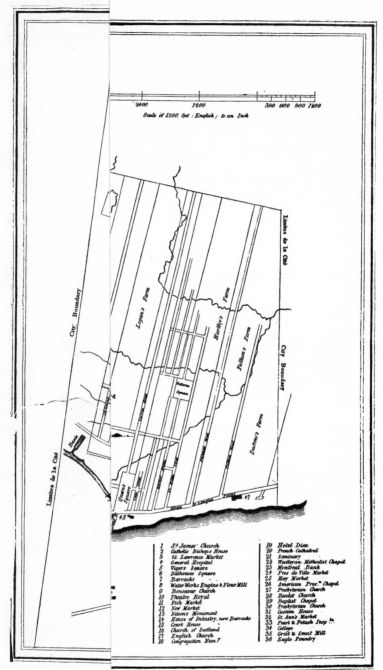

Scale of 1200 feet (English) to an Inch

1	St James' Church	19	Hotel Dieu
2	Catholic Bishop's House	20	French Cathedral
3	St. Lawrence Market	21	Seminary
4	General Hospital	22	Wesleyan Methodist Chapel
5	Vigers Square	23	Montreal Bank
6	Dalhousie Square	24	Pres de Ville Market
7	Barracks	25	Hay Market
8	Water Works Engine & Flour Mill	26	American Pres.ⁿ Chapel
9	Bonsecour Church	27	Presbyterian Church
10	Theatre Royal	28	Recolet Church
11	Fish Market	29	Baptist Chapel
12	New Market	30	Presbyterian Church
13	Nelson's Monument	31	Custom House
14	House of Industry, now Barracks	32	St. Ann's Market
15	Court House	33	Pearl & Potash Insp.ⁿ
16	Church of Scotland	34	College
17	English Church	35	Grist & Smut Mill
18	Congregation Nun.y	36	Eagle Foundry